GAMES AND GAMING

Berg *New Media* Series

ISSN 1753-724X

Edited by Leslie Haddon, Department of Media and Communications, London School of Economics and Political Sciences, and Nicola Green, Department of Sociology, University of Surrey.

The series aims to provide students with historically grounded and theoretically informed studies of significant aspects of new media. The volumes take a broad approach to the subject, assessing how technologies and issues related to them are located in their social, cultural, political and economic contexts.

Current titles in this series include:

Forthcoming titles in this series will include:

GAMES AND GAMING

An Introduction to New Media

Larissa Hjorth

Oxford • New York

English edition
First published in 2011 by
Berg
Editorial offices:
First Floor, Angel Court, 81 St Clements Street, Oxford OX4 1AW, UK
175 Fifth Avenue, New York, NY 10010, USA

Berg is the imprint of Oxford International Publishers Ltd.

Library of Congress Cataloging-in-Publication Data

A catalogue record for this book is available from the Library of Congress.

British Library Cataloguing-in-Publication Data

A catalogue record for this book is available from the British Library.

ISBN 978 1 84788 492 3 (Cloth)
   978 1 84788 491 6 (Paper)
e-ISBN 978 1 84788 839 6 (Institutional)
   978 1 84788 838 9 (Individual)

Typeset by Apex CoVantage, LLC, Madison, WI.
Printed in the UK by the MPG Books Group

www.bergpublishers.com

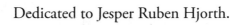

Dedicated to Jesper Ruben Hjorth.

CONTENTS

ACKNOWLEDGEMENTS

I would like to thank the wonderful series editors, Leslie Haddon and Nicola Green, for all their words of wisdom, advice and friendship as well as the great team at Berg—especially Tristan Palmer—for their professionalism and support.

I would also like to thank colleagues Adriana de Souza e Silva, Katie Salen, Susana Tosca, Ingrid Richardson, Stephanie Donald, Stefan Greuter and the RMIT games program staff. In addition, I thank the Australian Research Council (ARC) for the invaluable fellowship that allowed me the time to write this book.

The research in China was kindly supported by The State Innovative Institute for the Studies of Journalism & Communication and Media Society at Fudan University and I would also like to thank my research assistant, Chu Yuewen. For assistance with fieldwork in the Asia-Pacific, I would like to thank Li Ting Ng, Bora Na, Airah Cadiogan and Yonmi Kim.

Lastly, I would like to dedicate this book to my son, Jesper Ruben. I can only imagine what types of games and technologies his generation will use. This book is a historical study for you and your generation.

1 INTRODUCTION

In China, millions play the cute farm online multiplayer game *Happy Farm,* with some keen players setting their alarms in the middle of the night so that they can steal other (sleeping) people's virtual chickens. Far from being a preoccupation of the young, these casual, cute online games are being embraced by older generations— much to the dismay of their children. In the Philippines, the playing of games such as *DotA* (*Defense of the Ancients,* a custom scenario for the real-time strategy game *Warcraft III: Reign of Chaos*) has been replaced by *Mafia Wars,* a phenomenon sweep- ing other locations such as Singapore and Melbourne. Around the world, iPhone users in urban settings are joining the world of gamers with the 'filling in' activity of playing games transforming into a hobby. But how the games are played, how they are accessed (via personal computer at home/work/internet café, the iPhone or on the mobile phone) and what these games and their attendant gameplay mean to individuals and their communities differ greatly. The uptake of gaming—and types of associated gaming cultures in each location—is influenced by a wide variety of factors, from the nature of the technological infrastructure to linguistic and socio- cultural considerations.

Reflection: Place and Gameplay

How do you think place informs the types of games we play? Consider some of the games you play and how this relates to location. You may wish to do a compare and contrast between locations and the types of games played. Reflect upon how linguistic, sociocultural and technological factors influence games and gameplay.

Despite these aforementioned disparities, one constant can be noted: the phenom- enal rise of gaming globally. From the growth in diverse game consoles such as the haptic Nintendo Wii and the iPhone—along with the emergence of new genres— gaming is no longer the activity of young males or *otaku* (Japanese media-obsessed fans) but is now an integral part of global popular cultures partaken by the young and the old, male and female. This has made gaming, and the types of gaming cultures they produce, a vehicle for understanding new media more broadly. It is not by accident that as games have emerged globally, the study of them has become increasingly prevalent. Indeed, over the preceding couple of decades, and especially since the beginning of the twenty-first century, the rigorous and interdisciplinary nature of gaming scholarship has aptly addressed many issues around new media, narratology (the study of narrative), interactivity and active audiences—bringing in-depth approaches to the creative industries and global studies and in rethinking popular culture.

More recently, with the rise of convergent, networked social media (characterized by internet media such as Facebook and YouTube), the role of online communities and localized sociocultural practices such as massively multiplayer online games (MMOs) like *Lineage* and *World of Warcraft* (WoW) have given rise to ethnographic empirical research and area studies examining gaming communities. By focusing upon gaming cultures we can gain insight into these burgeoning transnational communities and creative industries of the twenty-first century. If TV, in the late twentieth century, was the popular vehicle for exploring debates around media consumption and production that led to new models of spectatorship and authorship, then in the twenty-first century it is indeed game studies where the new media models and practices are being explored.

Reflection: Examples of User Created Content (UCC)

Can you give some examples of what you think might be meant by the concept of UCC? Given that UCC is different than user generated content (UGC) that tends to refer to less involvement and creative participation on the part of the user, can you think of examples that are UCC and contrast them to UGC? Have you made some UCC? In particular, have you made game-related UCC like computer modelling (modding)?

This book provides a critical space for students to explore the role of games through a variety of approaches, whilst also being mindful of the changing nature of global popular culture and notions such as 'participation' and 'engagement' in an age of Web 2.0 and 'conversational media' (Jenkins 2005). That is, rather than media being unidirectional as in twentieth-century models, twenty-first-century media are characterized by a discursive dynamism, reflected in user created content (UCC)—a phenomenon marked by conversational, vernacular features. In short, mass, broadcast media have been redefined by narrowcasting. Through the portal of *Games and Gaming*, students will think critically about the new media and popular culture that pervade their everyday lives, particularly through the book's case studies, which aim to develop students' reflexivity and creative abilities to tackle new media without being consumed by their 'newness'. Given that the used-by date for much of this material is increasingly exponential, this book is mindful that all-pervasive media— such as social networking sites (SNSs) like Facebook and UCC vehicles such as YouTube—that are currently helping to shape the nature of games within everyday life are in a constant state of transition and transformation. Thus *Games and Gaming* provides students, for many of whom the internet and mobile phones have always been part of their lives, with an analytical space to stand back and contextualize such phenomena as part of broader global media shifts from the late twentieth century and into the twenty-first century.

Drawing from micro ethnographic studies and macro political economy analysis, *Games and Gaming* proposes an inclusive model for thinking through the politics of gaming production, representation and consumption. The book provides a broad backdrop for students entering the topic from a variety of disciplines and knowledge bases. By no means exhaustive, *Games and Gaming* offers inroads into the subject for students studying game theory and practice.

Games and Gaming, like the field of game studies, employs interdisciplinary frameworks drawing upon theoretical analyses ranging from media sociology (in the analysis of ads and brand identities), ethnography (in case studies of locations, empirical studies of players and studying the virtual and digital worlds as cultures) and cultural studies (in the critique of the industry rhetoric proclaiming user agency) to media and communication (examining the creative industries, the impact of games on other industries such as film and the relationships between online communities and social capital). This book locates gaming cultures not just as a symbol of lifestyle orientation, but also as cultural practices involving new media. Gaming cultures are as much a *cultural process* as they are media practices. *Games and Gaming* views contemporary culture as a series of techno-cultures, i.e. cultures that are saturated by and with technologies. Here, technology is not defined as merely functional, but rather, as it operates upon both the symbolic (immaterial) and material levels within our everyday lives.

Thus, *Games and Gaming* aims to reconnect the sociocultural, as well as political and economic, dimensions of gaming with new media theory and practice. It intends to revise current models of global gaming studies while providing a sound and logical outline of the major debates, theories and phenomena associated with gaming theory and practice today. In order to do so, each of the book's chapters proffers a different way in which to contextualize and conceptualize game studies and gaming. From historical to discipline-specific, each chapter aims to provide students with another perspective on game studies by locating viewpoints within the various gaming cultures.

AN OUTLINE OF THE FOLLOWING CHAPTERS

In Chapter 2, entitled 'The Histories of Gaming', we consider the ways in which game studies has multiple histories—particularly dependent upon what discipline and approach one takes. In this chapter we explore these various histories and potentialities of gaming through a cursory overview of video games such as *Pong* to consoles such as Nintendo Wii and location-aware gaming such as *Pac-Manhattan*. Beginning with one of the defining moments in game studies—the ludology versus narratology debate—Chapter 2 complicates this history in an age of social and 'participatory' media (Jenkins 2006b) such as UCC. As we will see, ludology supporters argued that narrative was not the driving force in games—thus making games distinctive from other media—whereas narratologists forwarded the premise that games, like all other media, needed narrative (abstract or linear, inherent in the story or projected by the user).

Here, we consider how games borrow methods and styles from other, older media (such as narrative from film) as well as employing forms of engagement, or media consumption, that are distinct to games and media properties, such as interactivity. This chapter situates the popular cultures of gaming within the context of gaming history, theory and practice as well as broader global political economies. Moreover, 'The Histories of Gaming' highlights the limitations of so-called global studies: many Scandinavian and American theorists have claimed to be providing universal accounts of gaming when, in actuality, they are demonstrating the way in which gaming is increasingly becoming determined at the level of the local. In sum, this chapter encourages students to think about the different sociocultural, political and linguistic issues informing 'global gaming' and how they relate to localized play practices.

In Chapter 3, 'Games as New Media', we conceptualize games as new media. In what way does this limit or expand upon the potentiality of both realms—games and new media—within twenty-first-century media contexts? And how does thinking about games as new media revise twentieth-century media practices? Are new media theories such as 'remediation', posed by Jay Bolter and Richard Grusin (1999), useful for game studies? In 'Games as New Media', we consider the way in which games have been differentiated from other new media practices, particularly in terms of the 'what is gameplay?' debate. For a ludologist, what distinguish games from other media are the roles of interactivity and simulation—two concepts important to the relationship between storytelling, narrative and gameplay. This chapter explores these concepts in the context of emerging types of gameplay (particularly around Nintendo Wii and online gaming) and relates them to debates in new media. The chapter will pose questions for class debate such as: how do we define gaming? Are there types of activities that are not part of the ethics of gameplay, such as cheating? What are some of the distinctive characteristics of gameplay? Are games really 'interactive'? How are our definitions of digital storytelling changing?

Convergent media, Web 2.0 and social media are all continuing to have an impact upon gaming. In this chapter, Chapter 4, we consider how this rise of Web 2.0, UCC and full-time public intimacy (Berlant 1998) is altering the role of online gaming. Here, 'Web 2.0, Social Media and Online Games' explores some of the challenges and adventures for gaming in an age of convergence and divergence (Jenkins 2006a). By questioning the impact of the rise of Web 2.0 SNSs like Facebook, this chapter assesses how these new social media are affecting new forms of gameplay. We consider: how does the emergence of UCC and the idea of the user as what Axel Bruns (2005) calls the 'produser' (a conflation of 'user' and 'producer') form new agendas for the future of gaming?

In Chapter 5, 'The Politics of the Personal: Avatar Representation, Identity and Beyond', we investigate the ways in which representation, identity and identification are being performed and transformed through avatars (online characters). With the debates surrounding the relationship between online and offline worlds raging— particularly in terms of early cyberspace feminist debates and, more recently, the network versus community model of the internet—methodologies and approaches have continued to be revised and challenged. This questioning has undoubtedly informed debates around identity and representation in virtual and offline spaces a practice that imbues the degrees of participation and immersion in online games. So what are some of the questions for identity and subjectivity within Web 2.0 and what is the impact upon gameplay? As Web 2.0 and forms of virtuality increasingly become part of everyday life, what influence is this having on the role of representation? Why are some types of avatars popular in certain regions (such as cute characters in Asia) and not in others? This chapter explores some examples of particular avatars and what types of identification—and thus gameplay—they establish. In this chapter we also consider the relationship between aesthetics, ethics and sociocultural identities. Class discussion involves a debate about the politics of representation and the ethical dimension of game design and aesthetics.

Chapter 6, 'Glaze Cultures: Urban and Location-aware Gaming', explores the emergence of gaming as a new sensory experience, given that urban games take players away from the 'gaze' cultures of film and the 'glance regime' of TV and into the space of the haptic (touch) dimension of gameplay. Drawing on console games cultures, Australian new media theorist Chris Chesher (2004) identifies three types of 'glaze' spaces—that is, an engagement in between the gaze and the glance. For example, Chesher discusses the integral role haptics play in the visual engagement with console games. In 'Glaze Cultures', we consider the role of urban mobile gaming as a site for challenging conventional ways of reading and experiencing games, play and urbanity. We explore the different types of urban mobile games and how these can transform how people and place are negotiated. For new media artists such as Rafael Lazano Hemmer, it is the play between the cerebral and the haptic, the virtual and the actual, which is the important component of urban play. As gaming expert Frans Mäyrä (2003) argues, what is missing from much gameplay today is its most significant component, a sense of place. This chapter considers some of the experimental types of gameplay such as location-aware mobile gaming and how they bring gaming 'back to the future' by deploying older, physical game tactics through new technological infrastructure such as GPS (Global Positioning System). 'Glaze Cultures' provides examples of these types of projects, from Blast Theory to *Pac-Manhattan*, and includes some exercises for students to explore these types of haptic gameplay.

One area in particular in need of examination is the historical and contemporary impact of the games industries and cultures in the Asia-Pacific region. Including countries such as South Korea, China and Japan, the region has played an important role in the history of gaming—both in terms of hardware and software production as well as in terms of developing modes of consumption such as eSports ("electronic sports"—that is, professional leagues for players). Much of current literature on games in English has focused upon Anglophonic paradigms, neglecting the significance of the sociocultural dimensions of games. Few 'global' game studies have actually engaged with the industry on a global level. Also, if the sociocultural dimension of gameplay is negotiated, it is often purely from an ethnographic context (i.e. T. L. Taylor) that neglects to address the economic and political elements of the games industry.

Chapter 7, 'Gaming in the Asia-Pacific: Two Futures for Gaming—Online Gaming versus Electronic Individualism', speaks to this aforementioned oversight in game studies by tackling one of the booming and innovative regions for gaming both historically and now. By providing a context for the following chapter's case study of two centres for global gaming directions of online games (South Korea) and consoles (Japan), this chapter explores the multiple political and economic, sociocultural and linguistic dimensions of the global games industry. Through investigating a context outside the well-known and frequently cited locations such as the US, students can gain a clearer understanding of the complex ways in which games reflect social, cultural, economic and political spaces. Discussing non-Anglophonic examples can make us reflect upon some of the cultural assumptions we make around the notion of the 'global' games industry. Specifically, 'Gaming in the Asia-Pacific' explores the popularity of haptic mobile games consoles from Nintendo DS, PlayStation Portable (PSP), and Nintendo Wii on the one hand, and online multiplayer gaming on the other hand, all within the context of the global market.

In this concluding chapter (Chapter 8), 'Gaming in the Twenty-first Century', we summarize the book's key themes and then reflect upon the potential futures for gaming in the twenty-first century. Here we consider the role of Web 2.0, SNSs and mobile gaming in the context of potential futures. We reflect upon a series of future possibilities of gaming in the light of contemporary directions such as: what are some of the ways in which the current proliferation of divergent online multiplayer games subgenres will grow? How has the success of Nintendo Wii with its haptic gameplay transformed one future of games? How is convergent mobile media such as the iPhone changing the accessibility and playability of games?

These various chapters provide students with the foundations for understanding game studies. *Games and Gaming* is not meant to be exhaustive. Instead, it proffers examples, case studies and references for students to engage with and reflect upon as they, with their various backgrounds and cultural contexts, develop their own interpretation of game studies. The book, in particular, does not report the most cited examples or case studies. Rather, this book tries to focus on some of the gaps and still-emergent areas so that students can think through the challenges that face game studies for future generations. Some of these examples were emergent as this book was being written, but by engaging with such contemporary, dynamic and evolving case studies, this textbook illustrates how, through the lens of game studies, we can learn much about the study of contemporary cultural practice—both the limitations and the possibilities.

Summary

- Game studies has emerged from an interdisciplinary background. There are many ways to analyse games, gaming cultures and gameplay.
- Gaming, like play, is informed by various factors such as socioeconomic, political, techno-national, cultural and linguistic influences. Global gaming is characterized by divergent localities, communities and practices.
- The role of networked, social media and convergent haptic technologies such as the iPhone and Nintendo Wii are having an impact upon the ways in which games are experienced and consumed.

2 THE HISTORIES OF GAMING

Games have come of age. Over the three decades since the 1970s, games have transformed and transgressed genres and associated player stereotypes to become one of the dominant media cultures of the twenty-first century. Just as the range of gamers playing 'casual' and 'serious' games has expanded to encompass young and old, male and female, individuals and families, so too has the capacity of games to address various forms of media literacy, platforms, contexts and practices burgeoned. Despite the economic downturn of 2008, the games industry (including hardware and software) globally drew an annual profit of US$49.9 billion (Screen Digest 2008). Whilst games have continued to grow towards the mainstream since the 1980s, it was not until the dawn of the century that games started to take centre stage in global popular culture, maturing from a subcultural activity partaken by boys and *otaku*. Games are no longer mere child's play. *Let the games begin.*

Thus, games can be 'read' (or understood) as cultural artefacts, industries, social communities, material cultures (i.e. the psychological dimension of objects as part of one's cultural identity) and media practices—to name but a few possibilities. Video games in their increasingly various convergent formats—computer, online, console—have continued to grow since the 1980s to become one of the central forms of entertainment in the twenty-first century. From MMOs and consoles such as Sony PlayStation 3, Nintendo Wii, and Microsoft's Xbox to the rise of mobile gaming on devices such as the iPhone, video game content, genres and platforms have expanded to reflect the burgeoning diversity and heterogeneity of player demographics.

Over the decades since the inception of games in the 1970s—intensifying since the beginning of this century—the rigorous and interdisciplinary nature of gaming scholarship has aptly addressed many issues around new media, narratology, interactivity and active audiences. As we shall learn in the following chapters, game studies, like new media (which encompasses the rise of digital and networked media in the twentieth century), has borrowed, adapted and reinvented various cultural and media precepts. From narratology (the study that all media can be analysed in terms of narratives) to the cultural studies shifts from textual analysis to audience-focused ethnographies, game studies has been both shaped by and also shaped these approaches.

Since its inception, gaming has developed in two strong directions—handheld mobile console and online gaming. This latter lineage has intensified with the recent growth in the social, online community elements of gaming—as evidenced in MMOGs like *StarCraft, Lineage* and *WoW*—in which the context for understanding games has begun to focus around Web 2.0 (that is, the dimensions of the internet focused around UCC, collaboration and community) and its associated networked publics. With this emergence of social media we can see the necessity for and rise of empirical, ethnographic and area studies (i.e. cultural contexts) approaches to understanding gaming communities (Taylor 2006a; Hjorth 2008a).

Indeed, the expansion of gaming as one of the dominant entertainment industries of the twenty-first century has been accompanied by the proliferation of convergent media. As Henry Jenkins (2006a) notes, convergence occurs across cultural, economic and technological levels that have, in turn, revised twentieth-century models of consumption and production that were characterized as 'packaged media' (Jenkins 2006b). If the twentieth century was marked by non-discursive media models, then the twenty-first century—symbolized by interactive media like games—has been defined by 'conversational' media. In the case of the games industry, participative media have seen an erosion between old distinctions, such as those between casual games (i.e. puzzle and mobile phone games) versus serious games (i.e. role-playing games), in what has been called a 'casual revolution' (Juul 2009). The uptake of games on the centre stage of popular culture by players from various demographics has seen a major revision of game genres, platforms (i.e. consoles) and gameplay.

Accompanying these changes, the relationship between players and makers has become increasingly dynamic with the rise of player-driven game activities such as modding (computer modifications of existing games), machinima (cinema using game engines) and ancillary gaming cultures like cosplay (costume play) and eSports. Within these new gaming social 'cartographies' (i.e. spaces mapped by the social), players through their labour—also characterized as 'playbour' (Kücklich 2005)—can be seen to have become co-producers or 'produsers' (Bruns 2005). We now address these transformations in the games industry.

First we will briefly discuss game studies in relation to models of social and domesticated technologies. This context helps to locate game studies within broader traditions for understanding social technologies and ICTs (information and communication technologies). Then the chapter looks at the invention of video games through its hackivist history. The initial stages of game development can be seen to have been led by hobbists and scientists who explored the limits of the emerging digital age through games. This genealogy is important to reflect upon in the light of current debates around the rise of produsers in which amateurs become professionals. We then move on to the debate that helped secure game studies as a distinct area of study as compared to other media studies—ludology versus narratology. While ludologists (Juul 2001; Frasca 1999) argued that what distinguished games from other media was the central role of the *ludus* (game) in which such issues as narrative were of little consideration, narratologists (Aarseth 1997; Murray 1997) forwarded the argument that all media were determined and defined by narrative—whether abstract or realistic.

Histories Rather than History

From the outset it is important to note that this mapping of the history of gaming is but one in many. Game studies, as an interdisciplinary area of study, is marked by contested definitions and genealogies—making it an exciting but also a complex realm. The use of the plural 'histories' in the chapter title is intended to highlight the fact that there are many histories of gaming. Indeed, dependent upon cultural context and disciplinary background, gaming has many genealogies.

Along with understanding the history of games as multiple and contested through the concept of histories, we also need to consider how games and gameplay are influenced by different contexts. In particular, games are shaped by techno-cultures, that is, the notion that contemporary culture is saturated by, and with, technologies (Green 2001). Moreover, these technologies are not merely functional. Rather, their importance lies in the fact that they are sites for cultural practices as well as being cultural artefacts that are shaped by, and also shape, people's experiences of the world.

APPROACHES TO SOCIAL TECHNOLOGIES

Games, like other popular media such as TV, have often attracted moral panics. In particular, as a form of 'youth media', games have borne the brunt of concerns about a variety of social problems, and their 'effects' have been framed within simplistic definitions of childhood (i.e. children being seen by adults as vulnerable and passive). Specifically, much of the debate around the role of violence in games has been embroiled within technological determinist approaches to understanding the consequences of, for example, various media. These approaches assume that technologies in some straightforward manner affect and change 'us'.

> ## Reflection
>
> Can you think of some examples of media stories in which the reportage implies that game playing affected a person's behaviour? Consider what factors the story is neglecting to address such as the socio-economic and the sociocultural context.

In such models, 'us' is viewed as homogeneous, fixed and without agency—implying that media dictates ideologies to us that we just passively consume without interpretation or filtering. This not only ignores the diversity of experiences that we bring, as readers, to a text but also the way in which context (place, time, etc.) affects how we participate and engage with certain media. Indeed, one history of media could chart how new media perpetually becomes a scapegoat for wider social issues. If only things were that simple. If only the various wars and violence that have been part of the rise of humanity could be blamed upon *Grand Theft Auto*. This technological determinist, naïve and crude understanding of media (and their relationship to audiences), which in the context of media analysis is also known as the 'media effects' model, assumes either that media unthinkingly change our behaviour, as in the case of copying violence, or else imposes ideologies and beliefs upon the consumer/audience/user.

Of course, this 'substantive approach' (a subset of which is technological determinism)—substantive in the sense of its focus on the idea that technologies affect us, rather than us influencing technology—is far from new and has remained persistent since the introduction of domestic technologies; from the TV to, more recently, video games. The study of the rise of new media technologies within popular culture can be mapped back to two key figures in the 1960s—British cultural theorist Raymond Williams and Canadian media theorist Marshall McLuhan. Both scholars were the first to study the 'new medium' of the time, TV, highlighting the significance of this new media as a lens for analysing contemporary culture. Williams founded the tradition that would be known as cultural studies through the Birmingham School of Cultural Criticism (BSCC), while McLuhan became a popular media figure by way of his skill for coining key phrases that would become part of English colloquialisms.

McLuhan's substantive approach, often dubbed technological determinist, was the one that made studying new media accessible to the general masses through car salesman–like sayings such as 'the global village' and puns like 'the medium is the message/massage'. Arguing that technologies extend our senses, McLuhan's work provided useful ways of understanding the role of technologies within different forms of human expression. A telephone, for example, extended the ear. However, this substantive view of technology has been criticized for its inability to take into account the complexity of human agency and the fact that technologies are as much shaped by the cultures that house them as they shape cultural practices.

Williams's work, alternatively, forwarded a social constructivist approach towards technology, in which the agency and power of the user and culture were given greater attention. For Williams, media such as TV needed to be understood as being embedded within a particular techno-culture in which users (or in the case of games, players) shaped the medium as much as the medium shaped their experiences. Williams's work, by focusing upon the ways in which technologies were consumed within specific cultural practices, informed what would become the social construction of technology (SCOT) approach (MacKenzie and Wajcman 1999).

Substantive versus Social Constructivist Approaches

McLuhan and Williams represented two very different approaches to technology and new media—substantive and social constructivist. The former has often been associated with the quantitative analysis of media and technologies and has a strong tradition in US-based media and communication, and journalism departments. The latter attempts to capture a more dynamic model of culture, as a living and ever-changing space, by focusing upon the micro level and using qualitative methodologies. The social constructivist approach can be found in anthropology, culture studies and sociology.

Three subsets of social constructivism are the domestication approach, virtual ethnography (i.e. studying the internet as a culture [Miller and Slater 2000; Hine 2000]) and digital ethnography (i.e. studying the social and new media surrounding the internet, as exemplified by YouTube studies [Wesch 2008]). The domestication approach has British and Norwegian origins. The British tradition (Silverstone and Haddon 1996), from which the term 'domestication' first arose, was founded by Roger Silverstone (extending upon Williams's work), and grew out of media studies and an interest in consumption studies (Miller 1987) and cultural studies (Hebdige 1988). It also drew upon anthropology, especially in the discussion of the symbolic nature of technologies in the context of material cultures (i.e. the study of how objects reflect the user's identity and social context [Miller 1988]). The Norwegian version had this origin, and in later work it engaged with the social shaping of technology discussions. These different approaches were subsequently deployed in the evolution of game studies, helping to locate games within broader cultural and technological practices. However, these methodologies and traditions have been adapted and repurposed within game studies.

Games can be conceptualized more broadly in terms of being ICTs and new media. Studies stemming from them, which highlight the social rather than functional nature of technology, have developed their own traditions and approaches that have often been deployed within a generally interdisciplinary game studies. Within the realm of social and cultural technologies, we have discussed two out of the three main approaches—substantive, social constructivism. The third approach is the study of technology's affordances (MacKenzie and Wajcman 1999). The first two approaches have been most influential in game studies. The substantive approach, whose publicly popular face was in the form of technological determinism or 'media effects' was criticized for its simplistic understandings of technologies and users. In particular, it failed to appreciate the multidimensional agency of the user—in other words, ignoring the context in which the technologies/media were deployed and how this impacted upon the active ways in which the user participated in, or even ignored the media. While this model has gained currency again with the rise of cyberculture studies, it was inadequate for exploring how and why users engaged in media in complex and diverse ways. In order to address the problems associated with the first approach, the inverse model that emerged was outlined above—social constructivism.

As technologies have become increasingly more integral in social relations and a defining feature of the user's identity and lifestyle, so too have the models through which to conceptualize the dynamic relationship between the user and their technologies needed to become more complex. Technologies operate across various levels encompassing both the symbolic and material. They extend existing rituals of social interaction whilst also providing new forms of expression and media literacy. With this in mind, theorists such as Bruno Latour (1986) developed an approach that extended the substantive and social constructivist models—actor network theory (ANT)—whereby both technologies and people are seen as 'actors'. Users affect the technology just as the technology impacts upon the user in a dynamic and ongoing relationship.

The affordances approach, developed by Donald Norman in *The Design of Everyday Things* (1988), has been widely deployed in the fields of interaction design, cognitive design and human-computer interaction (HCI). Deemed an 'ecological approach' by Norman, the human-centred design method tries to consider not only the physical capabilities of the actors/users but also their motivations, plans, values and history. Focusing upon a relational rather than subjective or essentialist approach, the affordances approach has become a dominant consideration in the development of practical design within an increasingly HCI environment.

Meanwhile, the domestication approach noted earlier (Silverstone and Hirsch 1992; Silverstone, Hirsch and Morley 1992; Miller 1987) focuses on technologies after acquisition, technologies in everyday life and their *symbolic role*. The word 'domestication' itself comes from 'taming the wild animal', and this was then applied to describing the processes involved in 'domesticating ICTs' when bringing them into the home (Silverstone, Hirsch and Morley 1992). The ongoing influence of the domestication approach attests to its importance as a tool for comprehending the sociocultural and symbolic power of commodities, especially communication technologies, as re-enacting older rituals and cultural practices. For example, games and play can be found in all cultures across history, and video games draw from these models and practices. The technological function of artefacts pales in comparison to their symbolic weight and power. As Silverstone and Eric Hirsch observe in their pioneering work into the area, contemporary technological artefacts must be viewed as essentially material objects, capable of great symbolic significance, investment and meaning, while domestic technologies are 'embedded in the structures and dynamics of contemporary consumer culture' (1992: 20). In order to fully understand games, we need to analyse the context in which they are framed.

In particular, the domestication approach focuses on the meanings that individuals and cultural contexts give to technologies, thereby extending the ways in which users perceive them. A key feature of the domestication approach is that it explores the interaction between the user and the technology as an ongoing process, as well as addressing the ways in which technologies such as the mobile phone can function symbolically as indicators of the user's tastes, values and cultural and social capital. These notions of social and cultural capital refer in turn to French sociologist Pierre Bourdieu's important study *Distinction* (1979[1984]), which sketched some new ways for thinking about the ways in which people's tastes are formed and how they can themselves be turned into resources, or capital. For Bourdieu, capital was a form of 'knowledge' that helped produce and naturalize (or normalize) taste. While cultural capital refers to one's history, upbringing, education, etc., their social capital can be built up through interaction with friends, family and acquaintances. Games (and game consoles) are not only a symbolic repository for the user's social capital but also signals to other certain unspoken clues about the user's identity and social status.

Reflection

How do the games we play reflect our values and identity? Why do some people choose some types of consoles such as Wii over Xbox? Make a list of the some game genres and the associated players and then discuss in a group to move beyond the stereotypes (i.e. despite being deemed a 'male genre', first person shooters [FPSs] are also played and enjoyed by women). Also, what do the different types of consoles (mobile phone, PC, Wii, PSP, etc.) and their branding say about the ideal user? Reflect and discuss.

As an interdisciplinary framework, the domestication approach identifies new technologies as having become embedded in everyday life and household social relations (i.e. family power relations). This results in new technologies and media not only being a site (a space or context) for making meaning but also a place in which meaning can be gleaned. In other words, objects have their own meanings and histories that are then put into the dynamics of cultural practice, which, in turn, redefines the meanings. For example, an old retro games console like Atari holds a particular position in games history, but it also has multiple individual histories that relate to specific users. This is why objects take on different meanings dependent upon context. Groundbreaking case studies, such as Paul du Gay et al.'s *The Story of the Walkman: Doing Cultural Studies* (1997), although not specifically using the domestication framework, are indicative of how pivotal deploying this approach was for understanding the various dimensions of lifestyle technologies within contemporary life.

There have been a variety of reworkings of the domestication approach in the context of game studies—in particular, see Jon Dovey and Helen Kennedy's *Game Cultures* (2006) and detailed studies or ethnographies of online gaming communities (Taylor 2006a). Simon Egenfeldt Nielsen, Jonas Smith and Susana Tosca's *Understanding Video Games: The Essential Introduction* (2008) fuses cultural with literary studies approaches and provides a good summary of game studies models from some of the most regarded researchers, such as Susana Tosca (who is also editor of the key online journal *game studies*). Aphra Kerr's (2006) important work combines cultural studies with a study of the creative industries by analysing both games as texts and the various features of the games industry. She applies and revises du Gay et al.'s 'circuit of culture' (1997)—a framework for thinking about the different ways in which we can analyse, in this case, technologies. In the circuit of culture, designed when twentieth-century 'packaged media' was prevalent, we see various interrelated 'nodes' such as the representation of technologies (e.g. how they are portrayed in the media or advertising), their consumption, the ideology associated with the product and their production.

As each node was altered, this affected the other nodes in the circuit. However, games complicate this model as they are one of the first examples of 'participatory media' (Jenkins 2006b), and so distinctions between audience and producer/designer, consumption and production are blurred. This is identified by Kücklich's (2005) aforementioned 'playbour' notion in which the labour (creative, social, affective and emotional) of the player (in his example, the modder) becomes an integral part of the game culture surrounding a games text. In other words, the player utilizes his or her creativity and social knowledge to make a mod, as well as investing the mod with their own emotions and affectivity. This is a complex composition of different skills and knowledges invested by the player which is, in turn, deployed within the gaming community and supports, and is supported by, the industry. Moreover, this labour is encapsulated by Bruns's (2005) notion of the 'produser' that we explore in more detail in Chapter 4. First, let us just recap games studies within these broader traditions before moving on to one case study of gaming history and then the ludology debate.

CONTEXTUALIZING METHODS IN GAME STUDIES

Game studies, like media studies (Morley 1992; Ang 1985), has seen the rise of textual, and then ethnographic (Taylor 2003a, 2006a), approaches to understanding games that have complicated, if not challenged, the substantive model of analysis. Textual analysis saw games as being 'texts' which could be 'read', in the same way as the contents of books, television or films could be interpreted by an (ideal) reader or viewer.

Reflection

As an exercise in textuality (reading a text), imagine a game (either an esoteric one not known by many or one that you have made up) and outline how you would summarize and explain it to someone not familiar with the game. In the summary you need to not just describe the goals, genre and what happens next in the story, but also try to convey the essence of the gameplay.

When conducting textual analysis one needed to be mindful of the fact that texts have contexts (the historical, social or physical environments in which the text, in this case game, exists) and that text and context are interdependent; every new context can give rise to a different reading of a text. The work of Dovey and Kennedy, in *Game Cultures* (2006), revises game studies within the cultural studies tradition by deploying a textual and ideological focus, while Stephen Kline et al.'s *Digital Play* (2003) focuses upon both the ideological and labour practices constituting the games industry.

Building on the textual studies that dominated the 1980s and early 1990s, a more contextually rigorous model of ethnography, which shifted the focus away from the 'text' and onto the readers (or, in the case of games, players), started to appear and gain more weight in game studies. Key examples of these forms of ethnography—especially virtual ethnography—include T. L. Taylor's pioneering work on online multiplayer games that explored the multidimensions of games as social and cultural spaces and the growing agency of the player, as a diverse and participatory practice. This similar pathway by which methodologies changed when examining games and TV is, in part, due to the history of video games on personal computers that, like TV, inhabit domestic spaces.

Games can be seen as playing an important part in the rise of ICTs in domestic spaces through this shared history with personal computers. There are also parallels to be found between the interrelated growth of mobile phone gaming devices and portable gaming devices from the 1980s onwards. Indeed, even when these ICTs physically leave the home (i.e. mobile phone or mobile game console), their usage is still very much linked to one's sense of home and the private. Our experiences and memories, both inside and outside the game, inform our gameplay. This is why in some cultural contexts such as South Korea, where a sense of the close-knit family is the metaphor for national identity, 'community', guild-based (akin to kinship) MMOGs have succeeded; while, in other contexts such as Japan, it has been argued that the triumph of the individual console game (such as PSP and Nintendo DS and precursors such as Game & Watch) is characteristic of a techno-national policy and industry that emphasize 'electronic individualism' (Kogawa 1984).

'Mobile Privatization'

This mobile phenomenon (on the console or phone, particularly 'networked' ones) can be viewed as an extension of what Williams defined as 'mobile privatization' (1974). While Williams coined the term to describe the then-contemporary vehicle for popular culture, the TV, he identified this phenomenon as part of a boarder 'unique modern condition' that was 'unprecedented' (1974: 29). Utilizing the metaphor of car traffic, Williams painted a scene of modern dislocation to characterize contemporary 'mobile privatized' social relations. As Williams observed in the case of the television, the mass media promoted an idea of mobility in which geographic movement could take place from the comfort of one's lounge room. This concept has haunted the ubiquitous rise of ICTs, in which private, domestic spheres have spilled over into the public parallel to the conflations between work and personal life (Wajcman et al. 2009) in which devices such as mobile phones make it impossible to leave work. Work can follow you everywhere, defusing itself temporally and spatially, behaving like a 'wireless leash' (Qiu 2008).

While semi-public versions of gaming could be found in arcade games—with more recent guises in the form of PC rooms—much of the rise of gaming has been orchestrated around the ubiquity of domestic technologies within contemporary lifestyle narratives. Like domestic technologies such as mobile phones, game consoles allowed users to move both inside and outside the home. The 'home' for playing games can also be outside the actual 'homes' where people live (i.e. the physical domain of the domestic sphere)—as evidenced in the rise of PC rooms in which guilds play online in the same offline space together, as well as the emergence of what has been characterized as the 'casual', mobile games market. Interestingly, both of these aspects (online and mobile) have captured the attention of predominantly female players for their casual and social dimensions.

Games extend the existing transformation and diffusion of boundaries between traditional private and public spheres through the ability to move *geographically* (in the case of mobile devices) as well as *psychologically* (in the case of online social worlds in which game spaces operate like mini-worlds for the players from different locations). One can see that games are creating new forms of geo-social imaginaries (i.e. becoming part of popular culture vernacular and imagery). Here, notions such as 'home', even if it is not the home where one lives, are integral in informing people's gameplay and their sense of identity within the game. This is why approaches such as the domestication approach have been so useful in conceptualizing games within broader techno-cultures. However, it is also important to understand what makes the genealogy and rise of gaming and games studies so unique. In the next section we explore one history in gaming, followed by the ludology debate.

HACTIVISM: THE BIRTH OF GAMING

Gaming has many histories, dependent upon what discipline and approach one takes. This interdisciplinary background—drawing from film and TV studies, literary and art theory, as well as approaches from media, communication and cultural studies—makes game studies both fascinating and perplexing.

Given that play is one of the most creative, innovative (Sutton-Smith 1997) and yet most misunderstood notions, it is not by accident that the birth of video games began with hackers, i.e. the preoccupation of computer scientists and hobbyists interested in pushing the possibilities of technology (Haddon 1999). This history has helped to shape the development of games into one of the most dominant global popular cultures, one that has been marked by subversive and independent subcultures. The invention of video games can be linked to the founding of computer science as a discipline in the 1950s and 1960s at MIT—secured by the investment of US military funding in areas such as artificial intelligence (AI). The establishment of MIT's computer science lab granted then-student Steve Russell with the technological opportunities for his group, the Tech Model Railway Club (TMRC), to create the first game, *Spacewar*, in 1962. This first incarnation of *Spacewar* was designed for the PDP-1 computer at MIT and was not capable of simultaneous two-player interaction. It was in 1971 that Nolan Bushnell took *Spacewar* and transformed it into one of the first arcade games, under the title *Computer Space*. Bushnell went on to make the popular *Pong* and establish the legendary Atari game company that dominated the 1970s entertainment industries, and he was also responsible for spearheading the shifting of games into the arcades.

The significance of the US military funding was also pertinent in the conception of the video game as domestic technology. The defence company Sanders Electronics was responsible for developing the first game technology for the TV in 1972 with the Magnavox Odyssey machine. The Odyssey was the first home console and featured twelve games, such as puzzle and maze games. One key game was Ralph Baer's *Tennis for Two*, which was later adapted by Atari and released in 1975 as *Pong*. By 1976, consoles contained microprocessors allowing them to be programmable—in short, hardware and software could be separated. This meant that games, like other popular media such as vinyl records, could be 'brought, collected, and compared' (Haddon 1999).

The late 1970s and early 1980s saw the games industry going from strength to strength. In 1979, Atari released its global success story *Space Invaders*. The early 1980s saw the introduction of many home consoles from Atari, Nintendo, Sega, Microsoft and Sony. This phenomenon was concurrent with the beginning of personal home computers such as Commodore 64, Apple II and the Sinclair Spectrum that also allowed users to experiment, hack and make their own games.

The histories of gaming can be mapped through various shifts across hardware and software, industry and academia. One genealogy of gaming could be in terms of industry-technology shifts that can be broadly categorized into seven generations (see Table 2.1). The first generation (beginning in 1971) saw the dawn of the arcade game and console gaming (the Magnavox Odyssey system in 1972). The rise of both university mainframe computers and home computers helped ensure the further development of games. In 1976, the introduction of the ROM cartridge format was spearheaded by the release of the Fairchild Video Entertainment System (VES), and Atari's Video Computer System (VCS, later called Atari 2600) in 1977 marked the birth of the second generation of gaming. By the early 1980s, often known as the 'Golden Age of Arcade Games', the once burgeoning games industry began to experience a slowdown. This period also fostered the rise of two of the most enduring directions in gaming—online and mobile/portable gaming.

Table 2.1: Gaming generation denoted by industry shifts

Gaming generation	Approximate dates of epoch	Key industry shifts
First	1971–7	Introduction of arcade game and console gaming (Magnavox Odyssey system 1972). Advancement of university mainframe and personal computers. In 1976, the introduction of the ROM cartridge format was spearheaded by the release of the Fairchild Video Entertainment System (VES), while Atari's Video Computer System (VCS, later called Atari 2600) in 1977 marked the birth of the second generation of gaming.
Second	1977–83	Characterized as both the 'Golden Age of Arcade Games' and also the rise of the handheld (Game & Watch), this period of growth met a disastrous finish with the video game crash of 1983.
Third	1985–9	This epoch was marked by the death of public gaming in the form of the arcade game and rise of the private characterized by Nintendo's release of the 8-bit console Famicom (or Nintendo Entertainment System [NES]).
Fourth	1989–96	Major advancements in graphics and memory, dramatically improving the visual quality and potential longer, more complex gameplay through the introduction of CD-ROM drives and 3D graphics such as flat-shaded polygons.
Fifth	1994–9	Marked by the failure of Nintendo as they made the choice to move from CD-ROMs for the cheaper-to-produce cartridges (Nintendo 64). This saw major companies such as SquareSoft move their games to PlayStation, making it the dominant console of this generation. The end of this generation was marked by the significant rise of mobile/portable in the form of PlayStation Portable [PSP] and Nintendo DS.
Sixth	1999–2004	Sega leaves and Microsoft enters the games market. Online gaming burgeons as does the mobile/portable market (especially supported by major shifts in mobile phones from mere communication portals to sites for mobile media).
Seventh	2004–present	The market for mobile media continues to expand and attracts new audiences to gaming. So too does the online market with online games increasingly becoming casual.

Source: For more information, see http://en.wikipedia.org/wiki/History_of_video_games.

Early online gaming could be seen in the form of dialup Bulletin Board Systems (BBSs—a precursor to Web 2.0 social networking sites), which allowed for some of the first examples of MUDs (multi-user dungeons) and basic, textual, fantasy role-playing games that would eventually evolve into MMORGs (massively multiplayer online role-playing games). Concurrently, we could see the rise of mobile, handheld gaming in the form of Nintendo's Game and Watch (initiated in 1980)—the spirit of this phenomenon can be seen in the recent success of Nintendo DS portable and Wii. This second generation was marked by one of the defining periods in the games industry—the North American video game crash of 1983. The crash was marked by the unsuccessful adaptation of blockbuster films into games, most notably the video game version of Steven Spielberg's film *E. T.* (1982). Not only was it dubbed as the 'all time worst video game in history' but it also marked the beginning of the end of Atari with its biggest commercial failures. Tens of thousands of *E. T.* game cartridges were buried in a New Mexico landfill—a symbolic grave not only for Atari but the games industry as well. After the software and hardware peak of 1982, the boom was over—suddenly, production dwindled and declined.

After the crash of 1983, the gaming industry was partly resuscitated, marking the third generation (1985–9) with Nintendo's release of the 8-bit console Famicom (or Nintendo Entertainment System [NES]). The 1990s saw the decline and death of arcade gaming in the face of the rise of handheld gaming and MMOGs. Known as the fourth generation (1989–96), this epoch saw the introduction of CD-ROM drives and 3D graphics such as flat-shaded polygons, which enabled more memory, sophisticated graphics and immersive gameplay. The fifth generation (1994–9) saw Nintendo's departure from CD-ROMs for the cheaper-to-produce cartridges (Nintendo 64) with disastrous consequences. Given that CD-ROMs could hold more data than the cartridges in a time where games were increasing their graphics (requiring more memory), companies such as SquareSoft (producers of the legionary *Final Fantasy* series) quickly shifted from Nintendo to PlayStation platforms. By the end of the fifth generation, PlayStation led the market globally, whilst Nintendo only had success in Japan.

At the end of this period, two key features became apparent—the growing significance of the portable (mobile) game systems (Sony PlayStation Portable [PSP], Nintendo DS) and the rise of the online and networked UCC in the form of game modding. The integral role of the player—and their 'playbour'—in the production and consumption of gaming cultures can be found in the modding of games such as *Counter-Strike*, *Half-Life*, *Unreal Tournament* and *The Sims*. Game companies began including customizing tools in games packages and online downloads as a part of this playbour phenomenon. The sixth generation (1999–2004) saw the exit of Sega, Sony gaining an increasing stronghold over the market and the entrance of Microsoft. During this time, online gaming continued to burgeon, whilst 'casual gaming' shifted from consoles to the PC.

Along with the growth in portable (handheld) game systems was the rise in games for mobile phones. As mobile phones shifted from being extensions of the landlines to third Generation ([3G] i.e. mobile phone with internet connection) media convergence par excellence—incorporating Web 2.0 features of social media such as YouTube, Flickr and Second Life—games were pivotal in this transformation. In Japan, the main telecommunications provider, NTT DoCoMo's i-mode, featured numerous games aimed at audiences from diverse backgrounds not normally associated with gaming. In South Korea, companies such as GOMID (now defunct) made haptic (movement activated) games exclusively for the mobile phone. Within the Western world, Nokia's N-Gage phone, whilst not hugely successful, marked the shift as mobile phones became mobile media platforms. This transformation was marked by mobile phones increasingly becoming devices for hosting media (i.e. entertainment portals) and no longer just for communication. The huge expansion of mobile phone games was spearheaded by the launch of Apple's iPhone in 2007- by 2008, more than half of the iPhone's applications being sold were games. As of the end of 2008, iPhone App Store has over 1,500 titles to choose from—from independent games to big global companies such as Electronic Arts. Over this time period—known as the seventh generation (2004–present)—the market for mobile game consoles became a war between Sony PSP and Nintendo DS. Nintendo managed to gain control by its introduction of the haptic console, Nintendo Wii.

Since 2000, the increasing dominance of games within the popular culture imaginary has become evident. This period was also marked by the rise of game studies as a serious discipline and a pivotal lens for analysing contemporary models of digital media literacy in an age of the networked social media outlined earlier. There are various ways in which games can be studied—as a history (social and art/design), text/cultural artefact, socio-technological phenomenon, industry and in terms of the experiences of fans/players/audiences, to name but a few. As a history, games can be discussed from a visual arts perspective (Flanagan 2009), in the context of design (Salen and Zimmerman 2003, 2005), play (Taylor 2006a; Flanagan 2009), cultural studies (Dovey and Kennedy 2006; Swalwell and Wilson 2008), new media (Darley 2000; Jenkins 2006b), formalism (Juul 2005) and social worlds (Taylor 2006a; Boellstorff 2006; Pearce 2009).

Key Texts

Disciplines such as literature, history, computer science, media studies, anthropology, sociology, psychology, education and art/visual culture have all played a part in the rise of game studies, and developments in game cultures have, in turn, informed the directions of analysis and research in some of these areas. In particular, for gaming practitioners, the two anthologies by Katie Salen and Eric Zimmerman, *Rules of Play: Game Design Fundamentals* (2003) and *The Game Design Reader* (2005), have become mini-bibles for students. For theory students, such texts as Simon Egenfeldt Nielsen, Jonas Smith and Susana Tosca's (2008) *Understanding Video Games: The Essential Introduction* (which is very useful for students interested in educational games) and Jon Dovey and Helen Kennedy's (2006) *Game Cultures: Computer Games as New Media* are also very helpful.

One of the key factors in understanding gaming and new media literacy has been the concept of play (Ito et al. 2008; Salen and Zimmerman 2005). Thus, it is not by accident that one of the key game studies debates, ludology, interrogated the notion of play. In the rise of divergent gaming cultures, the notion of play has come under radical revision through game studies. In order to understand play, we need to acknowledge that game studies draws from a rich history of studies around play from disciplines such as anthropology and psychology. But first we need to appreciate how play has been characterized by those specializing in this field. One of the key anthropologists in the area, Brian Sutton-Smith (1997), argued that play activities can be categorized within four 'play' groups: learning, power, fantasy and self. While each of these areas are interrelated, play often draws on one or more of these facets at different times. Observing that 'play can cure children of the hypocrisies of adult life', Sutton-Smith (1997) saw play as an integral part of socialization.

Pioneering play expert Johan Huizinga noted that play shapes, and is shaped by, social rituals. Although part of the socializing process that prepares children for dealing with risks that can be found later in adult life, Huizinga contends that play creates its own 'magic circle' by operating as 'a closed space' that is differentiated 'either materially or ideally ... from the everyday surroundings' (1938: 38–9). The implication is that games afford a type of role-playing situation that can be useful for learning skills for real-world scenarios. Meanwhile, Mary Flanagan differentiates a type of play in terms of the 'critical' (2009). She states that 'critical play' occupies 'play environments and activities that represent one or more questions about aspects of human life' (2009: 6). Flanagan adds, 'Critical play is characterized by a careful examination of social, cultural, political, or even personal themes that function as alternatives to popular play spaces' (2009: 6). This complex notion of play clearly repositions it away from its non-serious connotations.

When we turn to the contributions of games studies, for virtual ethnographer Celia Pearce, online games are best understood in terms of being 'communities of play' rather than 'communities of practice' (2009)—the distinction suggesting that play is a more useful concept for engaging with gaming cultures. In game studies, the ongoing revision of play has provided a rich site for understanding gaming cultures. Indeed, the notion of play (*paidia*) was central in one of the defining moments in game studies, the ludology versus narratology debate noted earlier. There are as many various play cultures as there are game cultures. And yet there is a difference.

As an interdisciplinary area of research drawing on numerous research traditions, the particularities of games and their attendant gaming cultures are marked by some distinctions that separate them from previous media. Despite these synergies with other domestic technologies, as highlighted above, games differ dramatically from other media such as TV in terms of two key attributes—*interactivity* and *simulation*. These unique features led to the development of game studies in the form of the ludology versus narratology debate heralded by three theorists—Gonzalo Frasca, Jesper Juul and Espen Aarseth—in the early 2000s.

LOCATING GAME STUDIES: THE LUDOLOGY VERSUS NARRATOLOGY DEBATE AND BEYOND

Given that game studies draws from a variety of disciplines and media, an important part of defining the field came from trying to differentiate what constituted 'games' as opposed to other media. How are games similar to other media? How are they different? As mentioned, two key features separated games from other media such as TV and film—interactivity and simulation. These two elements, central to gameplay and the various genres and platforms for gaming, became key in the late 1990s as game studies started to forge itself through the ludology debate. In this section we will explore the emergence of this debate and the key players who helped shape this discussion. As we will observe, the deeply flawed debate enabled game studies to differentiate itself from other media traditions and approaches.

Drawing researchers from predominantly literary studies and, to a lesser degree, visual culture, new media and internet studies, the ludology debate explored ways to study the new phenomenon of game studies. In particular, the rise of interactive and online media extended Theodor H. Nelson's 1960s notion of hypertext as a new form of textuality characterized by 'nonsequential writing'—'text that branches out and allows choices to the reader, best read at an interactive screen. As popularly conceived, this is a series of text chunks connected by links that offer the reader different pathways' (Nelson 1980: 0). In 1997, *Cybertext: Perspectives on Ergodic Literature* saw Norwegian scholar Espen Aarseth link hypertext to games, arguing that games such as MUDs (multi-user dungeons) provided new ways for readers and texts to interact. Also in 1997, Janet Murray published *Hamlet on the Holodeck: The Future of Narrative in Cyberspace*—a work that linked contemporary narratives and forms of readership to earlier models found in literature and older media. These two publications were pivotal in shaping what would become the ludology versus narratology debate. It is important to note that both drew from literary studies and this should be acknowledged when understanding how narrative was being conceptualized and how this formed the limitation of such a debate.

Reflection

How do you clarify the difference between narrative and play? One way to consider the differences is if you think of two games where the narrative is very different, but the gameplay is very similar. Or alternatively, you may wish to think of two very similar games in which the gameplay is different.

Narratologists argued that narratives underpin all types of media—from literature and film to games. From the Latin word for 'game' (*ludus*), ludology aimed to establish a discipline that studied game and play activities (Frasca 1999, 2003). Ludology has been ascribed to the scholarly study of game and play activities. Ludologists such as Juul argued that whilst narratives do operate within games, they are almost *incidental* to the specific interactive and simulative dimensions of gameplay. As Juul explained, narratives are not essential to games, and the 'strength' of a game is that it 'doesn't tell stories' (2001: 86). This can be seen in the game genres that have been predominantly defined around player interaction (i.e. first person shooter, role-playing games), rather than in relation to this underlying narrative of the game. But, of course, part of this debate is determined by how loosely one defines a 'narrative'. Indeed, some would argue that it is impossible not to have a narrative—even readers bring their own narratives, their understandings, to abstract texts in order to make sense. We narrativize our life in order to make sense of what can sometimes be quite arbitrary or contingent events.

For key theorist Frasca (1999), one way to understand the difference between ludology and narratology is vis-à-vis *ludus* (game) and *paidia* (play). Traditionally in the context of children, *games* are conceived as having rules while *play* does not.

However, Frasca highlighted how even forms of child's play still have rules and con-ventions (i.e. if one is playing being a bird then one does not run around sounding like a car). Thus, if both *play* and *games* have rules, the difference lies in their result—games define a winner or loser, play does not. Although puzzle and traditional video game genres such as FPSs (first person shooters) had a pre-designated goal, more recently, with the rise of 'sandbox' online social games such as *The Sims*, gameplay increasingly moves towards notions of play rather than being framed in the game modality.

As Frasca argued, computer games are simulations and are thus narratives based on 'forms of the future'—that is, given that games are interactive, the possible nar-rative outcome is determined by the player's moves. In 'Simulation versus Narrative: Introduction to Ludology' (2003), Frasca noted that the simulation and the futural, temporal mode of the user (player) engagement are different for narrative and drama that are based on the past or present. According to Frasca, the interactive simulation model is based on a future-directed modality that will affect the way we view the future of new media forms and digital culture. This proposition provided a healthy debate but was limited in grasping the agency of the player and the way in which previous experiences (both inside and outside the game space) inform how the game text is played and interpreted.

Reflection

Reflect upon how a previous experience, including experiences of playing other games, has affected how you played a new game. For example, think about a driving game and how your experiences of driving—both in-game and non-game spaces—have influenced the way you play and feel about the game.

Alternatively, think about games you did not want to play because you thought it was something similar to what you know, or perhaps because you did not like something about the ideas built into the game. Discuss and compare.

Whilst games are different from traditional narrative, they have been important in reshaping how narrative is conceptualized beyond literary traditions. It is also im-portant to note that ludology did not argue that games had no narrative, but rather that narrative was not central to games. As Frasca noted:

> Ludology can be defined as a discipline that studies games in general, and video-games in particular . . . Ludology does not disdain [the narrative element] of games, but claims they are not held together by a narrative structure. (2003: 212)

Juul was most vehement in his opposition to traditional narrative in the context of games. His precocious master's thesis, 'A Clash Between Game and Narrative' (1999), spearheaded the extremities of the ludology position in which he argued that not only was narrative a minor element in games, but also that games without narrative are some of the best examples of games. It is questionable whether such as concept 'without narrative' is possible, especially given that players apply their own narratives of experience to the game as a sense-making mechanism. While Juul's argument was somewhat over-zealous, it did help to distinguish and secure ludology as the study of games and play. This position was furthered by Juul's *Half-Real: Video Games between Real Rules and Fictional Worlds* (2005), in which he developed some of the emerging formal characteristics informing games and game studies. For Juul, contemporary games were defined by their 'half-real' features. As Juul posited:

> Half-Real refers to the fact that video games are two different things at the same time: video games are real in that they consist of real rules with which players actually interact, and in the winning or losing a game is a real event. However, when winning a game by staying a dragon, the dragon is not a real dragon but a fictional one. To play a video game is therefore to interact with real rules while imagining a fictional world, and a video game is a set of rules as well as a fictional world. (2005: 1)

According to Finnish games researcher, expert and founder of DiGRA (Digital Games Research Association) Frans Mäyrä, there are at least three main areas for methodology within games studies. In his concise *Introduction to Games Studies*, Mäyrä observes:

> The first area is research that principally aims to study games and their structures; the second kind of research is mostly focused on understanding game players and their play behaviours; a third distinctive area involves research game design and development—even if in reality there is much overlap and interaction between and within the research done in all these three main areas. (2008: 156)

In Mäyrä's opinion, these areas draw their methodologies from a few key traditions—humanities, social sciences, design research and game playing (2008: 157–66). The various methodologies, models and approaches deployed within game studies make it an area that is rich in new models of research and analysis. It is not surprising that areas of new media and new technologies such as internet studies are borrowing from lessons learnt in game studies. As one of the most innovative and pioneering areas for studies of interactivity and participation, gaming has provided a platform for contemporary discussions that are, more broadly, about the rise of convergent and social media—as will be outlined in the next chapters. But it is important to recognize that the realm of games—whilst converging with other disciplines and practices—still occupies a particular space and culture that no other areas encompass.

CONCLUSION

This chapter has outlined some of the many ways that game studies, and the histories of games, can be conceptualized. Although this summary has been by no means exhaustive in its approach, it has located various points in the ever-changing body of game studies. Just as its histories, methodologies and traditions are interdisciplinary and multivalent, so too does the future of games look divergent and multidirectional. These possible futures will be discussed throughout the book's chapters. In particular, the impact of networked, social media, as well as the rise of convergent mobile media, are two key areas discussed. This does not mean they are the only areas. Rather, this book provides case studies that can help to understand the complexity of gaming and its attendant cultures in ways that are novel. But in doing so, they are just examples of the broader landscape of game studies and should be acknowledged as such. Moreover, given the ever-changing nature of gaming and new media, this book tries to resist much of the star-gazing hype surrounding the present and the future of games. By understanding where games have come from—its hackivist and domestic ICTs genealogies as well as games studies' multidisciplinary background—we can gain insight into the future of this field. As media cultures increasingly become networked and convergent (across platforms), games are being transformed by what has been called a 'casual revolution' (Juul 2009).

Indeed, with the rise of technological convergence, game genres are hybridizing and proliferating. Many of the traditional genres were defined around gameplay interaction—such as FPS, RPG (role-playing game), MMORG and MMO. Labels such as 'mobile gaming' have grown to no longer encompass just casual, 2D flash puzzle games. From networked multimedia devices such as Nintendo DS and PSP to mobile phones such as iPhones, the types of gameplay, graphics and social online possibilities are expanding. In turn, the rise of urban mobile gaming—which deploys mobile technologies to create gameplay within urban and online spaces—is becoming a viable area for education and experimentation. From 'big games' or 'urban games' (UGs) to location-based mobile games (LBMGs) and hybrid reality games (HRGs), we can find a plethora of new forms for circumnavigating and experiencing urbanity (de Souza e Silva and Hjorth 2009). As we explore in Chapter 6, the relationship between domestic ICTs of gaming and mobile media has led to new ways of conceptualizing the study of ludology—especially within the context of networked, hybrid reality games that blur online and offline worlds.

Every time a new invention or gaming culture emerges, it shapes and shifts how we read the histories of games. But undoubtedly one of the key factors is the rise of gaming into one of the most popular media in the world, along with its deployment in increasingly networked, online environments. The influence of convergent and 'participatory' media (Jenkins 2006b) cannot be underestimated. Indeed, this shift makes a major paradigm change in the way in which media are being used and evaluated from the twentieth-century package media (e.g. TV) to the twenty-first-century conversational media (e.g. social media like YouTube). The rise of gaming, as one of the first interactive media, can be seen as both concurrent to and pivotal in this shift. Such a change, in an age of convergent, networked and participatory media, has unquestionably altered how we view, experience, interact and define new media—an impact that will be discussed in greater detail in the next chapter.

Summary

- There are two main approaches to technology and culture—the substantive, symbolized by technological determinism, and its inverse, the SCOT (social construction of technology), characterized by social constructivism. The former has often been associated with quantitative analysis of media and technologies and has a strong tradition in US-based media and communication, and journalism departments. The latter attempts to capture a more dynamic model of culture by focusing upon the micro and qualitative. There is a third minor approach (not used in games) called the affordances model which explores human-centred design. Three subsets of social constructivism are the domestication approach, virtual ethnography and digital ethnography.

- Like disciplines such as TV and film studies, game studies has adopted various approaches to the study of games. Initially, studies from literature and substantive models dominated, but there has been a move towards more culturally specific, qualitative studies, especially those deploying ethnographic and domestication approaches.

- Whilst there are multiple ways in which to understand the histories of game studies, one of the most defining moments was with the ludology debate of 1999. Whether one takes a position of ludology, narratology or somewhere in between, this debate helped to distinguish the specificities associated with game studies as opposed to other media such as film and TV. Ludology has been ascribed to the scholarly study of game and play activities.

- Games have a history that predates video games, and appreciating this background is useful for understanding the ways in which games can teach and inspire creativity as well as sociality. Exploring older games can help us grasp the importance of games within cultural practices. Moreover, by conceptualizing games within the context of play, we can examine some of the rules and rituals that inform and bind us to particular meanings. One way to examine this is through the analysis of *ludus* (games) and *paidia* (play) more broadly.

3 GAMES AS NEW MEDIA

In the transformation of the global games industry, the possibilities of games as a site for artistic and independent (indie) experimentation and exploration have blossomed. As gaming has become increasingly mainstream, it has at the same time fostered innovative forms of new media practice that merge media arts and game art. This can be witnessed in the mounting divergence and contestation around what constitutes 'digital art', both within and outside of the games industry.

Parallel to the shifting notion of 'new media', gaming, as an art form, has evolved to encompass both interactive and non-interactive genres. Indeed, much of game art precariously straddles the two worlds of new media and contemporary art, occupying a satellite discourse that has the capacity to critique and challenge both worlds. In a period marked by convergence, gaming has merged with, and informed, networked social media. Given these changes, one is left to ask: what is the 'art' of gaming? Game art? What are the differences and overlaps between game art, new media art and contemporary art? How does gaming change how we define and conceptualize new media? And what does the phrase 'new media' mean anyway?

In this chapter we explore some of these questions surrounding gaming as new media. We will see that gaming provides new insights into conceptualizing new media, and vice versa. In order to do so, this chapter will first outline what new media means, followed by a discussion of some of the ways in which new media and gaming have converged. We then move on to some examples of game art such as machinima ('machine cinema', i.e. movies made from game engines).

WHAT'S OLD IS NEW AGAIN: GAMES AND NEW MEDIA

New media calls for a new stage in media theory whose beginnings can be traced back to the revolutionary works of Harold Innis in the 1950s and Marshall McLuhan in the 1960s. To understand the logic of new media, we need to turn to computer science. It is there that we may expect to find the new terms, categories, and operations that characterize media that became programmable. *From media studies, we move to something that can be called 'software studies'—from media theory to software theory.* (Manovich 2001: 48: author's italics)

According to one of the key new media theorists, Lev Manovich, we could learn about new media through computer science. However, what constitutes new media has remained a hotly contested topic. Like game studies, new media is interdisciplinary and draws from a variety of traditions such as sociology, anthropology, computer science, visual culture, media and communication studies, to name but a few. Both game studies and new media can be traced back to roughly the 1960s, with both being highly influenced by technological advancements, especially around ICTs. The realm of Web 2.0 has had a major impact, not only upon how games are played (i.e. increasingly networked such as MMOGs) and shared but also upon how notions of community, collaboration, identity and authorship are conceptualized and practised. This, in turn, has complicated how digital art, game art and new media are defined and where the boundaries exist between the three areas.

Like all new media, game and digital art are perpetually haunted by the ghosts—either through content or philosophies—of older media. This has resulted in a multitude of challenges surrounding the aptitude of the 'new' in new media—indeed, at the turn of the twenty-first century, many theorists were asking, 'what is *new* about new media?' (Flew 2002). This question is particularly pertinent when we look at many new media artists such as Lee Bull, Bruce Nauman or the late Nam June Paik, who deployed often-older technologies to reflect upon contemporary, techno-cultural practice in order to highlight that the 'new' in new media was frequently a misnomer. Pioneering cultural and media theorists such as McLuhan in the 1960s were quick to identify the difference between 'new media' and 'new technology'—an issue that still prevails today. For Australian new media theorist Darren Tofts, the 'new' in new media is not about new technologies per se, but rather about utilizing various technologies (old and new) in order to comment on technology as a social practice. He argues:

> For years I've been railing against the continued use of the term 'new media', arguing that it is no longer a viable category. Video art's grown up. Mixed media's looking decidedly old. Computer and art, new media? Forget it. (Tofts 2004: 23)

This ongoing debate of the deployment of 'new' has dominated much of new media literature. There has been much work conducted around conceptualizing the new as not a break from but rather an extension of media genealogies. Indeed, much of the content and exploration of new media are often those of the earlier technology (McLuhan 1964), as can be seen by the introduction of TV that utilized the genres and modes of address of radio (hence 'radio with pictures'). As media theorists Bolter and Grusin (1999) note, 'remediation' is a reworking of McLuhan's (1964) argument that the content of new technologies is that of previous technologies. Thus new technologies are not seen as 'separate' from culture as a technological determinist may argue, but, rather, new technologies are a recombinant of previous technologies and ideologies.

Reflection

Can you think of examples where relatively 'new' innovation (perhaps a website or application online) makes use of some older elements? Perhaps a website that has the look and feel of an old book? Or perhaps a new game that deploys retro features in its appearance and gameplay?

The introduction of new technologies sees not only the new remediating the earlier media but also vice versa. A key example is the way in which 'online content' industries such as journalism have reworked the significance and role of a hard copy medium like newspapers. The impact of online journalism on offline media such as newspapers and radio is unquestionable and companies such as BBC have been quick to harness cross-platforming services to cater to the different media and associated contexts. For Australian media and communications scholar Terry Flew, like Tofts, there is little 'new' about new media. Rather, new technologies often rehearse and adapt older practices of communication and representation in which 'the lines between "new" and "old" media are hard to draw' (2002: 11). Flew observes:

> The idea of 'new media' captures both the development of unique forms of digital media, and the remaking of more traditional media forms to adopt and adapt to the new media technologies ... The content of new media such as on World Wide Web sites is frequently recombinant—derived from already existing media content developed in other formats (printed text, photographs, films, recorded music, television)—and reproduced in a digital format rather than involving the generation of new content. (2002: 11)

The cyclic nature of technologies has been discussed in the context of the domestic technologies approach in Chapter 2. Indeed, parallels can be made between domestic technologies and new media approaches with both methods teaching, and learning from, the other (Hjorth 2007). Domestic technologies can learn about the artistic dimensions, whilst new media can grow to encompass the sociocultural factors. As Erkki Huhtamo (1997), an influential Finnish theorist in the field of media archaeology, has argued, the cyclical phenomena of media tend to transcend historical contexts, often placating a process of paradoxical re-enactment and re-enchantment with what is deemed as 'new'.

On the one hand, the project of examining new media entails observing the remediated nature of new technologies and thus conceptualizing them in terms of media archaeologies (Huhtamo 1997). On the other hand, new media's re-enactment of earlier technologies is indicative of its domestic technologies tradition that extends and rehearses the processes of precursors such as radio and TV. As Huhtamo observes, media archaeology approaches are 'a way of studying recurring cyclical phenomena that (re)appear and disappear over and over again in media history, somehow seeming to transcend specific historical contexts' (1997: 222). For Finnish media researchers Jussi Parikka and Jaakko Suominen, the procedural nature of media archaeology means that 'new media is always situated within continuous histories of media production, distribution and usage—as part of a longer duration of experience' (2006: n.p.).

Despite the overlaps and synergies between game studies and new media, there is still much more research needed in this area. Each discipline neglects to fully engage and challenge the other, even in the face of the realities of the synergies. This quandary thus becomes one of the major problems with conducting a literature review of the convergences between gaming and new media—depicted most aptly in the debates surrounding game art and digital art; i.e. the terrain is continuously evolving and changing. For example, digital art has two traditions: one specifically within game studies, in which it is viewed as synonymous with game art, and another that links game studies to new media and media arts practice—a phenomenon that is overlooked by many publications in both the game studies and new media literature.

Cultural Studies and Games

One of the key publications to explore the connection between game studies and new media—through the lens of cultural studies—is Dovey and Kennedy's *Game Cultures: Computer Games as New Media* (2006). Much of this comprehensive analysis draws from cultural studies textual history. The one missing element is the deployment of an ethnographic analysis—particularly salient when tackling notions of community, social and creative convergences of games in an age of Web 2.0. Melanie Swalwell and Jason Wilson's anthology *The Pleasures of Computer Games: Essays on Cultural History, Theory and Aesthetics* (2008) provides further insight into game studies via cultural studies and new media lenses. Although drawing from a diversity of approaches—including politics and political economy—it does little to explore the art and gaming connections and issues.

Outside the realm of game studies, there are various new media or visual cultures books that engage with the synergies between game studies, art and new media. Perhaps the most successful engagement with games and art is that of aforementioned artist and game designer Flanagan in her *Critical Play: Radical Game Design* (2009). Spanning the twentieth century, Flanagan's historical study examines alternative games and modes of play deployed by artists and activists. In this wonderful revision of art history through the lens of games and play, Flanagan highlights the important role that artists/activists have played in shaping game culture. By exploring alternative games, *Critical Play* provides new ways of thinking about game design and play—specifically in an avant-garde context.

Flanagan's focus on 'artistic, political, and social critique or intervention' (2009: 2) clearly connects the ongoing underlining relationship between politics, play and games. Drawing upon and inverting the art history canon, Flanagan 'outlines how play has influenced the history of creative exploration of the social and the political' (2009: 2). Contrary to Manovich's call to understand games in terms of computer science, as noted in this section's opening quotation (2001: 48), Flanagan argues the need to 'ground contemporary gaming in creative and aesthetic origins rather than a primarily technological context' (2009: 2) as well as connecting the often-overlooked correlations between games and art. Flanagan's focus upon 'artists using games as a *medium of expression*' (2009: 3: author's italics) has been central in the rise of art, indie and political games. As she notes in *Critical Play*, 'activist approaches to media are important to the study of digital culture precisely because of the media's inherent imbalances' (2009: 13). Through canvassing avant-garde movements such as Surrealism, Dadaism and Fluxus, Flanagan highlights the pivotal role games have played. Thus she explains:

> In the early part of the twentieth century, World War I, scientific developments, and the increasing influences of the writings of Sigmund Freud brought new interest in the unconscious and new experiments with play. Games became an important part of this exploration of the internal life, as games consistently reflect both the culture in which they were created and, through play, the present context as well. Artists have used game as a medium of exploration and expression for over one hundred years. Like art, games tend to reinforce larger cultural influences. Artists, especially those who followed the Surrealist and Fluxus movements, also tend to be especially critical of the ways games are tied to social structures, economies, and ideas of their times. (Flanagan 2009: 88)

Despite such a rich history, few studies have explored in detail this ongoing affair between art, politics and games. Much of the study of games outside the area of game studies or design is from new media—an area that, like games, should acknowledge its history and genealogy within the arts. In Matt Hanson's *The End of*

Celluloid (2004), game studies and new media are viewed as having twin histories. Hanson takes Bolter and Grusin's notion of remediation to reflect upon new media convergences within gaming and film. Hanson's book is useful in thinking about art and popular new media. However, he neglects to fully engage with the politics of creativity and authorship in an age of Web 2.0. Moreover, whilst *The End of Celluloid* is good for pushing game studies beyond the late 1990s 'ludology versus narratology' debate, it does little to acknowledge the specific ways in which game art can challenge new media and contemporary art conventions. Indeed, the volume functions more as a textbook for students of film rather than of game studies.

Egenfeldt Nielsen, Smith and Tosca's *Understanding Video Games: The Essential Introduction* (2008) provides a wonderfully concise and rigorous study of game studies approaches—particularly from the influential Scandinavian context (and specifically the influential Center for Computer Games Research, IT University, Copenhagen). However, the connection between game art, indie gaming and new media is overlooked. Many other edited collections have focused on offering broad theorizations of games as a significant aspect of new media studies (e.g. Waldrip-Fruin and Harrigan's anthology *First Person: New Media as Story, Performance, and Game* [2004]) and on providing collated overviews of key paradigms specific to game studies, but they too have neglected to address the relationship between game art, new media and media arts within this phenomenon.

Salen and Zimmerman's two key texts—*Rules of Play: Game Design Fundamentals* (2003) and *The Game Design Reader* (2005)—undoubtedly occupy a significant place in the hearts and minds of many games graphic design, game studies and digital art students, but not of new media or media arts practitioners and theorists. Salen and Zimmerman's two anthologies have been key textbooks for game artists and designers, working well in unison for games design students. However, for game artists and digital artists, the readings are very design focused and neglect to flesh out the implications and possibilities for game art and new media—both in and outside of games.

While books oriented to game studies seem to not fully engage with new media and media arts, new media textbooks do little to tackle game art. In Andrew Dewdney and Peter Ride's *The New Media Handbook* (2006), we are presented with a wide-ranging book that brings together case studies of new media practices and concepts, theories and histories of new media. Although the book is well grounded in the practical application of new media technology, and is of value to new media practitioners, it does not deal with issues of UCC or game art but instead looks at new media producers as artists or professionals. Martin Lister's *New Media: A Critical Introduction* (2002) is aimed at new media theorists and, whilst it provides a good model for deploying interdisciplinary methodologies and case studies, the book has not dated well (i.e. in its discussion of the virtual). Although it proffers a good historical case study, it is not adequate for someone wanting to know the state of new media now, let alone the connection between game art, new media and media arts.

Manovich's *The Language of New Media* (2001) is a pivotal work from a theorist who is viewed as the godfather of new media studies. His earlier work pioneered the way to think about new media as interrelated to old media, especially in terms of digital art being very much informed by the aura of the analogue (i.e. analogue twentieth-century media like photography and film that can be witnessed in digital art software programs such as Photoshop, and Final Cut Pro). Manovich's *The Language of New Media,* along with Bolter and Grusin's (1999) *Remediation,* set the tone for new media debates at the turn of the millennium. However, given the rise of Web 2.0 and the types of creativity, collaboration and authorship heralded by the UCC revolution, these texts have on going relevance and yet limited application.

In particular, according to Catalan-born, US-based Manuel Castells' (2001) pioneering work on the 'networked society', *The Internet Galaxy: Reflections on the Internet, Business, and Society,* the increasing role of the internet within everyday life has been accompanied by both 'customization' and 'standardization'. Manovich identifies this argument in his summation of new media in which 'new media follows, or actually runs ahead of, a quite different logic of post-industrial society—that of individual customization rather than mass standardization' (2001: 30). With the lack of dialogue between game studies and new media, despite the apparent need for such conversations, it is perhaps in the area of game art that we can explore the prevalent issues.

GAME ART: COLLISIONS BETWEEN NEW MEDIA, GAMES AND CONTEMPORARY ART

Machinima is just a medium, neutral as any other medium. Yet, as any other 'remix' practice, it has an enormous potential that emerges when the existing material is used to convey a meaning that conflicts with its own source. The video becomes a kind of prosthetic narrative, which extends the game's narrative in an unpredictable direction. And that, sometimes, rejects the body it was designed for. From cut-up theory to culture jamming to Nicolas Bourriaud's 'postproduction' model, many great theorists have discussed this potential: what is interesting to me is that, when it comes to games, your appropriation is not only dealing with 'existing cultural material', or with a medium, but with your own life, the life you lived inside the game. (Quaranta 2009: n.p.)

Given the pervasiveness of games as both a cultural practice and artefact, they have become tools of experimentation for such new media groups as UK's Igloo (i.e. Swan Quake) and US artists Cody Arcangel and Brody Condon. Moreover, the integral role that hacking has played in the birth and growth of gaming can be found in the variety of player-driven UCC genres such as machinima and modding.

An Example of Machinima

One of the key features of early machinima—illustrated by the work of machinima guru Rooster Teeth (specifically *Red vs. Blue*, which was adapted from the *Halo* game engine http://www.roosterteeth.com)—is the deployment of postmodern techniques such as irony, intertextuality, pastiche and parody. Rather than performing the typical FPS features of *Halo*, *Red vs. Blue* consists of the characters trying to be sensitive, reflexive, almost new-age types—the antithesis to *Halo's* avatar shoot-'em-up roles. In this way, machinima proffers a space to critique and challenge notions such as violence in games, a fact that is relished by both game players and developers.

So, given this phenomenon of game art, how can we understand gaming if it is framed in terms of new media? In what way does this limit, or expand upon, the potentiality of both realms within twenty-first-century media contexts? And how does it provide a lens for reframing the twentieth-century media practices? As one of the dominant forms of popular culture, games are a fecund site for critiquing consumer culture. As noted earlier in the work of Flanagan (2009), avant-garde art movements have historically seized upon the power of games to find and critique political intervention. As such, there has been a rise in the use of game art as a form of cultural critique.

Reflections

Think about a game you know and how it could be redesigned so the player would think more critically about the themes and genres of the gameplay.

Game art takes two forms—interactive and non-interactive. Some genres draw their techniques from new media art; the others deploy more conventional visual art strategies from disciplines such as sculpture, painting and video art. Machinima constitutes a great deal of the non-interactive form of game art, with much of the field dominated by one of the key features of games—interaction. Examples of machinima artists exploring the boundaries between art and new media include Swedish artist Tobias Bernstrup (http://bernstrup.com/) and American artist Condon. The work of Arcangel (http://www.beigerecords.com/cory/), like Condon's, deploys both the interactive and non-interactive in his installations to explore the nexus between game art, new media and contemporary art. Here, the deployment of installational practice clearly highlights the reference to art and the art context. Arcangel's examples include the hacked (non-interactive) console mods of Mario Brothers, along with an interactive hacking of *Hogan's Alley* in which the aim of the game was transformed into a shooting Andy Warhol exercise (in *I Shot Andy Warhol*). Within the realm of interactive game art, we find in-game invention and performance, site-specific installations and site-relative mods, hardware mods, generative art mods, and real-time performance.

In-game Interventions

In-game interventions involve, as the title suggests, interference in online game spaces in order to upset game norms. One of the key examples of this online intervention genre is *Velvet-Strike* (http://www.opensorcery.net/velvet-strike/) by Anne-Marie Schleiner, Brody Condon and Joan Leandre (an invention within the game *Counter-Strike*). Another example is Eddo Stern's *Runners*—an online intervention where three players run around endlessly in the world of *EverQuest*. Stern's political commentary is strongly voiced in his real-time performances, including *Tekken Torture Tournament* (http://www.c-level.cc/tekken1.html), which 'immerses' the players by giving them electronic shocks every time onscreen damage occurs. In his collaborative work with C-Level (Peter Brinson, Brody Condon, Michael Wilson, Mark Allen, Jessica Hutchins), the tragedy of the Waco massacre is turned into a game space where every player is David Koresh (who was the leader of the cult). Thus, the aim of *Waco Resurrection* (http://waco.c-level.org/) is that all players compete to die and become a martyr.

In the case of Stern, his background of serving in the Israeli army before moving to the United States is enlightening in terms of understanding the motivations behind his work. Having experienced much of the violence and bloodshed first-hand, he is critical of the relationship between media depictions (in game spaces and in the media in general) and the real world itself. This stance was evident in his first machinima in 1999, *Sheik Attack*—a palpable depiction of Israel's bloody history. For Domenico Quaranta (2009), Stern's work is best understood not by the portmanteau of 'machinima', but rather as 'machine animations'. As Quaranta argues, Stern's work functions to break with the magic circle of gameplay and, instead, reminds viewers of the crude realities of violence. This violence is not so much the product of games, as media effects models claim in their depiction of children and violence. Rather, games draw from one of the biggest reservoirs for such material—the real world. Quaranta observes:

> If videogames, through photorealism and immersion, employ considerate effort to make the player forget the machine, Stern returns the machine to the forefront. This could be unpleasant for both gamers and non-gamers, but it's the only way to escape the magic of so-called virtual worlds and start making works that are critical of self. As Eddo Stern, who spent 2,000 hours in *World of Warcraft*, knows quite well, the machine is the only frame between you and the game reality, and the only way to break the illusion is to make it more visible, in your face. So, if his videos can be described as prosthetic narratives, his installations can be described as prosthetic machines; both of them introduce a feeling of alienation, the first using the games in ways they are not meant for and inserting reality into them, the latter bring(s) the games to reality, in a way that makes their fictional constructs apparent. (2009: n.p.)

Many of the site-specific installations (that is, installation in relationship to a specific site or gallery context) replicate game world environments within the art gallery context—operating to challenge and undermine boundaries between new media and contemporary art, game and non-game spaces. Generative and hardware mods deploy the real-time capacities of games to produce works that continuously evolve. Julian Oliver's *ioq3aPaint* (http://julianoliver.com/), a generative painting system modded from the game *Quake III*, is an excellent example of this genre.

Another genre where games, art and new media collide and collaborate is mobile gaming. This will be discussed in detail in Chapter 6 where I outline the various types of mobile gaming, from games on the mobile phone to location-aware gaming. Indeed one of the emerging industries seized upon by developers is the mobile phone game market. Given that most large console games take around two years to develop and complete, and entail a huge investment of money and labour—along with the fact that in many countries the majority have a mobile phone—mobile games are a much easier way for game designers and developers to get games out into the general public. They can also be a site and platform for indie game developers to create alternative content quickly and economically. Moreover, the fact that mobile phones are

---

Indie Games

See http://www.indiegames.com/ and festivals such as *The Annual Independent Games Festival* (http://www.igf.com/) for examples.

all-pervasive means that they can also attract non-traditional gamers—the considerable 'casual' market (Juul 2009). And this 'casual' market consists of predominantly female users with multiple demographic backgrounds.

The global trend towards mobile gaming (and online gaming) has occurred in partnership with the transformation of mobile phones from communication devices to multimedia devices par excellence. With the success of the iPhone in Anglophonic locations such as the United Kingdom, the United States and Australia, games on mobile phones suddenly no longer needed to be 2D flash games. Instead, mobile games can follow the same trajectory as other 3G (mobile phone with internet capacity) and 4G mobile phone locations such as South Korea and Japan in which 3D graphic, networked games can be played. This has meant that the old gaming adage of 'casual versus serious' games blurs as mobile games become no longer simple and online multiplayer games increasingly display more sandbox genre (that is, games with no final goal but focused upon procedural play) characteristics.

Sandbox Games

Sandbox games are said to mirror life insofar as they are open-ended and often flow in non-linear gameplay. It is a genre in which the player can freely roam in an online space. Key examples of sandbox games are *The Sims*, *SimCity* and *Grand Theft Auto*.

In addition, with the growth in Web 2.0 customization, the spaces of gaming and other social sites like SNSs also progressively converge. In locations such as South Korea and China, SNSs like Cyworld minihompy and QQ obfuscate distinctions between game and non-game avatars and customization.

Mobile games have become a vehicle for experimentation around new forms of media literacy and digital storytelling within urban, ubiquitous environments. Utilizing game authoring tools and GPS, location-aware games can deploy various new and old technologies to provide insight and generate interest in public sites such as museums and educational contexts (see Chapter 6 for examples). Here the role of gameplay—where the magic circle of gameplay begins and ends—is complicated by such urban, location-based (LBG) and HRG games. Indeed, such experimental gameplay, whilst far from being profitable as yet, is on the increase as games become progressively promoted as educational and 'hacker' tools (de Souza e Silva and Hjorth 2009). We will discuss this matter in more detail in Chapter 6.

With the move towards cross-platforming and user-driven sandbox media, along with indie gaming, the hybrid possibilities and alternative games are further being explored. In particular, gaming environments can be used as tools to teach as well as contexts for reworking older content for younger generations. Games make great spaces for alternative digital storytelling, a notion that has not been lost on the creative industries. Moreover, these new forms of media practice can be used to excite and generate interest among young people in issues such as heritage.

Digital Storytelling and Heritage

As Theodor G. Wyeld, Brett Leavy and Patrick Crogan (2009) discuss in their paper on the Australian indigenous cultural perspectives of place and space in the *Digital Songlines (DSL)* project, games can be used for new forms of pedagogical content. *DSL*, a 3D computer game, was developed to replicate the modes and mores of Australian Aboriginal spirituality—'Dreamtime'—in which knowledge practices are embedded in movement and through an appreciation of the landscape. Here we see one example of games as a vehicle for providing alternative forms of digital storytelling and as a way of exploring cultural heritage. This work highlights the rise of educational games, which have been joined by politically orientated ones. In Australia we can find *Escape from Woomera* (http://www.escapefromwoomera.org/) and *Street Survivor* (a game based on young homeless people's lives). Internationally, the collaborative work of Frasca in his 'water cooler' games (http://www.bogost.com/watercoolergames/) is exemplary of this developing field. One example is the game *Sept 12* (http://www.newsgaming.com/games/index12.htm), made after the September 11 Twin Towers event, which consists of a village of Muslim civilians and terrorists in which you try to kill terrorists and inevitably kill more civilians who then become terrorists. This provides the game's moral content. The game clearly illustrates that violence plus violence doe not result in peace—demonstrating how games can be political tools for raising social consciousness.

The spirit of hacking and the indie gamer has continued throughout the rise of gaming and its maturation in mainstream culture. As discussed earlier, examples such as modding and machinima highlight the strong drive exhibited by players and the value of their labour practices. Festivals such as *Indie Games Con* (http://www.indiegamescon.com) have been important for bringing together programmers, artists, designers, musicians and produsers to foster independent discussion and debate around the games industry. Indeed, the future of Game 2.0 seems to offer multiple possibilities that could teach us about new forms of media consumption and production in the twenty-first century.

THE ART OF GAMING: CONCLUSIONS ON GAMING AS NEW MEDIA PRACTICE

Convergence is often misunderstood to mean a single solution, but in fact, as these technologies appear, they remediate each other in various ways and in various ratios to produce different devices and practices. Convergence means greater diversity for digital technologies in our culture. It may always be true that, by bringing two or more technologies together, remediation multiplies the possibilities. For the remediation at least spawns one new technique while leaving the two others available for cultural use. (Bolter and Grusin 1999: 225)

With the rise of the twin forces of convergence and divergence across technological, sociocultural, political and economic domains, games have been key players in this mediation phenomenon. As a repository for numerous genealogies from art history to social technologies, games provide a great example of remediation processes. Games—as a set of cultures, practices and communities—offer much room for artistic creativity both on behalf of the general player and the artist's community. And yet, despite this rich and divergent background, the 'art' of gaming, and its relationship to new media, still needs much refinement. As we will explore in the subsequent chapters (especially Chapters 4 and 5), there are various ways in which games provide insight into new ways of conceptualizing new media and vice versa.

This chapter has provided a rudimentary outline of some of the ways in which games have been defined as new media. It has argued, in tune with Flanagan, that there needs to be more of a discourse between art avant-garde history, games and new media. Moreover, games and new media need to appear in more in-depth discussions rather than games just operating as a mere example of new media within new media studies, as well as regarding new media as synonymous with cultural studies approaches within game studies. The chapter has highlighted the fact that there are various modes of analysis—such as the domestication of technology tradition, the social construction of technology (SCOT) and the media archaeology practice in new media—that echo many of the same concerns and use related methods. Within the study of games, such approaches can be synthesized and built upon.

In this chapter we have also identified some of the factors affecting how games and the games industry are being transformed. As the games industry becomes more mainstream and an integral part of global popular culture, so too are we seeing a rise in indie and art games. This phenomenon serves as a reminder of the fact that the history of games, like personal technologies, was forged through hacking (Haddon 1999). As such, games and the role of the player have always been at the forefront of innovative consumer practices. Indeed, the model of the games industry is an example of emerging twenty-first-century models of participatory/conversational media in which relationships between the consumer/user/player and the production process are blurred. As will be discussed in more detail in Chapter 4, games are illustrative of new types of creative labour practices that recruit the social, emotional, affective and creative skills of the player—that is, 'playbour' (Kücklich 2005). These new types of uneven collaboration highlight an ongoing relationship between power and play as the games industry evolves.

One area impacting upon the direction of games is the massive expansion of online social media and the 'wireless leashes' (Qiu 2008) of ICTs. As we will explore in the next chapter, the rise of this media is leading not only to the conscription of new players who at one time would never play games but also to a major revision of game genres. Online multiplayer games, once the prerogative of the hardcore gamer, are now amassing huge enrolments from casual gamers. Meanwhile, mobile games, once regarded as casual and somehow less sophisticated, are, through the growth in location-aware and educational games, also becoming the preoccupation of serious gamers.

Players are becoming part of the game production process—a trend embraced by the industry. The rise of player-driven social narratives in sandbox games, such as *The Sims*, is indicative of the ways in which games are making room for player creativity. The fact that games are coming with their own modding tools, which allow players to customize the game space to make game art such as machinima and upload and share on sites such as YouTube, reflects how the games industry has experienced some changes in how it addresses players. These shifts include not only acknowledging the history of gaming as emerging from hacking but also the realization that providing players with more agency and avenues to participate ultimately feeds back into the popularity of gaming cultures and industry.

Games are indicative of the new roles and 'circuits of culture' (du Gay et al. 1997) whereby older models of consumption and production are revised by the dynamics of twenty-first-century conversational media. This undulation of cultural precepts and practices is particularly apparent in the changing boundaries between fans, players and creative producers in which Toffler's (1980) 'prosumers' (consumer as part of the production process) transform into what Bruns's (2005) calls the 'produser'. The participatory nature of contemporary online media is affording some types of players and produsers with new forms of expression, agency and visibility.

As players become produsers in the world of game cultures, and as discourses such as game art (i.e. machimina) merge and evolve with new media practices, definitions of gaming are being contested. As media consumption and production spaces and practices transform within the first decade of the twenty-first century, gaming provides us with new ways of imaging, constructing and representing our stories, experiences, memories and politics. So too, game worlds can help us connect to both new and older forms of engagement and agency as we partake in the so-called participatory media proffered by contemporary culture. In the next chapter we explore the terrain often defined as 'Web 2.0' and social media that have shifted the course of online games from being the preoccupation of 'hardcore' gamers playing MMOGs to now tapping into former non-game players across the world. From *Mafia Wars* to

Happy Farm, the young and the old are now developing a taste for online gaming as a form of everyday socializing through the convergence of gaming and social media.

Summary

- Games can be understood as a form of new media. However, given the changes in games and game studies, there needs to be a revision of the relationship between games and new media approaches.
- Also, games are the product of art, new media and media arts discourses. They inform, at the same time as they are informed by, these practices. Despite this, an exploration of the relationship between these three areas is still relatively overlooked in the literature.
- Just as the 'new' in new media can be read as a misnomer, so too is it important to understand games within broader media histories. Games, like new media, should be conceptualized as being remediated; that is, there is a cyclic relationship between old and new technologies and content.
- Game art can provide a form of cultural critique, extending this role from avant-garde traditions such as twentieth-century art. There are various forms of game art, both interactive and non-interactive. Some genres include: machinima, in-game invention and performance, site-specific installations and site-relative mods, hardware mods, generative art mods and real-time performance instruments.

4 WEB 2.0, SOCIAL MEDIA AND ONLINE GAMES

Games as popular art forms offer to all an immediate means of participation in the full life of a society, such as no single role or job can offer to any man. (McLuhan 1964: 238)

Important matters concerning present developments in communication, politics and culture centre on the question of participation. This is especially the case with the constellation of technologies, cultures, new concepts of the social, and new forms of politics that are variously referred to as Web 2.0, user created content, social networking systems and social media. (Goggin and Hjorth 2009: 1)

In the rise of 'participatory' and 'networked' social media such as Web 2.0 and online gaming, we are seeing emerging, and yet remediated, forms of new media. Through the rubric of online gaming communities we can begin to reconceptualize what these emergent modes of participation, engagement, creativity and collaboration entail. Beyond all the rhetoric about participation, how are new voices being articulated in online gaming worlds?

The contested notion of 'participation' has become a central tenet in defining contemporary, convergent, online media practice (Jenkins 2006a). It occupies a curious position in the rise of interactive media such as games. What constitutes participation varies greatly, and requires us to unpack notions like engagement and agency. Phenomena such as Web 2.0 and social media have hijacked this term as part of their socio-spatial architecture. Whether we choose to call it Web 2.0 or not, the impact of advancements in the internet—from accessibility to sociability—is immeasurable in affecting not only how games are played and shared (e.g. in increasingly networked contexts such as MMOs) but also how notions of community, collaboration, identity and authorship are conceptualized and practised.

In this chapter we turn to one of the burgeoning areas of gameplay—the online. We consider how players and playing are transforming the online communities they inhabit and what this means in terms of the Web 2.0 rhetoric of participatory, cross-platforming and collaborative media. From the outset, we should acknowledge the inadequacy implied within a term such as 'Web 2.0'. In particular, much of the discussion surrounding Web 2.0 has occupied the realm of techno-cultural fetish with its overdetermined user empowerment rhetoric. As the internet is transformed by the creative social networking potentialities of Web 2.0 localities, the fact of techno-social inequalities and the role of power collectively problematize a 'bottom-up' egalitarian model that participatory online popular culture claims. In this chapter we will explore some of the ways in which games are impacting the social fabric of the online, and how media such as SNSs are recruiting new players, at the same time as converting the types of games played.

Once the preoccupation of 'hardcore' gamers, MMOGs have now become casualized (Juul 2009) and part of the daily diet of many millions of SNS users. In Singapore, Facebook users are now becoming synonymous with *Mafia Wars* players; in China, Renren (formerly Xiaonei) and Kaixin users are constantly keeping an eye on their farms and livestock in *Happy Farm*. Indeed, online games are recruiting the young and the old as key forms of everyday sociality and play. This phenomenon indicates that convergent social media have had a dramatic influence on games and their role in everyday life globally. But behind this rise, we must also consider the types of labour that players/users/produsers are performing as part of broader shifts in consumption/production paradigms. In particular, this chapter aims to consider the increasing role of the player in the production and reproduction of games, and how this type of labour can be conceptualized beyond an unproductive empowerment versus exploitation model.

Indeed, behind the rhetoric of the internet affording new forms of democracy, e-participation, digital storytelling, trans-media and netizen (internet citizen) e-politics, the so-called social networked revolution has far from eroded vertical models of imposed power. New digital divides are no longer between the have and the have-nots, but rather, as Jack Qiu notes in his study of the new Chinese working class, degrees of 'have-less' (2008). No one person, community or culture experiences the internet in the same way, and many fascinating techno-cultures have emerged around 'making-do' practices.

Despite the increasingly mainstream preoccupation with games as part of popular culture, it is not by accident that inequalities (gender, class, generational, ethnicity and context) around technology still prevail. Far from the internet becoming an imaginary space that bears no resemblance to the offline, increasingly, as social media burgeon, we are also met with new forms of online usage that are about offline politics. An example is Dean Chan's (2009) excellent study on in-game protests in China. Regarding Web 2.0's multiple internet localities—which traverse trans-media, trans-cultural and trans-community differences—this chapter will consider new forms of engagement, agency and empowerment, as well as residual modes of exploitation and misuse in online spaces. These issues are no more apparent than in the dynamics of game players playing within online communities.

FROM WEB 1.0 TO 2.0: SOCIALIZING THE INTERNET

Web 2.0 is not a technology, it is an attitude. (O'Reilly 2005: n.p.)

'Web 2.0' is a weird phrase. It began as the name of a conference, but the people organising the conference didn't really know what they meant by it. Mostly they thought it sounded catchy. However, 'Web 2.0' has since taken on a meaning. There are some interesting new trends on the Web, and it's the nature of a phrase like that to adhere to them. (Graham 2006: n.p.)

Nobody really knows what it means … If Web 2.0 for you is blogs and wikis, then that is people to people. But that was what the Web was supposed to be all along. (Berners-Lee 2006: n.p.)

As Tim Berners-Lee's observation aptly signals, the rhetoric behind the so-called Web 2.0 revolution is nothing more than an extension of the internet's intention all along. While for such figureheads as Tim O'Reilly, Web 2.0 has provided new ways to conceive of the internet in terms of economic value (Allen 2009: 17). According to Web 2.0 subscribers, Web 2.0 does not refer to any changes in the internet's architecture; rather, it refers to the types of software employed, and changes at the level of user practices. For Ethan Zuckerman, in his E-tech paper entitled 'Cute Cat Theory of Digital Activism', 'Web 1.0 was invented to allow physicists to share research papers and Web 2.0 was created to allow people to share pictures of cute cats' (2008: n.p.). Whilst this somewhat facetious comment could be read in light of the shift towards experiencing and conceptualizing the internet as a social space, it also highlights that, behind the often-banal activities of users, new forms of affective sharing and communities are emerging. As Zuckermen observes, while Web 2.0 'was designed for mundane uses, it can be extremely powerful in the hands of digital activists, especially those in environments where free speech is limited' (2008: n.p.).

However, we could say that the personalization of technology had been occurring long before Web 2.0, mobile media and the 'cute cat' phenomenon. Indeed, countries such as Japan have excelled globally in their ability to spearhead the 'personal technologies' revolution from the Sony Walkman onwards. Mizuko Ito (2005), for example, argues that it is the notion of the 'personal'—along with pedestrian and portable—has characterized Japanese technologies for decades (Fujimoto 2005; Okada 2005). Part of the success has been their deployment of high-level customization, particularly apparent in what anthropologist Brian McVeigh has called 'techno-cute', that is, the usage of the cute to make 'warm' and 'friendly' the coldness of new technologies (2000). Given this, one could argue that Web 2.0 is somewhat hindered in its understanding of the genealogies of ICTs and especially the internet, particularly from non-Western or Anglophonic points of view (Goggin and McLelland 2009). This sentiment is shared by World Wide Web (WWW) pioneers such as Berners-Lee who define Web 2.0 as little more than a 'piece of jargon' (2006: n.p.)—and he is far from alone.

Whether we think about the internet and its attendant online localities and communities as Web 2.0 or not, its role in everyday life—especially outside of Western or developed cultural contexts—has expanded dramatically. This phenomenon is inseparable from the uptake of online games as a form of global popular culture. For example, South Korea has become a global centre for online gaming, and has simultaneously initiated and expanded into ancillary sectors such as eSports and pro-leagues (players who have cult followings, like car drivers, and who can earn up to US$1 million by competing in publicly staged events). This has been achieved because of the role of techno-national policy that secures it as one of the most broad-banded countries in the world (OECD 2006; West 2007), but it is also a result of the significant role of the community room, *bang*, in ensuring the success of online games (Chee 2005; Hjorth 2006a; Huhh 2009). This example of online gaming will be discussed further in the section 'Game On' below, and in Chapter 7.

So what is Web 2.0? The term has often been attributed to the aforementioned O'Reilly and his *O'Reilly Media Web 2.0 conference* in 2004, wherein he and John Battelle defined Web 2.0 as a platform in which customers play an active role in building one's business. O'Reilly's language and position epitomize the shift of focus away from conceiving the internet as a technological space and, instead, towards it being embedded within the social (and, in O'Reilly's case, with particular focus upon the commercial). Signposting the already emergent movement of UGC, they posited that such activities could be 'harnessed' to create value for businesses. Here we can already start to see that part of the architecture of Web 2.0 is a tension between the creative practices of the users and corporations hijacking this creative labour to reap financial remuneration. However, in the growth of both UGC and UCC, the latter suggests a model for production and consumption of content that disrupts traditional unidirectional flows of media whereby corporations are able to gain hegemony over various forms of capital.

Reflection

What types of Web 2.0 practices do you use—SNSs, online games, etc.? What types of content do you generate (e.g. uploading pictures onto your SNS, building a community in an online game)? How does this content actually affect corporate-produced content?

Having given your practices some thought, do you think arguments such as O'Reilly's are valid and realistic? Why?

More recently, it has been recognized that the term was first deployed by Darcy DiNucci in 1999 to describe a new type of 'fragmentation' that would occur with the rise of ubiquitous media in the form of mobile web devices. DiNucci observes:

> The Web has already become an almost iconic cultural reference—ubiquitous and familiar. We think we know what it is by now. The Web we know now, which loads into a window on our computer screens in essentially static screenfuls, is an embryo of the Web as we will know it in not so many years ... The first glimmerings of Web 2.0 are now beginning to appear, and we can start to see just how that embryo might develop ... The Web will be understood, not as screenfuls of text and graphics but as a transport mechanism, the ether through which interactivity happens. It will still appear on your computer screen, transformed by the video and other dynamic media made possible by the speedy connection technologies now coming down the pike. It will also appear, in different guises, on your TV set (interactive content woven seamlessly into programming and commercials), your car dashboard (maps, yellow pages, and other traveler info), your cell phone (news, stock quotes, flight info), hand-held game machines (linking players with competitors over the Net), maybe even your microwave oven (automatically finding cooking times for the latest products). (1999: n.p.)

In DiNucci's somewhat science fiction tone of future gazing, she is linking Web 2.0 to the rise of ubiquitous computing. In her vision, the spectres of Mark Weiser's (1991) prescient words about the importance of context awareness and embeddedness within the constitution of ubiquitous technologies can be felt. DiNucci's focus is, however, from a designer's point of view rather than, as the term later gets recruited, from a business perspective. Her deployment of the term 'fragmented' to describe the shifts and expansion in hardware devices can be contextualized more broadly in the evolution of the internet by reflecting upon Castells (1996, 2001). In his influential notion of the internet as a 'network society', Castells represents one side of one of the great debates in internet studies—whether it should be conceptualized as a network (Castells 1996) or a series of communities (Arnold 2007).

One of the most important developments in the evolution of the so-called Web 2.0 and debates around network versus communities is the rise of social media in the form of SNS. From Facebook, Xiaonei (now Renren), MySpace, Flikr, YouTube, LinkedIn, Twitter and Cyworld, to mixi and QQ/Tencent, myriad active SNSs continue to burgeon globally. Digital ethnographers such as Ito, danah boyd and Heather Horst have particularly explored new forms of youth-driven sociality within the rise of networked social media (Ito et al. 2008). In this evolution, SNSs have become no longer just the prerogative of Western youth. Rather, the SNS has become part of many people's lives in both developing and developed cultural contexts. In fact, the use of SNSs by the middle-aged is becoming increasingly prevalent. In this phenomenon—encompassing new means of media literacy, creativity and collaboration—the deployment of 'vernacular creativity' (Burgess 2008) in UCC within specific communities becomes apparent.

Social networking literature is replete with references to the role of the SNS in establishing and maintaining—as well as weakening—links. From bridging and bonding ties, cultural movements, learning communities, communities of practice to employment opportunities, civic engagement and social participation, SNSs have been argued to develop a more nuanced, participatory form of democratic involvement. SNSs are both cultural practices *and* cultural artefacts; they are both commercial *and* cultural; they manifest the identity of a network *and* a community; they are present in our online relations *and* structure our offline relations; and they manifest both hierarchical *and* horizontal structures. Whether conceived as a set of networks or communities, SNSs epitomize the tensions between the twin forces identified by Castells as the 'standardization'/'customization' paradox. This is apparent with the concurrent rise of convergence with its opposition, divergence (Jenkins 2006a).

Reflection

Consider the types of SNS practice you participate in. What of the aforementioned characteristics (e.g. new forms of community, democratic practice, civic engagement) do you engage in? If they are 'new', how are they new (i.e. are they different from offline practice or what was done on the internet previously)?

Alternatively, if you do not engage in these types of practice, why not? What are the arguments against them, and are they different or of any use at all?

In the games industry, the tension (both productive and unproductive) around standardization/customization is played out in new forms of labour—what has aptly been defined by Kücklich's aforementioned (introduced in Chapter 2) notion of 'playbour' (2005). For Kücklich, a critique of Web 2.0 and the 'ideology of play'— playbour—has its roots in the hacker culture that accompanied the dotcom bubble, whereby 'you don't actually differentiate between your private life and your working life, because most of your friends work where you work, or in a similar area' (2005, n.p.). Drawing on the example of the growing interrelationships between modders (as discussed in Chapter 2) and the games industry, Küchlich observes:

> The precarious status of modding as a form of unpaid labour is veiled by the perception of modding as a leisure activity, or simply as an extension of play. This draws attention to the fact that in the entertainment industries, the relationship between work and play is changing, leading, as it were, to a hybrid form of 'playbour'. (2005, n.p.)

Kücklich highlights that in an age of convergent and participatory media, intimacy has become a public activity (Berlant 1998). Intimacy—and the associated involvement of the emotional and affective—has become part of the creative UCC practices within networked spaces. As Kücklich's example of the modder illustrates, the modder has to call upon the various forms of labour (social, creative, affective, and emotional) that reflect their community and the associated modes of knowledge. This process is an integral part of the gaming communities—a labour of love that is supported and then turned into profit by the industry. Media such as SNSs and mobile media operate to exploit a type of full-time intimacy in which work and life boundaries blur. This phenomenon can be seen in the rise of multiplayer online games in which the maintenance of the social in a sense of community, along with the deployment of creative and affective labour, is integral to gameplay. Playbour hits a chord in the politics of UCC labour practices; it highlights new forms of emergent affective, emotional, creative and social labour that are being deployed by users/players as they transgress conventional consumption and production divisions through their produser agency (see Chapter 2 for a description of Bruns's 'produser' [2005]).

Reflection

As mentioned, Kücklich's notion of playbour defines the players' various forms of labour (creative, social, affective and emotional) through the example of modding. Can you think of some other examples in which the players' labour is used? Is this tension productive or counter-productive tension between the players and the industry? Why?

Alternatively, Bruns's notion of the 'produser' (producer plus user) was originally defined in the context of blogging. How do the 'produser' practices between bloggers and players differ? How are they similar?

This labour involves a type of investment on behalf of players (involving time, creativity, social and cultural capital) in which remuneration can take various forms, but is rarely financial. Hence, as much as O'Reilly might suggest that Web 2.0 is an attitude and not a technology, it is still very much the case that the profit is often made by the company and not the people making the UCC. While for many, financial rewards are not desired and would be seen to muddy the pleasures of the activities, for those who do seek pathways to cross from produser to producer, the economic distinction remains elusive. It would be too easy to define this situation in terms of exploitation—indeed to focus just upon old models of exploitation versus empowerment would keep the conversation unproductive, and simply overlook some of the complex motivations, agencies and engagements operating around these new UCC practices. One could say that the jury is still out as to how much twenty-first-century media differs, in terms of participation and new produser practices, from twentieth-century models.

For Australian new media theorists Anna Munster and Andrew Murphie (2009), the confusion around rhetoric that has to do with Web 2.0, and the type of attendant agency it affords, is due to the fact that its semantics have been misunderstood. They argue that O'Reilly got it wrong:

> Web 2.0 is not an 'is', or not only this. Web 2.0 is also a verb or, as they taught us in primary school, it's a *doing* word. Here's a list of some web 2.0 things to do: apping, blogging, mapping, mashing, geocaching, tagging, searching, shopping, sharing, socialising and wikkiing. And the list goes on. Yet as the list goes on it becomes apparent that part of what web 2.0 does, while doing all the things on this list and more, is colonise everything in the network. It seems that there is no part of networked thought, activity or life that is not now web 2.0 ... Anything can become or be 2.0 as long as it demonstrates or is affiliated with a certain set of qualities. A list of typical Qualities 2.0 might look something like this: dynamic, participatory, engaged, interoperable, user-centred, open, collectively intelligent and so on. Clearly an 'attitude' can go a long way. (Munster and Murphie 2009: n.p.)

As Munster and Murphie note, '2.0' characteristics include 'participatory', 'dynamic' and 'user-centred'—features that are integral to Kücklich's notion of playbour in modding or gaming. This model of user/produser labour is vital in the reconceptualization of 'gaming cultures' in an age of Web 2.0 and social media. New forms of UCC labour and playbour are transforming gaming cultures—as a set of industries, practices, communities and localities. With the growth in player agency and ancillary discourses (see Chapter 8)—from cosplay (the Japanese-inspired 'costume play' [see Chapters 5 and 8]) to eSports (that is, playing of games competitively [see Chapter 7]) to LAN (local area network) gaming to in-game protests—the politics, modalities and rubrics of gaming cultures and genres are transforming.

One of the ways in which this transformation can be understood is by investigating the rise of 'community' within online gaming cultures in the face of the community versus network paradigm that is prevalent in internet studies. In the following section we explore online gaming and how it is being conceptualized in game studies, particularly in terms of new ethnographic approaches that are shedding light on notions of 'community' in game cultures. Game cultures, like all cultures, are characterized by lived experience, and game studies approaches to online games have seen revisions of the models of ethnography deployed by Web 1.0 research (Turkle 1995; Hine 1998; Bell and Kennedy 2000), virtual ethnography (Mason 1996; Hine 2000; Miller and Slater 2000) and digital ethnography (Wesch 2008). For Christine Hine, virtual ethnography embeds the technology 'within the social relations which make it meaningful' (1998)—in other words, it renders games spaces into lived techno-cultures. Some view the notion of 'virtual' to be too overdetermined in conceptualizing the internet and have sought to coin neologisms to address this burgeoning field of techno-cultural ethnographies. For Celia Pearce, deploying the term 'cyberethnography' (2009) avoids the somewhat prescriptive nature of the 'virtual' that is implied by 'virtual ethnography'. All these different subgenres of ethnography have been useful in the development of methodologies for online gaming. With the rise of networked gaming within SNSs, these methodologies will undoubtedly come under further revision, which, in turn, will impact upon internet studies more generally.

Subgenres of Online Ethnography

There are various forms of online ethnography—'virtual ethnography' (Hine 2000; Miller and Slater 2000), 'online ethnography' (Cornell 1995), 'netnography' (Korinets 2009), 'cyberethnography' (Pearce 2009) and 'digital ethnography' (Wesch 2008). The rise of online gaming has seen the growth in ethnographic approaches in order to understand the associated communities of practice. See T. L. Taylor and Celia Pearce for examples.

In the following discussion, we first briefly sketch the architecture of what constitutes a community in online games and social media. We then consider revisions around notions of 'social capital' (Bourdieu 1979). In the subsequent section we then explore how game studies has deployed virtual ethnography and taken it into new terrains in the pursuit of defining online gaming cultures.

GAME ON: ONLINE GAMING COMMUNITIES

Cultures … [do] not hold still for their portraits. (Clifford and Marcus 1986: 10)

The haunting and persistent image of smoky, dark rooms filled with males sitting like mushrooms in front of their computers playing online games for hours on end is beginning to subside as games become increasingly part of global popular culture. As I will discuss in Chapter 7, online gaming centres such as South Korea have been dramatically transformed with the impact of cross-platformed and social media. Many of the most popular online games, now based in Seoul, are the casual games used by an increasingly female demographic of players. In order to fully comprehend the shifts in online gaming in Seoul, we need to understand the various techno-national, sociocultural and economic factors. Spaces such as *bangs* (rooms) in Korean everyday life—from the PC *bang* (PC/game room) to the DVD *bang*, *noraebang* (music room) and *jimjilbang* (hot room)—play a key role in this uptake (Chee 2005; Hjorth 2006a; Huhh 2009). The *bang* highlights the specific characteristics and importance of 'community' in everyday Korean life. Communities are informed by various factors—locality being one. Let me turn to another example of an online community, this time in China, to highlight the significance of the local within communities of practice.

Techno-nationalism

This conflation between technology and the national gained much currency late in the twentieth century to describe the impacts of technology upon society and vice versa. The concept reflects ideological and regulatory relationships between government policy and industry in the construction of the local. The term has been particularly attributed to the policies and practices of newly industrialized countries (NICs) in Asia like South Korea as well as technological superpowers such as Japan. See Chapter 5 for Japanese and Chapter 7 for South Korean examples.

In China, we can see two very different but interrelated phenomena evolving around online gaming communities—one highly political, the other exceedingly social. On the one hand, there has been the phenomenon of in-game protesting (Chan 2009) that has highlighted the role of the internet as a form of public sphere for political agency (especially apparent in the blogging culture). On the other hand, the rise of simple, childlike games such as *Happy Farm*, played through SNSs such as Xiaonei (now Renren) and Kaixin, have seen millions of young and old participating in their attendant communities of practice.

This latter phenomenon, whilst highly social, also demonstrates changing attitudes to both the online and gaming. The main aim of the SNS game *Happy Farm* uses a quasi–101 model of capitalism whereby the player acquires, raises and sells produce, and one of the key—albeit subversive—factors of the game is to steal other people's produce when they are offline. A slightly damning condemnation of the morals (or lack thereof) of capitalism, it is commonplace to see *Happy Farm* players with the game open on their desktop whilst doing other activities (such as work) to avoid being robbed. Some have been known to set their alarms for the dead of night so that they can go online when everyone is asleep in order to steal. Stealing is part of the gameplay. Those who are stolen from gain 'pious' points. The success of the game in China has very much to do with China's own recent embrace of capitalism. With the backdrop of communism and the works of Karl Marx (vis-à-vis Mao) still part of core educational material, this game reflects a specifically mainland Chinese love for games, and a healthy understanding of the pitfalls of capitalism. Moreover, in locations such as Shanghai, where spiralling real estate has meant that many cannot afford to purchase their own home, *Happy Farm* provides a place for nostalgia in which you can own your own farm and build capital through working hard (synonymous with the amount of time you spend online).

Interestingly, the growing population of users migrating to these types of online games are not the obvious demographic—young students. Rather, it is their parents and even grandparents who are often being taught to use the internet by their children, who are living away from home for study or work (Hjorth 2010). This cross-generational new media literacy emerging in China's increasingly mobile population (i.e. migrating to cities like Shanghai for work or study) sees social media such as QQ (the largest and longest running SNS in China) and online games as helping to alleviate the negative effects of cross-generational class mobility by maintaining kinship relations.

Just as migrant workers—or what have been called the 'floating population' (Wei and Qian 2009)—use new mobile technologies to reinforce social networks and kin relationships in practices called 'communities of the air' (Wei and Qian 2009), the usage of SNSs and online games by university students is marking new forms of media literacy. These new modes of media literacy are striking in the ways in which the students transfer their new media knowledge cross-generationally—helping to bridge the gap as they migrate, via education and IT policies, into new lifestyles (Hjorth 2010). So much so that, often, students in focus groups (June 2009) have noted that their parents play more games than they themselves do, and that they are recruited into playing games to appease their parents and maintain contact. For one female respondent, aged 25, the significant time she spent playing online games such as mah-jong (an online version of a traditional Chinese board game) was because her mother liked to play them with her. She said, 'The more I play, the happier my mother is. I like to make her happy' (Hjorth 2010).

Another female respondent, aged 20, complained that she believed her father to be addicted to playing games. She said, 'He has so much time on his hands, he just wastes it on gaming. Our generation don't have time.' Here we see an interesting role reversal in the stereotypes associated with age and media practice. Rather than it being youth that are 'wasting' their time with new media, instead we see it is the parents and even the grandparents who are doing so. In interviews with parents and their university children, what constituted 'wasting' time online varied greatly between the generations. The students tended to rationalize their online time and were often very mindful of the way in which the online can absorb many hours, whereas the parents and grandparents tended to be less strict and conscious of the time spent online (Hjorth 2010).

In these two very different examples, provided by South Korea and China, we can see how communities of practice are informed by various factors—cultural, generational, linguistic (vernacular in particular), socio-economic and technological. Just as the rise of networked computing has seen the rise of multiple, heterogeneous internets, the role of community and play is also divergent and perpetually contested. Central to the emergence of multiple intimate publics online is Benedict Anderson's notion of 'imagined communities' (1983). This concept can be extended to 'imaging communities' (i.e. UCC practices) online (Hjorth 2009a). These 'imaging' practices involve not just the visual but also the textual and aural whilst deploying the creative, social, affective forms of the user's labour. From mobile (phone) multimedia images to guilds and avatar maintenance, the practices of imaging communities reflect forms of intimacy, labour and creativity, which provide ways for configuring, and intervening in, a nation's and a region's 'imagined community' (Anderson 1983).

Rather than the Asia-Pacific being a sum of Anderson's 'imagined communities'—that is, nations formed through the birth and rise of print capitalism and print media—the rise of networked social media and online gaming is best conceptualized as a series of ongoing, micro 'imaging communities'. These communities, like the media they deploy, span visual, textual and aural media forms, and can encompass scales of sociality from the intimate through to community, regional, national and global interactions. Contrary to Anderson's imagined communities, in which the rise of the nation leads to the demise of the local and vernacular, imaging communities further amplify the local and the colloquial at the same time as they reiterate national sentiments. This can be seen in the types of vernacular being deployed by various guilds to demark their community's symbolic terrain. For example, SNSs Renren and Facebook are almost identical in design, outline and functionality. Except one is in English, the other in Chinese. These linguistic differences reflect sociocultural disparities in their communities.

In the case of imaging communities, each community shares, stores and saves their media in diverse ways, reflecting localized gift giving rituals and practices. The emergence of new forms of gift giving and favour trading and norms of etiquette, social obligation and expectation are all pivotal in understanding online gaming and its attendant forms of shared sociality, creativity and politics. These imaging communities are also deeply implicated in emerging forms of gendered social labour, intimacy and networked sociality.

Conceptualizing Communities

As Pearce (with Artemesia, her online avatar) notes in *Communities of Play: Emergent Cultures in Multiplayer Games and Virtual Worlds* (2009), the notion of 'community' is a contested one. In particular, she argues that many of the issues arise with the open nature of what constitutes 'communities of practice'—a term often linked with research in anthropology, internet studies and computer-mediated communication (CMC). Instead, Pearce deploys the notion of 'communities of play', both as a specific domain of practice as well as a term that does not bear the weight of previous debates, particularly within internet studies. Drawing on German sociologist Ferdinard Tönnies's definition of community (*Gemeinschaft*) as 'an association of individuals with a collective will that is enacted through individual effort' (Pearce 2009: 5), she notes that 'a community of practice is defined as a group of individuals who engage in a process of collective learning and maintain a common identity defined by a shared domain of interest or activity' (Pearce 2009: 5). 'Communities of play' are one form of these 'communities of practice'.

The rise of social media and online gaming can also be understood through changing notions of 'social capital', as briefly discussed in Chapter 2. Coined by Bourdieu in his pioneering *Distinction: A Social Critique of the Judgment of Taste* ([1979]1984), this term was conceived as a way to make sense of how 'taste' was made to feel natural or normal rather than, as it is, constructed. For Bourdieu, capital was a form of 'knowledge', and it was capital that helped produce and naturalize taste. Interviewing 1,200 French people from varying class backgrounds about their tastes in art, music and popular culture, Bourdieu deployed the lens of capital to discuss three significant influences—cultural (informed by education and upbringing), social (community and networks) and economic. These factors, along with the individual's own habitus (the regular patterns of everyday activity), were the contributing elements in determining one's identification with a particular lifestyle niche.

Bourdieu's social capital took on new significance when it was reworked by James Colman (1988) to imply a more ego-centred concept, echoing Ulrich Beck's argument of globalization increasing processes of individualization (Beck and Beck-Gernsheim 2002). It was Robert Putnam, in his savage exposé on the declining role of community and social welfare in the United States entitled *Bowling Alone* (2000), who characterized social capital as socially orientated activity based upon notions of trust and reciprocity.

These theories on social capital have ongoing significance in understanding online gaming communities. Through the model of online gaming communities we can see the need to continuously revise our definitions of social capital. In MMOs we can find one sort of social capital evolving, in SNS online games we can see other examples. Indeed, through the variety of online gaming communities on offer, we can find a plethora of different instances of social capital that highlight the need to revise models provided by Bourdieu and Putnam.

Reflection

What types of social capital are produced in the online games you play? If you play more than one online game, compare and contrast.

Alternatively, if you do not play online games, how do you perceive the difference between social capital in online and offline spaces? Can you think of some online examples (e.g. like the social capital involved in your SNS community)?

TEXT ME: ETHNOGRAPHY AND ONLINE GAMING

With its proliferation of personal web sites, blogs, photo sites, forums, and Web 2.0 applications such as YouTube and MySpace, as well as online games and virtual worlds, the Internet is perhaps the largest stage in human history ... Online games and virtual worlds, with their fantasy narratives and role-playing structures, are arguably the most dramatic instantiation of the digital stage. While all the *real* world may not be a stage, it can be argued that all virtual worlds most definitely are ... Virtual worlds present us with a unique context for ethnographic research because they are inherently performative spaces. Unlike traditional ethnography, one cannot enter into an online game or virtual world without joining in the performance. There is no defined distinction between performer and audience; they are one and the same. (Pearce 2009: 58–9)

In anthropology, the writing up of fieldwork is called ethnography. Since its inception at the beginning of the twentieth century, anthropology has, like notions of culture, come under radical revision. Initially ethnocentric and consisting of predominantly Anglophonic readings of 'other', non-Anglo contexts, by the mid-twentieth century there grew many offshoots that challenged such 'colonial' and 'modernist' views of culture. In particular, the growing focus upon the ethnographer's self-reflexivity, and the role they 'played' in the study (i.e. that perhaps the study of a culture said more about the ethnographer's values and tastes than the actual object of study), resulted in a disciplinary transformation that saw many ethnographers turning to their own cultures, rather than to the 'exotic' other, as a source of meaning. They shifted their focus and analysis onto their own mundane and familiar environment and its atten-dant material cultures. They deployed the premise that social life is a negotiation of meanings and that cultures can be seen as various systems for, and of, meaning, that are shaped by the ethnographer as types of 'knowledges'. One of the key anthropolo-gists to mark the shift towards hyper-reflexive, poststructural approaches to culture was Clifford Geertz. Reading 'culture as a text', Geertz posited the idea that the role of ethnography was to provide a rich, 'thick description' of the field whilst acknowl-edging the embedded role of the ethnographer (1973).

With the burgeoning of technologies as part of everyday life, ethnographers turned their gaze to the symbolic and cultural elements of technologies. They trans-formed conceptions of technologies as merely functional into *sites for cultural practice* as well as *cultural artefacts*. Viewing technologies as part of the everyday vocabulary of material cultures, ethnography promised to bring much insight to the rise of ICTs such as the internet, beyond viewing technologies as merely functional. By emphasizing the sociocultural dimensions of the internet, ethnography rendered it as a series of dynamic cultures, practices and rituals. In these emerging studies, as-sociated with the shift from cybercultures to internet studies, both the internet and ethnography were transformed.

As noted earlier, some of the subgenres consisted of 'online ethnography' (Cornell 1995), 'virtual ethnography' (Hine 2000; Miller and Slater 2000), 'netnography' (Korinets 2009), 'cyberethnography' (Pearce 2009) and 'digital ethnography' (Wesch 2008)—all similar in their perception of the internet as a cultural space, but differing slightly in their specific methods or focus. One of the key ongoing factors, of which ethnographers need to be continuously reflexive, is their role *as participants*. As James Clifford and George Marcus (1986) have observed, there is often a precarious rela-tionship around the ethnographer's participation in a culture, and their ability to maintain analytical focus. Noting that, 'since Malinowski's time, the "method" of participant observation has enacted a delicate balance of subjectivity and objectivity', Clifford and Marcus argue that while the ethnographer's experiences, unquestionably informing their participation and empathy, 'are central', 'they are firmly restrained by the impersonal standards of observation and "objective" distance' (1986: 13).

Thus, it comes as no surprise that the relevance and contribution of ethnography have been concurrent with the call for examining and interrogating the various modes of 'participation' within current debates around Web 2.0, social media and online games. For example, how much can ethnographers immerse themselves before they become unable to successfully analyse the culture in which they are participating? How long should an ethnographer play and participate in an online game community before impartiality gives way to what Bonnie Nardi has defined as 'me-ethnography' (2009)? At what point does reflexivity become nihilism? This ongoing interrogation of methods and reflexivity around the role of participation is central to the prevalence of ethnographic studies in online gaming.

The negotiation of reflexivity and participation is epitomized by Pearce's detailed discussion of her avatar, Artemesia, as 'neither entirely "me", nor entirely "not me," but a *version* of me that only exists in a particular mediated context' (2009: 119). This in-betweenness, or liminality (Turner 1982), occupied by the avatar can be seen as parallelling, and being informed by, the 'performances of everyday life' (Goffman 1959). Here, the notion of identity is viewed as a series of maintained, repeated and regulated actions and performances, and has been discussed by pioneering sociologists such as Erving Goffman. More recently, the concept has been reworked by theorists such as Judith Butler, a poststructuralist who used the notion of performance to conceptualize gender not as innate, but rather as ordered by way of a set of repetitions and regulations—what she called 'gender performativity' (1991). Understanding notions of identity and performance are important if we are to comprehend the role of participation in online gaming cultures. Online ethnography—with its various subsets—has been useful in conceptualizing the communities of practices and social capital involved in online gaming. In the next chapter we will elaborate upon notions of performance and identity politics and further consider its significance in the constitution of gaming.

CONCLUSION: GAME 2.0

In an age of cross-platformed 'participatory media' (Jenkins 2006b) such as Web 2.0, games are providing a variety of alternative and mainstream forms of storytelling. Relationships between players and industry are no longer distinct as modes of playbour become increasingly pervasive. With games moving into centre stage as a dominant form of creative and social media, the demographies of players have dramatically expanded to include young and old, male and female.

Given the impact of Web 2.0 and social media on the changing architecture of online games—especially in terms of the types of access and participation employed by traditionally non-game players, or the shift in genre from hardcore to casual modes of gameplay—this chapter has attempted to shed some light on the often-overused and misunderstood notion of Web 2.0. We have explored some of the many debates surrounding the applicability of 'Web 2.0' as a rubric for current forms of online storytelling, playing, communities and participation. Far from being a fait accompli, definitions and arguments still surround Web 2.0. However, through the lens of online gaming, we can see how Web 2.0—like Web 1.0—is constituted by many diverse cultures, practices and communities that, in turn, bring new understanding to the 'network versus community' debate that has continued to persist.

In this chapter we have also explored the changing nature of what constitutes community, and attendant concepts such as social capital, in an age of social media and online gaming. We have investigated the pivotal role that ethnography has played, not only in online gaming and game studies but also how these studies have informed other disciplines such as internet studies. There are now numerous subgenres of ethnography that all explore online games as cultural practices. Central to the study of online gaming has been the role of participation on behalf of the researcher. These questions about participation, agency and engagement reflect broader concerns that underlie research on social media. In this way, the studies conducted on online gaming can provide much insight into general research on SNSs and emerging techno-cultures. In the next chapter we will continue to think about community and participation, as well as emerging notions of identity and performativity, in the context of the politics of increasing personalization.

Summary

■ Drawing from the tradition of anthropology and its redeployment in internet studies, ethnography has become a dominant model for studying online games. Ethnography conceives of technologies as embedded in social and cultural practice, what can be understood as 'techno-culture'. Through this type of qualitative research, game studies is informing new models of ethnographic practice. Some researchers have coined their own terms—such as cyberethnography (Pearce 2009)—to account for this shift.

■ The debate over whether to conceptualize the internet as a series of networks or communities takes a particular role in online games studies. Online gaming practices, along with SNSs, are revising notions of community as first defined by Tönnies. Communities are informed by various factors such as locality and, like cultures, they evolve and change. Once associated with hardcore gaming, social media have transformed online gaming into a popular activity recruiting many non-traditional players.

■ Another notion being interrogated by online games and social media is the concept of social capital. As Pierre Bourdieu noted, 'capital' is a type of 'knowledge'. Thus when we think about the internet we should think about it in terms of knowledge rather than information. James Colman revised the concept of social capital to refer to social networks. Robert Putnam then used it to discuss the decline of social capital as social welfare in the United States.

5 THE POLITICS OF THE PERSONAL: AVATAR REPRESENTATION, IDENTITY AND BEYOND

The burgeoning of online and networked spaces such as online gaming and social media locales within the everyday is having a dramatic impact on how we are defining the relationship between online and offline spaces and identity. Since science fiction writer William Gibson referred to 'cyberspace' as a 'consensual hallucination' in his pioneering book *Neuromancer* (1984), the way in which the online has been conceptualized, imagined and practised has grown to encompass various communities and networks. As a metaphor for the internet, 'cyberspace' was often used to refer to the digital networked spaces of the online rather than the hardware and software that are also associated with the internet.

Since the debates of the 1990s in which poststructuralist feminists such as Donna Haraway, Sherry Turkle, Allucquère Rosanne Stone, Lisa Nakamura and Judy Wajcman identified the ways in which identity was constructed across online and offline spaces in the face of various inequalities, cyberspace's consensual hallucination has taken on numerous guises. As the internet has developed to become an integral part of everyday life globally, the online has evolved into a complex set of networks and communities that have challenged traditional notions of online/offline relations. One of the ways in which this transformation has occurred can be witnessed in the changing definitions of the political and the personal. In the rise of 'conversational media', the online has become a key space for negotiating these two salient ideas. In some locations, such as South Korea, the techno-cultural and governmental regulations in which users register using their citizen ID—along with one of the best broadband infrastructures globally (OECD)—have resulted in a seamlessness between the user's online and offline identities. Alternatively, in other locations, such as Japan, anonymity and divergence between the online and the offline are emphasized—demonstrated by the popular, anonymous BBS (a precursor to Web 2.0 SNSs) 2ch. These two cultural examples highlight how types of identity and performance reflect the offline context (with its particular cultural, economic and social conditions).

With the growth in the deployment of the internet in everyday life in both developed and developing countries globally, the place of the online is increasingly becoming an important site for defining one's self-expression, identity and community. The relationship between the online and offline is dependent on various micro and macro factors—from techno-national regulations and infrastructure to linguistic, sociocultural and socio-economic issues. For example, what is personal and political in one cultural context may not be viewed the same in another. In locations such as the Philippines, dubbed both the 'SMS' (Pertierra 2007; Rafael 2003) and 'SNS' (Universal McCann Report 2009) capital of the world, the 'people power' lineage and strong Catholicism inform a compelling model of the personal is political in users' deployment of the online—from SNSs such as Twitter and Facebook to games such as *DotA*.

As the implementation of the online expands within everyday offline contexts, notions of online identity, community and expression are changing—a phenomenon directly impacting game spaces. In this chapter we explore some of the ways in which identity and representation are being played out in current online spaces. Building on the discussion in Chapter 4 of Web 2.0, this chapter reflects upon some of the ways people are traversing the online and the offline, and attendant forms of representation such as the avatar. In light of the current two dominant directions for online aesthetics—in one direction, the ongoing significance of Japanese gaming and its cute characterization and avatars in online, networked communities in Web 2.0; in the other direction, the highly simulated realism of computer generated imagery (CGI) evoked by the US games industry—this chapter will focus upon the case study of the cute as occupying a particular role in the rise of personalization techniques and the avatar. In particular, as a persistent and accessible form of representation, cute character culture has been central in the recruitment of non-typical gamers—as witnessed in the rise of casual MMOGs such as *Kart Rider* and *Happy Farm,* and in the dominant visual economy of such 'family' consoles as Wii.

In this chapter, we first discuss some of the ways in which the personal and political are changing, and how this reconfigures the definitions of intimacy—both mediated and unmediated. Issues of intimacy are salient when thinking about the trust and ongoing investment of users, especially in the long-term involvement of players in online multiplayer guilds such as *WoW, StarCraft* or *Lineage,* and, more recently, in the often-unaccounted hours being consumed by the increasing prevalence of casual online games such as *Mafia Wars,* which draw on the player's existing social capital and networks, extending the role of their SNS such as Facebook. We then turn to one of the key repositories for negotiating identity between online and offline worlds, the avatar. We reflect upon how these forms of online personal identity have been defined, the motifs they have generated and how they help to maintain and expand upon what sociologist Goffman calls 'presentations of self' (1959).

Finally, we explore one of the most pervasive examples of personalization within the rise of personal technologies—cute customization. As a pivotal customization tool deployed by the Japanese in personal technologies and gaming cultures since the 1970s, the cute (*kawaii*) extends the 'glocal' (a conflation of 'global' and 'local' [Robertson 1995]) technique by fusing a number of conflicting forces—the new with the old, the familiar with the unfamiliar, the warm with the cold. This process, as noted in Chapter 4, was defined by McVeigh as 'techno-cute'; a process whereby the cute makes the coldness of new technology both warm and familiar (2000). Playing an integral role in the burgeoning of personal technologies in Japan from the 1970s onwards, the techno-cute is no longer the preoccupation of the Japanese. Rather, as demonstrated by games such as *LittleBigPlanet* and gaming consoles such as Nintendo Wii, the salience of cute customization has ensured the greater accessibility and uptake globally of these games and techno-cultures by both the young and the old. The cute, like the notion of the personal, is informed by various factors such as class, age, ethnicity, gender and cultural context. Through the example of cute customization, this chapter provides one way for understanding the politics of representation within the myriad histories and issues that accompany the user and avatar as they move between online and offline spaces.

INTIMATE PUBLICS: THE PERSONAL AND THE POLITICAL

Expressions, representations and 'presentations of self' online are undeniably informed by the user's offline identity and techno-cultural context. In an age where networked, social media is the norm, notions of intimacy and the personal are continuously coming under interrogation—especially through the co-presence of ICTs and online spaces. It is important to recognize that intimacy has always been involved in mediation and that, while face-to-face (f2f) proffers a complex series of sensory experiences that cannot be replicated in mediated environments, mediation plays an important part in maintaining a sense of the intimate and the personal. How we define intimacy is subject to numerous factors on both individual and social levels. Experiences, age, physical circumstances and socio-economic and linguistic factors all come into play in informing our definitions.

Indeed, each culture has its own etiquette and language surrounding intimacy. This is why various games 'make sense' in some cultures and not in others. For Michael Herzfeld, cultural intimacy describes the 'social poetics' of the nation-state and is 'the recognition of those aspects of a cultural identity that are considered a source of external embarrassment but that nevertheless provide insiders with their assurance of common sociality' (1997: 3). An example of 'external embarrassment' in a gaming context might be the acknowledgement by a hardcore gamer of the 'hardcore' stereotype constructed outside the gaming world. Whilst the hardcore gamer would no doubt differ from the 'typecast,' they—and their community of players—would also identify with it. It is through this negotiation between the personal intimacies and the socio-cultural intimacies that a sense of place and identity is constructed.

More recently, with the rise of social media and 'affective' technologies such as mobile phones and networked, social media, intimacy has undergone some changes. Writing before the onset of social media, cultural theorist Lauren Berlant observed that intimacy has taken on new geographies and forms of mobility, most notably as a kind of 'publicness' (1998: 281). As intimacy is negotiated within networked social media, the publicness—along with the continuous, multitasking full-timeness—of intimacy becomes increasingly palpable. These online communities are now *intimate publics*. For Arlie Hochschild, the rise of globalization can be seen through the role of service care industries (epitomized by Filipinos) whereby women, especially from developing contexts, are exploited for their emotional labour in the public sphere (1983, 2000, 2001, 2003). She notes that with the increasing commercialization of human feelings and the intimate, distinctions between work and home have blurred. Kücklich's notion of 'playbour' (2005), introduced in Chapter 2, is indicative of this commercialization of the intimate and the personal by rendering the affective, creative and social labour of the player as leisure, whilst the industry financially profits from such immaterial and material labour.

In the work/life blurring, ICTs are as much the repository as the vehicle (Wajcman et al. 2009). The success of ICTs has undoubtedly been their ability to deploy the affective and personal—so much so that SNS expert Clay Shirky (2008) has argued that the personal is no longer a space between people (whether in public or private realms). Rather, it has been hijacked by technologies. Personal technologies have almost become a tautology. This puts a new spin on the feminist adage of the 'personal is political', especially given that many forms of immaterial labour emerging around ICTs—affective, emotional, social and creative—are traditionally demeaned as women's, or domestic, work. For Spanish sociologist Amparo Lasén (2004), the increasing significance and prevalence of personal technologies—epitomized by the ICT revolution in which games have played a key role—are predicated on their role as 'affective' technologies in which emotional and affective labour become the dominant currencies. In this phenomenon, the role of customization (Castells 1996, 2001; Hjorth 2003a, 2003b) through the vernacular further links emotions with technologies. One of the dominant repositories for the negotiation of the personal and political in online spaces is the avatar.

This reworking of the personal and political can be seen in the rise of personalization—a phenomenon that can be mapped in terms of two, often-conflicting forces: industry and the user. Personalization was initially spearheaded in the development of the personal technologies industry from 1970 onwards. Initial models of personalized technologies pioneered by Japan in the 1970s, such as Game & Watch (Nintendo's precursor to the Game Boy) and the Sony Walkman, were demonstrative of an emerging industry technique in the form of 'glocalization'. While in the 1980s earlier models of personal technologies were characterized by industry-driven personalization, the rise of personal technologies globally can be noted by a shift from personalization being an industry-driven condition to being a subversive practice on the behalf of the user. This is exemplified in Japan by the rise of the high-school pager revolution (Hjorth 2003a, 2003b; Matsuda 2005; Okada 2005).

Glocalization

As a portmanteau of localization and globalization, 'glocalization' (from the Japanese word *dochakuka*, meaning global localization) originally referred to farming techniques. However, by the late 1970s it had been redeployed as a branding technique by business companies such as Sony to fuse global technologies with a sense of the local through providing many more options and choices to the user than had previously been on offer. This was one of the first examples of late-twentieth-century customization that would feature in the rise of personal technologies globally.

'Glocal' was later used in the English-speaking world by sociologist Roland Robertson (1995) to describe the dual and often-conflicting processes of globalization. As a cultural sociologist, Robertson deployed the term to describe global cultural flows. It has since been used by other theorists to describe processes between media, people and commerce.

Today, there is a productive tension between the top-down and bottom-up—industry versus users—processes of personalization. While social media critics such as Shirky (2008) may lament the hijacking of the 'personal' from the realm of people to technologies (epitomized by O'Reilly's [2005] adage of Web 2.0 being an attitude in which businesses recruit users to do the work), others such as Lasén (2004) are less convinced. Rather, they argue that the growing ubiquity of affective technologies marks the ways that the personal is becoming increasingly public—especially through social media like Facebook and Twitter that are often used as broadcast media.

Reflection

How do you 'personalize' your social media? List examples like editing profile and uploading images. Do you think your personalization is the effect of technology, or are you tailoring the media to your 'life-worlds' (Luckmann 1983)? Is personalization for you just a customization of the media channels for your own use, or are you creating something different?

The phenomenon of public intimacy (or what Berlant calls 'the intimate public sphere' [1998]) is acknowledged in the branding of YouTube as a way in which to 'broadcast yourself'. In contrast to twentieth-century models of broadcast media that were 'packaged' to the masses, contemporary broadcast media are characterized by the participatory, conversational role at the level of the local, micro and vernacular. These personalization practices are informed by the local and are, in turn, changing how we view, and participate in, news and the political. Examples include the death of Michael Jackson in June 2009 and the subsequent mass-but-individuated outpouring of emotion that heralded a very different form of public grief and confession than in the 1997 death of Princess Diana and its attendant packaged media.

One Example of Personalized Politics

In times of environmental crisis, such as the floods, typhoons and tsunamis that destroyed many locations in South East Asia in September 2009, social media becomes a site for 'netizen' (internet citizen) reports, as well as a vehicle for mobilizing global support and help. Here avenues for the personal become vernacular media for broadcasting. Picture profiles on SNSs such as Facebook were used to project political images in order to give further visibility to the user's cause. Indeed, we can find numerous examples of implicit and explicit forms of the personal is political being projected in online spaces. In Manila after the typhoon disaster of September 2009, social media like Twitter and YouTube were used to recruit help from abroad as well as keeping people (both abroad and local) abreast of events. Also, with the death of their much-loved former president Corazon Aquino (Cory) only one month earlier in August 2009, social media was deployed for public mourning. In this instance, the personal loss was *political* and the political loss was *personal*. These types of politics—whereby social media is used for the recruitment of civic engagement or social capital—have been evident in MMOG guilds and are, like games in general, becoming increasingly mainstream.

Hence, through a revised notion of the personal is political, we can gain much insight into the emerging and remediated practices that move beyond the empowerment versus exploitation 'participatory' paradigms often repeated in contemporary debates about social media. And one of the dominant symbols of, and vehicles for, negotiating participation between online and offline worlds is the avatar. Avatars have been central in the rise of online gaming, and have played a particular role in the shifting terrains of online spaces. In the next section we explore some of the ways in which the avatar has been defined, particularly in the context of online games. As Pearce notes, as a 'representation of yourself', 'avatars are also a prerequisite to being in a multiplayer world' (2009: 115).

GAMES OF THE SELF: AVATARS AND BEING ONLINE

The definition and role of the avatar have long been debated. As a portal, alter ego or a form of prothesis, the avatar not only operates as an online construction of self but also plays a part in the social fabric of the online game space. Once used to refer to Indian deities, the term 'avatar' was quickly deployed in early discussions of cyberspace. Now, avatars are defined as personal representations used by individuals in digital environments. For game designers and players, avatars are the most accessible and common form of character design. Often, people have multiple avatars that reflect different parts of their personality, different times in their lives, as well as their relationship to the techno-cultural fabric of the online space they inhabit.

Reflection

Do you have an avatar—either in a game or another online space? To what extent do they represent 'you'? To what degree are they 'you and not you' (see Pearce 2009)? What dimensions of self or identity do they express? How?

> Far from being singly a creation of the individual, the avatar is a mechanism for
> social agency, and the player's identity-creation will emerge in a particular social
> context through a set of interactions with a particular group of people. Ava-
> tars do not exist in isolation, and through this intersubjective co-performative
> framework players may discover sides of themselves that may not have avenues
> of expression in the other aspects of their lives, even sides of themselves of which
> they may not previously have been aware. At times, these forms of expression
> can be subversive, in both negative and positive ways. (Pearce 2009: 60)

As Pearce notes, the lens of 'intersubjectivity' is useful in thinking about the construction and maintenance of cultures. The culture of a game provides a particular 'social
construction of shared meanings between designers and players' (Pearce 2009: 52)
that inform what Thomas Luckmann called the 'life-worlds' (1983) of everyday
life. Intersubjectivity is a type of common sense constructed through social interactions and cultural context. For Pearce, the intersection between her and her avatar,
Artemesia, can be seen as what James Gee calls 'the third being' (2003)—'a new
creation that exists between the player and a fictional character whose agency she
controls' (Pearce 2009: 198). This construction and maintenance of the avatar, as an
intersubjective node between the online and player, take a particular route within
MMOGs. As Pearce observes:

> Massively multiplayer games tend to place not only character agency but also
> personality, including appearance, squarely in the hands of the player, given a
> designed and constrained kit of parts. Thus the player constructs her avatar char-
> acter through a combination of representation and improvisational performance
> over time, through play. Avatar development follows its own emergent patterns:
> just as there is a feedback loop between players in a play community, there also
> exists a similar feedback loop *between* the player and his or her avatar ... the
> avatar is an extension of the player's real-life persona, even if it instantiates
> in ways that digress significantly from her real-world personality or life roles.
> (2009: 198)

In this way, avatars are extending the performances of identity found in offline
contexts. Performance in this context is a reference to Butler's notion of 'performativity', as discussed in *Gender Trouble* (1991). For Butler, gender is not natural, but
rather informed and maintained through a series of performances that are regulated
by sociocultural factors. So while gender is viewed as a construction, this does not
mean that one's own gender performativity can be whatever one desires. Rather, it
is informed and structured by the 'life-world' of the individual. For example, norms
of women's behaviour are largely shaped by cultural precepts—what might be considered okay in one context could be viewed as inappropriate in another. The performativity of the avatar is shaped by not only the user's offline identities (gender, age,

ethnicity, class, etc.) but is also informed by the sociocultural fabric of the online world it inhabits.

For T. L. Taylor, avatars are 'intentional bodies' (2003), whilst for Pearce avatars are 'the primary forms of expression provided to players' (2009: 111). Your choice of avatar reflects your social and cultural capital, and informs your gameplay and interaction with the community. A successful avatar will provide the player with a sense of immersion in the game space, in turn playing back into offline notions of identity. This is illustrated by Pearce's choice to 'co-author' her *Communities of Play* with her co-researcher, avatar Artemesia (2009). For Pearce, she and her avatar, Artemesia, create a special relationship in a game space. As Pearce notes:

> When that context, and with it the avatar, ceases to be, that part of the self dies as well. That part of the self, expressed and projected through the avatar in a shared virtual world, is as much a creation of the group as the group is a creation of the individuals within it ... Thus, the avatar identity is what sociologists would call an 'intersubjective accomplishment,' the product of an ongoing and dynamic set of social transactions and feedback—in other words, emergence. (2009: 119)

For Cathy Cleland (2009), in her study of avatars in an age of convergent media, the affective role of the avatar differs between media, techno-cultures and sociocultural contexts. Cleland notes that users have been guided through the rise of social networked media by the avatar—this is why avatars have become even more pervasive in an age of Web 2.0. In Cleland's argument, the emergence of the pervasiveness of networked, online services has provided users with much more agency surrounding their 'impression management'. This optimistic view of online and offline politics and practice suggests that the online can liberate the user through the control of personalization techniques that are not available in their 'real-world' interactions. However, one must be mindful that a user's agency is negotiated through various online and offline 'life-worlds' (Luckmann 1983) in which they may not have total control or ability to fully participate. For Cleland:

> In personal home pages, blogs, and social networking sites like MySpace and Facebook, photographs and text can carefully be selected and edited to present the individual's desired persona within that particular environment ... With avatar identities, even more 'impression management' is possible, as the individual can control and transform his or her visual identity beyond their real-life specificities of age, gender, race, and appearance. In online environments, the individual's real-world physical appearance and physical environment can remain completely hidden 'back-stage' so that only the desired 'front-stage' avatar identity is visible. Individuals can also move seamlessly between different online 'windows' or 'social frames', where they can activate and play out different performative identities. (2009: 221)

Presentations of Self

Erving Goffman in *The Presentation of Self in Everyday Life* (1959) uses the image of the theatre to describe the role of human (specifically social) action. He distinguishes between the performance and front-stage. The social actor chooses all the props, costumes and actions he shows to the audience. Goffman's work is characterized by his emphasis upon the importance of position and situation in every interaction.

In order to understand the shifting function of the avatar, Cleland draws upon Goffman's discussion of performativity through the theatre analogy of 'back-stage' and 'front-stage'. In this analogy, Goffman focuses upon the positionality in terms of performance—a discussion not easily adapted to public/private spaces as indicated by Cleland. However, if we were to describe a positionality of performance for contemporary forms of 'public intimacy', we could argue that we now occupy the 'in between' curtain position in which they are both public and private and yet not fully both notions. This curtain location is undoubtedly the product of the fact that whilst privacy was born, as Shirky (2008) notes, out of inconvenience (that is, it was often too hard to find information on specific people), now, in an age of Web 2.0, knowledge about one's private life is too conveniently accessed—hence the increasing attention given to current issues around privacy and intellectual property.

Living in an age of Web 2.0 means grappling with revised notions of agency, engagement, authorship, collaboration and creativity. One way of understanding these revisions is in terms of the rise of customization characterized by the internet from Web 1.0 to 2.0, discussed in Chapter 4. Castells notes that as the internet becomes global, it is exemplified by two dialectical forces—'standardization' and 'customization' (2001). With the rise of UCC and new avenues and forms of vernacular creativity, the politics of personalization—for which the avatar is a vehicle—continues to be renegotiated.

In an epoch defined by personalization politics, avatars and online representation can be conceptualized in terms of Bourdieu's (1979) discussion of social, cultural and economic capital (or 'knowledges'—see Chapter 4). 'Cute' cultural capital has a particular currency within online spaces, calling on specific affective and emotional responses to the cute (which becomes embedded in the technology) dependent upon the user's 'life-world' context. Within many contemporary techno-cultures and online communities, the role of cute cultural capital as a form of affective and emotional language has become a key phenomenon—both *inside* game space customization (i.e. Nintendo Wii) and *outside* (social networking sites such as Cyworld minihompy)—within broader networked, social media. Far from being mere child's play, the cute has graduated into a dominant theme in the age of Web 2.0. It is integral in the politics of personalization in an age of affective technologies. In order to understand this transformation, we will therefore explore the context of cute cultural capital, within its Japanese genealogy, below.

CUTE@CAPITAL: CUTE CULTURE GENEALOGIES, PLAY AND THE POLITICS OF PERSONALIZATION

One of the defining features in customizing new technologies and gaming spaces is the role of cute aesthetics; throughout the world, the cute is all-pervasive and yet disjunctive in its meanings. The use of cute capital (i.e. cute characters) has long been viewed as a popular mode for both young and old to 'domesticate' (make familiar) new technologies in Japan (Hjorth 2003a, 2003b). This is a phenomenon that does not translate into other contexts such as the United States (Hjorth 2005). By investigating customization techniques (the politics of personalization) as indicative of the sociocultural context, we can understand the relationship between online and offline identity, and associated localized notions of individualism, community and social capital—important factors in the emergence of Web 2.0 and avatar culture.

Customizing encourages users to conceive of technologies as remediated (Bolter and Grusin 1999). Through the cute customization of mobile media and games in the Asia-Pacific region, new technologies are linked to earlier cultural histories and media archaeologies that are distinctive from European or American models. The notion of 'Asia-Pacific' means many things dependent upon the cultural context (Hjorth 2009a; Wilson and Dirlik 1995; Wilson 2000). Each location imagines the Asia-Pacific region differently; so too over time, the contested concept has shifted and changed to encompass many things. In this instance, Asia-Pacific includes Southeast (e.g. the Philippines, Singapore, Indonesia) and Eastern (e.g. China, Japan, South Korea) Asia along with the Oceania (e.g. Australia, New Zealand, Papua New Guinea). As discussed elsewhere, Occidental misinterpretations of the Asia-Pacific's obsession with cute customization, as an affectation of the region's feminine or childish qualities, can be found in online discussions about Asian cute games such as *Kart Rider* (Hjorth 2006a). This can be seen as part of broader processes of postindustrialism in which 'Asia' was deemed to be hyperfeminine (Truong 1999). The *kawaii* (cute) has provided a prominent avenue for women to become interested in gaming—so much so that an alternative history of the rise of women in games could be mapped through *kawaii* culture (Ito 2006). As Ito explains, there is an un-acknowledged and under-theorized history of females entering the games industry, initially as players of *kawaii* games. Ito observes:

> Although Japanese gaming has not been considered central to the girls' gaming movement, the role of Japanese gaming genres in bringing girls into electronic gaming should not be overlooked. Much as *The Sims* has provided a relatively gender-neutral avenue into gaming for women, *Pokémon* broke new ground for girls who subsequently adopted the Game Boy platform and trading card games. (2006: n.p.)

Just as the cute is no longer associated solely with Japan, so too is it no longer solely the preoccupation of females. Increasingly, versions of cute culture grace mobile and gaming spaces, socializing the technologies and contextualizing the new into the media histories of the region. Moreover, once identified as a form of Japanization both within the region and globally, cute culture has taken on various formations in different contexts. In locations such as South Korea, the deployment of the cute is distinctive to the Japanese *kawaii* form. This issue was evidenced in case study interviews with Korean users of the cute online community Cyworld minihompy, in which users claimed that the cute helped socialize the technological space (Hjorth and Kim 2005). From the cute avatar and mini-room (cyber-room) to the pages of customized photos performing and parodying 'cuteness', the cute is an integral part of socializing. This socialization and affective investment are pivotal in the deployment of cute culture—a phenomenon that is integral to the ongoing persistence of the avatar as an important lynchpin between the online and offline. The rise of the *kawaii* represents a specific relationship and engagement between the game space and the gamer, a particular kind of playful identification and affective representation that allows various atypical or casual players to enter into gaming.

To explore the *kawaii* in gaming and avatar politics, the discussion of its genealogy in Japan is unavoidable. However, to read the *kawaii* as merely a form of Japanese production of new media technologies is to undersell the growing complexity of the consumption of *kawaii* culture globally. Moreover, as *kawaii* culture takes on new vernaculars in game design outside Japan, we need to be able to conceptualize the new socio-aesthetic dimensions that are being constituted.

Once associated with child audiences in locations outside of Japan, the growth of *kawaii* culture globally represents a revision of categories such as children and adults beyond the model detailed by Philippe Ariés in *Centuries of Childhood* (1962), whereby childhood was defined as opposite to adulthood with the abolishment of child labour. Indeed, with a global phenomenon such as 'kidults'—adults challenging conventions about age and technology by consuming new media in ways associated with children or teenagers—such categories as *kawaii* cultures could provide much insight into the relationship between age and technology.

Reflection: Cute Character Culture and Games

Can you think of different examples of cute culture in games that are aimed at various age groups? For example, the Wii avatar is cute and is aimed at all ages. What about a game for children? Alternatively, what about a game with cute characters for adults? Consider the differences and similarities in aesthetics, manner, style, content and graphics.

Moreover, *kawaii* culture can be a site in which to explore nostalgia (for an 'imagined' childhood), emotion and localization. As Wai-ming Ng notes, in his eloquent analysis of consuming Japanese games in Hong Kong, 'consuming Japanese games in Hong Kong is not a form of cultural imperialism, because we have witnessed the making of a dialectical nexus between global (Japan) and local (Hong Kong) in terms of ongoing cultural hybridization' (2006: n.p.).

The evolution of the *kawaii* has a particular role in Japan's established technoculture. For Ito et al., the market success of Japanese new technologies—from the Sony Walkman, the Atari games console, the PlayStation, to the 'keitai (mobile phone) IT revolution'—can best be explained by three characteristics: Pedestrian, Personal and Portable (2005). The significance of these three P's is that they transform technological gadgets into sociocultural artefacts by relocating them into the dynamic space of cultural production. Tokyo, in the games world, is arguably the originator of gaming (along with the United States). This has also resulted in further enhancing Japan's 'soft capital' (that is, ideological power), or what Douglas McGray has called 'Gross National Cool' (2002), in which technology has been a key node in Japanese twenty-first-century nationalism (Matsuda 2005; McVeigh 2003)—what is often called 'techno-nationalism' (see Chapter 4 for definition). As a centre for gaming and media technologies deploying innovative 'electronic individualism' (Kogawa 1984), Japan has often provided a 'default sci-fi' (Nakamura 2002) backdrop for Western imaginings of the future. For many a player and maker of games, the consumption of Japan as the 'centre' is the standard rite of passage. As an aesthetic and a philosophy, the role of *kawaii* culture is pivotal in the rise of personalization.

Being a prominent example of the rise of subversive female subcultural languages in the 1970s, *kawaii* culture, in the form of 'kitten writing' (writing that plays with

Japanese characters—especially *hiragana*—and makes them into cute characters), has been linked to female and feminine cultures in Japan (Kinsella 1995), particularly in light of its role in customizing domestic technologies in the form of the 'techno-cute' (McVeigh 2000). Practices such as 'kitten writing' are examples of youths subverting Japanese concepts by intentionally misspelling words in acts of political neologism (Kinsella 1995); these were pivotal in the UCC and amateur *manga* (cartoon) phenomenon of the 1970s in which female produsers (Bruns's 2005 conflation of 'producer' and 'user') featured prominently (Napier 2001). More recently, this practice has been continued in the practice of *keitai shôsetsu* (mobile phone novels). Kitten writings can be seen as earlier examples of *emoji* (emoticons), before they were institutionalized by industry as part of built-in *keitai* customization. The various possibilities for women as players and makers is undoubtedly catered to, and addressed by, the *kawaii* within games cultures. As Ito notes in the case of American girls' deployment of Japanese games, 'from the perspective of style, Japanese media mix content is also distinctive because of the centrality of "*kawaii*" (cute) culture. Hello Kitty and Pikachu are the face of *kawaii* culture overseas' (2006: n.p.).

According to Sharon Kinsella's (1995) groundbreaking research, *kawaii* culture arose as a youth subculture in the 1970s for the purpose of self-expression and rearticulation, and as a reaction to the overarching traditions that were perceived as oppressive. Young adults preferred to stay childlike rather than join the ranks of the corrupt adults (Kinsella 1995). This phenomenon highlighted the way in which 'childhood', as a construct, is conceived and practised in locations such as Japan, with its premature adulthood, in contrast to the West (Ariés 1962; White 1993). The *kawaii*, while stereotyped as a young female's preoccupation, and thus associated with the feminine, was seen as traditionally asexual, that is, a gender without sex. Like the typical consumer, the *shôjo* (young female), the *kawaii* was a female without sexual agency in a society where the *oyaji* (salaryman) was the national symbol after World War II.

As John Whittier Treat (1996) perspicuously notes, the *shôjo* signified a sexually neutral, consumption-focused female. However, as *kawaii* culture married *keitai* scapes and was forged into virtual spaces, the *kawaii's* gender-without-sexual identity took on new characteristics (Hjorth 2003a). Most notably, the *kôgyaru* (fashionable female in her twenties) deployed ironic appropriations of *kawaii* to infuse the gendered commodities with sexual connotations, thus transforming the *kawaii* into a representation of gender *with* sexuality. This was predominantly enacted through *kawaii* customization whereby the cute was no longer deployed in an asexual manner.

Kawaii culture can be viewed as part of the growth in the personalization of new media spaces—a phenomenon discussed by Hirofumi Katsuno and Christine Yano (2002) in their study on the rise of the *kaomoji* (face marks in emoticons [*emoji*]) from early internet usage to pagers and then to *keitai*. Face marks are most commonly known in the form of 'smileys'. However, it is interesting to note that while in English, the smileys are vertical—i.e. :)—in Japanese they are horizontal—i.e. ^_^. This form of vernacular highlights the glocalization processes within online communication. With the proliferation of personalizing modes of signification through mobile e-mail, photo e-mail and the SNS, the growth of what Kinsella described as kitten writing is becoming a leading form of techno-cute customization of technological spaces.

Katsuno and Yano (2002) argue that the *kaomoji* is not a form of post-humanism but rather neo-humanism. Here, Katsuno and Yano highlight that much of the early discussion around internet studies explored post-human approaches. Humanism is a moral philosophy that places humans at the centre, a notion that is refuted by post-humanism (that is, after humanism). Throughout the variety of contested definitions of post-humanism, one thread remains constant—that is, it is the critique of the idea of humanism. Neo-humanism, that is, new humanism, can be seen as a return to humanism after the concept is no longer fixed. In this light, Katsuno and Yano's 'neo-human' (2002) *kaomoji* functions to domesticate, humanize and customize technological spaces, reminding us that technologies are shaped by cultural and social processes. Customization is a process that operates primarily upon emotional levels. One of the enduring features of Japanese customization is its role in creating emotion and affect as a type of warmness in the coolness of technological spaces. For Tomoyuki Okada (2005), this is characterized by the importance of *yasashisa* ('kindness'); for Anne Allison (2003), it is the *yasashii* ('gentle') that makes Japanese character culture so easily consumed both within and outside Japan.

In 'Portable Monsters and Commodity Cuteness; *Pokémon* as Japan's New Global Power' (2003), Allison eloquently outlines the phenomenon of *Pokémon* both in Japan and the United States. In doing so, she not only reinterprets the role of cuteness as a Japanese form of global commodity but also explains how this allows us to see Japan's changing role in the global economy. Taking *Pokémon* as a symbol of 'cuteness' (*kawairashisa*), Allison analyses how this translates for consumers— both Japanese and American. Drawing from focus groups and case studies, along with interview material with the designer of *Pokémon*, Tajiri Satoshi, Allison tries to explain and contextualize this growing commodity culture. Framing her arguments in terms of Japanization and the associated Japan-as-global-power rhetoric, Allison makes a claim for *Pokémon*'s fame as part of general global economic shifts whereby a 'decentering of cultural (entertainment) trends once hegemonised by Euroamerica (and particularly the United States)' becomes prevalent (2003: 394–5).

For Allison, cuteness is not necessarily linked to the cliché of girlishness and the 'feminine'. Cuteness is—as she finds in interviews with both Japanese and US youth consumers of Japanese commodities such as *Pokémon*—deeply embedded in the idea of *yasashii*, or gentleness (2003: 385). *Kawaii* culture is also, according to Allison, 'postmodern' in nature—'it is this polymorphous, open-ended, everyday nature of *Pokémon* that many of its Japanese producers or commentators refer to under the umbrella of "cuteness"' (2003: 384). Just as *kawaii* cultures have given rise to various forms of gender parody and irony (Miller 2006) that reflect new forms of femininity in Japan, this is even more amplified with gaming and *anime* (animation) contexts. The deployment of *kawaii*, for both male and female game characters in such key games as *Final Fantasy*, has afforded many 'flexible' modes of gender performativity (Butler 1991).

As previously discussed, Butler defines gender not as natural but rather as a construction that is continuously maintained through a set of regulations. *Kawaii*-inspired digital art can be viewed as a site for new localized female subjectivities and agencies that, in turn, provide new spaces for young females—both within and outside of Japan. It is not by accident that young women, migrating from game players to produsers to producers, have deployed the *kawaii* through participating in cosplay. For many, this emerging rite of passage allows them to enter, and find a sense of place in, the still–male dominated games industry (Hjorth 2009a). The importance of customizing and personalizing technology continued as the *kawaii* expanded into a broader form of aesthetics, prompting Allison (2003) to define the *kawaii* aesthetic as 'postmodern' (that is, culturally relative, and informed by contested interpretations) by way of its underlying mode of *yasashii* (gentleness) in techno-cute practices.

Cosplay (Costume Play)

Cosplay originated in Japan but has now become a worldwide phenomenon. Drawing from Japanese *manga* (comics), *anime* (animation) and games, cosplay as a form of 'costume play', involves fans spending much time and effort in perfecting their costumes and style. Initially associated with the youth of Japan's Harajuku, cosplay is no longer just a young Japanese subculture. While cosplay is global, many of the famous cosplayers have Japanese young women passionate about their subbcultural identity.

For artist Takashi Murakami, the postmodern—which he defines in terms of the 'superflat' (2000)—differs greatly from Allison's model. Superflat is a postmodern relationship to surface and commodity that Murakami argues has its origins within the traditional *nihon-ga* (Japanese narrative painting) of the seventeenth and eighteenth centuries. For Murakami, the 'postmodern' in Japan differs greatly from its ontology in the West. Murakami's (2000) argument for Japanese modernity parallels Kenichi Fujimoto's (2005) discussion of *keitai* customization and *nagara* mobilism (*nagara*, meaning 'whilst doing something else') as an extension of *shikōkin* ('pleasurable favourites') that can be mapped back centuries to the ongoing significance of tea ceremonies within Japanese life. These are but a few examples of the various ways in which notions such as the 'postmodern'—as with the cute—are contested.

Japanese customization like the *kawaii* can be seen as a form of what Koichi Iwabuchi calls 'odor' (2002). As Iwabuchi notes, the dissemination and indigenization of Japanese popular culture globally 'articulates the universal appeal of Japanese cultural products and the disappearance of any perceptible "Japaneseness"' (2002: 33). The 'odorlessness' of Japanese animation (*anime*) like *Pokémon,* for instance, is underscored by the characteristics of *mukokuseki* (statelessness), which Iwabuchi defines as 'the unembedded expression of race, ethnicity, and culture' that ensures that non-Japanese audiences are yearning for 'an animated, race-less and culture-less, virtual version of "Japan"' (2002: 33). For Iwabuchi, the dissemination of Japanese popular culture globally, specifically in relation to *Pokémon*, ensures an erasure of 'Japaneseness' that is, in itself, a type of 'Japaneseness', a process whereby the *mukokuseki* encapsulates a type of 'unembedded' culture that is undeniably linked to a virtual imaginary of Japan. In other words, Iwabuchi's notion of 'odorlessness' is, in itself, a form of odor.

Pokémon: Selling Japanese Popular Culture Globally

Both *Pokémon* and Hello Kitty have come to symbolize and evoke a notion of 'Japan' globally. Pointing to the history of *kawairashisa* (cuteness) in Japan as a site for the 'imaginary', as well as its link to traditional Japanese culture with its commodification in the 1970s with the likes of Hello Kitty, Anne Allison argues that 'the millennial play product[s] Japan is selling—and using to sell itself—on the popular marketplace of global (kids') culture' connects back to this genealogy (2003: 382). For Koichi Iwabuchi, the *Pokémon* phenomenon can be seen as an example of Japanese technology's global adaptation as 'odorless' (2002). This state of 'odorless' is marked by an 'unembedded' sense of cultural identity globally.

Iwabuchi sees phenomena such as *Pokémon* as selling a global image of Japanese technology as 'odorless' (2002). Iwabuchi's notion of 'odorless'—as a 'flavour' of Japanese cultural products at the level of global consumption—is both evocative and provocative, echoing as it does the essentializing 'Confucius capitalism' of the region at that time. As Arif Dirlik (1995, 1999) noted, 'Confucius capitalism'—that is, a particular adaptation of capitalism deploying 'Asian' morals towards modernization—could be witnessed throughout the region after the 1997 economic crisis. This phenomenon informed Iwabuchi's (2002) argument about the reinvention of Japan and selling Japan both within and outside the region. However, in contrast to Allison's ethnographic focus, Iwabuchi's model focuses on the production and industrial side of the 'circuit' of Japanese 'odorless' culture, and neglected to gain a sense of how consumers/users/players—at a grass roots level—negotiate this 'odorlessness' in everyday life.

As discussed in this section, the genealogy of the cute is far from simple, and is important in understanding some of the current politics of personalization. Far from the prerogative of the young or Asian, the affective nature of cute has been integral in the uptake of games by the mainstream as demonstrated by consoles such as Wii and the rise of convergent social media games like *Happy Farm* and *Mafia Wars*.

THE GAME OF IDENTITY: CONCLUSIONS ON GAMING AND IDENTITY

Through the portal or index of the avatar, we can negotiate relationships between online and offline spaces. How we define avatars—as presentations of and for the self, as well as part of the inflection of the player's 'life-world'—has come under revision. With the burgeoning of the online within everyday life, the avatar plays a crucial role in the meanings between the online and offline. In a period marked by changing definitions of the personal and the political, avatars can help us to understand some of the ways in which these cultural precepts are transforming. Through the case study of one of the dominant global visual economies that has accompanied the growth of games into the mainstream, cute culture can provide some insight into this phenomenon.

We have looked at one of the dominant areas of avatar/character design in the form of cute culture. By contextualizing it within its Japanese genealogy as the *kawaii*, we have considered how its dissemination and re-appropriation have been adapted by globalization. We have noted how the rise of personal technologies in Japan since the 1970s has been, not by accident, concurrent with the development of techno-cute. This can be seen as one form of personalization occurring across both industry and user levels—a process that informs the dynamics between user and industry within contemporary techno-cultures. Current forms of the politics of personalization within games can be seen in the practice of playbour as part of the games circuit of culture.

Despite the ubiquity of the online, and how this is affording emergent forms of identity and community, there is still much to be done in terms of the inequalities surrounding online and offline 'life-worlds' (Luckmann 1983). For Game 2.0 to be as successful in developing new avenues for creativity, authorship and collaboration for a variety of communities and individuals, it needs to make clearer inroads into addressing inequalities. Issues such as gender, age, socio-economic and cultural context all inform the types of gaming cultures emerging; and yet this diversity is still far from mirrored in the industry.

The rise in female game players and ancillary game cultures such as cosplay notwithstanding, there is a big difference between the communities of practice within online gaming, the associated representation and the way in which the industry is addressing this phenomenon. Avatar culture plays a central role in these politics of representation. On the one hand, the customization toolkits have often reinforced stereotypes. On the other hand, players have often deployed conventional identity tropes. But as customization increasingly expands, as demonstrated by the growth in this area in games from Wii to personalized-centric games like *LittleBigPlanet*, along with the player participation (i.e. playbour) and the converging with social media such as SNSs in the case of *Mafia Wars* and *Happy Farm*, we are seeing new forms of the personal and political.

Given that twenty-first-century media have heralded new forms of participatory, conversational media, we are witnessing new notions of the personal and political as the relationship between the online and offline have transformed. These shifts manifest in the games industry—from the growth in genres and subgenres to the expansive way in which avatars are being deployed. Online games have matured from their once 'hardcore' status to accompany these changes. As the internet increasingly becomes ubiquitous and all-pervasive, so too is the way in which online games are played and negotiated, with the offline radically altering. In this chapter we have considered but some of these changes through the lens of the avatar and the attendant visual economy of cute culture in this phenomenon. Another area that has radically transformed how the online and offline are negotiated is that of mobile gaming genres such as location-aware games. As we explore in the next chapter, the rise of this burgeoning field of gaming has impacted not only traditional dichotomies between hardcore and casual games; it also has the potential to transform how we experience, and define, a sense of place both online and offline.

Summary

- As the internet increasingly becomes part of everyday life, the relationship between the online and offline has been transformed.
- The avatar plays an important part in the construction and 'presentations of self' online. The avatar occupies a satellite space in between the player's sense of self and the community it inhabits.
- Concurrent and interrelated to the development of games into one of the dominant forms of popular culture globally has been the growth of social media. This synergy has seen the recruitment of new types of players as well as emerging forms of the personal and the political. In each location, the personal and the political take on different characteristics and definitions.
- One prevalent example of the avatar can be found in cute character culture. Over the course of three decades, the cute has developed its techno-cute aspects to accompany the rise of personal technologies globally. Once the preoccupation of Japanese (in the form of the *kawaii*) young females, cute culture has graduated to become one of the key signifiers in the shift of games to the mainstream.

6 GLAZE CULTURES: URBAN AND LOCATION-AWARE GAMING

> As mobile phones became popular, so too did 'mobile gaming'. Generally when the term 'mobile gaming' is used, it refers to games played on the cell phone screen. However, location awareness and Global Positioning System (GPS) devices embedded on mobiles turn them into interfaces to navigate physical spaces. When the mobile device knows where it is in public space, it might transform not only the relationship between users and places, but also among users themselves. By adding a digital information layer to places, mobile technologies might add value to physical spaces. For example, some location-based services (LBS) might attach "digital information" to specific places, such as the history of a building, or directions to the closest mall, so that if a user with a location-aware cell phone enters the range in which the information was 'attached', he or she can access it with their device. (de Souza e Silva and Hjorth 2009: 602)

Whereas in the last chapter we examined the ways in which modes of online representation—specifically through the discussion of avatars and cute culture—are changing as the internet becomes more pervasive in everyday life, so too are these shifts reflected within the emerging genre of mobile gaming. With the burgeoning of networked and ubiquitous technologies, how we experience a sense of place and locality is being redefined. Today, almost all mobile phones come enabled with GPS—highlighting a new relationship between the online and offline experience of place. Mobile, networked technologies not only transform how we understand place in everyday life, they also remind us that place is more than just physical geographic location. More importantly, places are constructed by an ongoing accumulation of stories, memories and social practices (Massey 1999; Harvey 2001; Soja 1989). This is particularly the case within the realm of urban mobile gaming, which seeks to challenge everyday conventions and routines that shape the cityscape.

Once associated with casual flash-based games (2D graphics) on mobile phones, or early generation mobile consoles such as Game & Watch or Game Boy, mobile games have now grown and developed into a variety of innovative game genres. These genres include urban ('big games'), location-aware (LAMG)/location-based (LBMG) and hybrid reality (HRG) games. For the purpose of clarity in this chapter, 'urban mobile games' refers to all these different and diverse types of games and gaming practices. Through advances in ubiquitous technologies, the rise of urban mobile games has been encouraged by ready access to geo-mobile applications that are available on most new mobile phones (third generation [3G]—known as 'mobile with internet'—onwards). The various types of geo-mobile software provide new ways of experiencing and defining the urban—transforming the familiar and everyday into new and exciting possibilities of play (Jungnickel 2004; de Souza e Silva and Hjorth 2009), as well as rendering the mobile phone user either a player or a game maker.

Apart from the obvious rapid expansion of mobile game applications for networked mobile media like the iPhone, mobile gaming has also expanded into other avenues for exploration and experimentation outside mainstream markets. In particular, location-aware mobile gaming—such as *Pac-Manhattan* (this urban game transforms the streets of New York into the retro 1980s game) and the pioneering work conducted by the UK collaborative group Blast Theory—has seen the emergence of types of games that reflect new possibilities for play between online and offline spaces. LAMG and HRGs highlight that urban spaces, and movement through them, can be inherently playful (de Souza e Silva and Hjorth 2009)—a feature that has often been forgotten in video games (Mäyrä 2003). This oversight has begun to be addressed through the rise of sandbox games (see Chapter 3) that seek to locate the social and community through a sense of place.

In this chapter we explore the various forms of urban mobile gaming, especially the experiential and experimental types such as LBMGs. In order to do so, we begin by outlining some of the ways in which the conceptual models and approaches are being deployed within urban mobile gaming research. We then go on to discuss the different types of urban mobile games, and some of the pioneering examples in these genres. This discussion concludes with a case study of an urban mobile gaming collective, the Korean group Dotplay, which provides us with a detailed example of the way hacking and subversion of place and politics are integral to urban mobile gaming tactics.

CONCEPTUALIZING APPROACHES TO MOBILE URBAN GAMING

As mentioned, apart from the obvious rapid expansion of mobile game applications for networked mobile media like the iPhone, mobile gaming has also expanded into other avenues for exploration and experimentation outside mainstream markets.

In particular, LAMG and HRG has grown—creating new possibilities for play between online and offline spaces. With the ability to negotiate simultaneously various online and offline spaces, along with senses such as the haptic (touch), mobile urban gaming is transforming how we think about gaming, play and mobility.

In this recent and quickly changing field of research, there is a need to conceptualize some of the ways in which urban mobile gaming is being discussed and contextualized. Some approaches have argued that play within urban spaces can best be understood with reference to three historical analogies (de Souza e Silva and Hjorth 2009). The first historical analogy is the transformation from the nineteenth-century formation of Charles Baudelaire's *flâneur* (the wanderer of the modern city) into what Robert Luke (2006) calls the 'phoneur' (the user as part of the informational network flows constituting contemporary urbanity). The *flâneur*, best encapsulated by German philosopher Walter Benjamin's discussion of Baudelaire's painting, has been defined as an important symbol of Paris and modernity as it moved into nineteenth-century urbanity. Thanks to the restructuring of one-third of the small streets of Paris into boulevards by Baron Hausmann, Paris of the nineteenth century took on a new sense of place and space. If the *flâneur* epitomized modernism and the rise of nineteenth-century urbanism, then for Luke (2006), the phoneur is the twenty-first-century extension of this tradition as the icon of modernity.

According to Adriana de Souza e Silva and Larissa Hjorth (2009), a second analogy that we might draw upon to understand gaming in urban space is to make reference to the 1960s Situationist International (SI) subversive activity of the *dérive*. For Guy Débord, *dérive* is a type of drifting through a geographic space that radically revises the usual motives and actions one generally uses whilst moving through urban spaces. This invention was an important strategy to challenge the increasing commercialization Débord viewed within everyday Parisian life. By disrupting naturalized notions of place, the *dérive* rewrites the experience of the city. In an extension of the *dérive*, contemporary urban mobile games can also be viewed as converting and altering the urban and the everyday.

Finally, de Souza e Silva and Hjorth (2009) suggest that we might understand contemporary mobile urban gaming by drawing an analogy with the spirit and practice of the contemporary French wall subculture called Parkour. Invented by David Belle in a revision of martial art and military moves, Parkour sees the city as a series of physical obstacles to be overcome. The art of Parkour—through the act of the traceur (the person doing Parkour)—can be a mode for new ways of experiencing a city and its temporal spatiality. These are the new exercises of the urban that challenge conventional notions of urban cartographies and bounded spaces. The radical re-inscription and rewriting posed by urban mobile games can be seen to parallel and enact Parkour through mobile media technologies. Through contemporary examples of urban games, LBMGs, and HRGs, we can learn much about changing definitions and experiences of the urban, mobility, and a sense of place.

By way of contrast with these three analogies that focus on the physical spaces of the city, other researchers have emphasized the interaction between the senses and media technologies. The title of this chapter—'Glaze Cultures'—was initially coined by Chesher (see Chapter 1). For Chesher (2004), gaming is not an engagement of the gaze, or the glance, but rather somewhere in between—what he characterizes as the 'glaze'. According to John Ellis ([1982]1992), twentieth-century media, like TV or film, were predicated on types of 'packaged media' engagement—in which TV was ordered around the domestic engagement of the 'glance', whereas film deployed the gaze.

Chesher (2004) argues that games call upon an in-between form of sensory experience, *the glaze*. As a conflation of the gaze and the glance, games straddle and remediate older media practices through their interactive, conversational form. Identifying three types of glaze spaces—the glazed over (game immersion), sticky (holding the player within a visceral immersion that is hard to interrupt) and identity-reflective (whereby the player can multitask, slipping between game and other worlds)— Chesher argues these three 'dimensions' of the glaze move beyond a visual orientation, also drawing upon the other senses such as aural (hearing) and haptic (touch). For example, console games are 'sticky'—that is, they hold the player to the screen via a visual link to a virtual space, while also emphasizing the link with a haptic attachment to the hand-controller and peripherals. Casual gamers must deliberately avoid this 'stickiness' so that they are perpetually ready to resume their temporarily interrupted activities. These different modes of engagement come into further question and expansion via urban mobile games. Indeed, there is still much to be elaborated upon within this area of research (de Souza e Silva and Sutko 2009).

Reflection

As mentioned, Chesher defines three types of glaze (game engagement) spaces—the glazed over (game immersion), sticky (holding the player within a visceral immersion that is hard to interrupt) and identity-reflective (whereby the player can multitask, slipping between game and other worlds). Can you think of some examples in which you have engaged in these game states? Do you agree with Chesher's argument that console games are 'sticky' and that casual gamers must avoid this practice? Why?

Alternatively, can you think of examples of 'glazing' in your mobile gaming practices? Or even 'non-mobile' gaming practices? Consider the different hardware/software/space/place configuration at play and the impact upon the gradations of glaze states.

The sensibilities of the *flâneur*, *dérive* Parkour, and the new media practices of the glaze come together in innovative mobile urban games-as-art. Much of the experimentation and exploration of mobile media artwork have taken the form of HRG and LBMG (de Souza e Silva 2004, 2006a, 2006b; Davis 2005) as they challenge the role of co-presence and everyday life, thereby forging questions around the boundaries between the virtual and actual, online and offline, haptic (touch) and cerebral (mind), delay and immediacy (Hjorth 2007, 2009a). Examples include *Pac-Manhattan* (US), Proboscis's *Urban Tapestries* (UK), Blast Theory (UK), aware (FIN), *Mogi game* (JP) and the INP (Interactive and Practice) *Urban Vibe* (SK). In these projects we can gain insight into some of the possibilities of games, which is to challenge our sense of place and play. These projects also highlight the relationship between games studies and new media discourses—a synergy exemplified by the work of aforementioned Mexican new media artist Lazano Hemmer. In the next section, we therefore explore different forms of urban mobile gaming and art, and consider the questions they raise for the development of mobile media gaming, and in turn, what this indicates about the possibilities and limits of games.

THE GAME OF BEING MOBILE: TYPES OF MOBILE GAMES

While the burgeoning of haptic technologies in networked mobile media such as the iPhone may seem recent, they actually have their basis in experimental urban mobile games genres such as LBMG and pervasive gaming. In this section we investigate some of the various types of urban mobile gaming, as well as explore some key examples. As an area often dubbed 'urban games', 'pervasive games' or 'location-aware gaming', mobile games such as LBMGs/LAMGs involve the use of GPS that allows games to be played simultaneously online and offline. As expert Mäyrä (2003) notes, gaming has always involved place and mobility, and yet it is precisely this key feature that is missing in most current video games, especially single player genres. Mäyrä points to the possibilities of pervasive (location-aware) gaming as not only testing our imagination and creativity but also questioning our ideas of what constitutes reality and what it means to be co-present and virtual. By using both online and offline spaces, pervasive games can offer new ways of experiencing place, play and identity. In this section we therefore explore the three main areas of urban mobile games following the model proposed by de Souza e Silva and Hjorth (2009). First, we begin with urban games (big games), then go on to consider LBMGs/LAMGs. The section concludes by considering the implications of HRGs.

Big Games

The notion of 'big games' does not so much relate to the game pieces being excessive in size, but rather has more to do with the role of people and the importance of place in the navigation of co-presence in urban spaces. These projects serve to remind us of the importance of locality and its relationship to practices of co-presence. Co-presence can entail people being in different spaces and states simultaneously—a phenomenon that ICTs help to further extend. The potentiality in contemporary media cultures of 'big games' to expose and comment on the practices of co-presence—traversing virtual and actual, here and there—has gained much attention. Big games highlight some of the key forms of co-presence of everyday life that have been exemplified in mobile media projects such as LAMG. The forms of co-presence include virtual and actual, online and offline, cerebral and haptic, delay and immediacy.

A New York-based game designer who has been involved in such pivotal projects as *Pac-Manhattan*, Lantz (2006) argues that location-aware mobile gaming—or 'big games'—will play a pivotal role in the future of gaming. Big games are, for Lantz, 'large-scale, real-world games that occupy urban streets and other public spaces and combine the richness, complexity, and procedural depth of digital media with physical activity and face-to-face social interaction' (2006: n.p.).

Art, Socio-political Change and Its Impact upon Gaming

As Lantz notes, the precursors to big games were undoubtedly the art movements of the 1960s such as happenings (impromptu art events in public spaces), and the Situationist International (SI) tactics such as *dérive*—discussed in the previous section—that served to interrupt/disrupt everyday practices. He also signposts the significance of the US version of the SI in the form of the New Games Movement. In response to the Vietnam War and the dramatic social and political changes of the 1970s (such as the energy crisis, civil rights and feminism), Stewart Brand and others established the New Games Movement. This movement, paralleled by environmental art projects such as Buckminster Fuller's *World Game*, Robert Smithson's *Spiral Jetty* and Christo's *Valley Curtain*, highlighted the important role that play and games served in political commentary and change.

Alternatively, the development of urban mobile games can be compared to the trend in contemporary art from the 1990s that French curator and critic Nicolas Bourriaud dubbed 'relational aesthetics' (2002). As Bourriaud observed, 'relational aesthetics' dominated the international art scene from the 1990s onwards, and emphasized locality, the de-institutionalization of installation and the 'international', in favour of the vernacular and local. These factors—vernacular and local—are central in the practice of urban mobile games.

Urban games use the city space as the game board by offering multiplayer games that are played out in the streets and city. Three projects that exemplify big games are *B.U.G.* (Big Urban Game), *Pac-Manhattan* and *Shoot me if you can*.

In *B.U.G.*, in 2003, the streets of Minneapolis and St. Paul became the game space. As a five-day event that spanned 200 square miles, *B.U.G.* pitted three teams against one another as they raced conspicuous 25-foot-tall red, yellow and blue in-flatable game pieces across the terrain to the finish line. Their game choices and moves were orchestrated by public decisions registered on the *B.U.G.* website. The aim of *B.U.G.* was for teams to visit all the sites in the 'game space' in the quickest time. The spectacle of the big inflatable game pieces created disruption wherever they went—akin to the *dérive* tactics of SI. People stopped and stared as streets, once full of movement, froze.

A key feature of big games is the way in which the game space interrupts the flows of everyday urban life. Colour, spectacle and movement come together in big games within the urban environment. One of the most infamous urban games was *Pac-Manhattan*. The original *Pac-Man* was a simple puzzle game involving Pac-Man being chased by ghosts whilst trying to eat all the fruit and get to the end. Based in New York in 2004, *Pac-Manhattan* drew on the retro power of *Pac-Man* outside his normal virtual world and placed him in the real-world context of New York urbanity. Consisting of a person dressed as Pac-Man (wearing yellow) trying to avoid being 'eaten' on the streets by other people ('ghosts') dressed in various primary colours and safely making it home, the task of the game was further complicated by the fact that the street runners were actually operating as avatars for virtual players located elsewhere. The avatar runners had walkie-talkies, via which they received directions by players elsewhere who were working from virtual maps (with GPS tracking). The disjuncture between the virtual and the actual game spaces provided great spontane-ity and further extended the sense of play and urban disruption—often involving passing pedestrians. Here we are reminded of parkour and *dérive* tactics in disrupting the urban. As with all the urban games, even when the same game is played again it will never result in the same gameplay; instead, it is at the mercy of the contingencies of place. Each place provides a different template with new temporal, spatial and eth-nographic flavours that mix to transform the gameplay. Each time the game is played it affords another route of urban traffic and pace through a specific social fabric that responds differently each time.

Shoot me if you can, in 2005, was part of a set of mobile games entitled *Urban Vibe* conducted by the Korean interdisciplinary collaborative group INP in Seoul. Or-chestrated through the South Korean new media centre Nabi, *Urban Vibe* presented a variety of games that drew from earlier board games such as chess. One particular project, a chasing game involving camera phones and MMS-ing called *Shoot me if you can*, consisted of two teams pitted against each other, in which the aim was to 'shoot' all the opposing team members without being shot yourself. Drawing from the video game genre FPS and previous offline activities such as paintballing, *Shoot me if you can* replaced the guns with the camera phone, and photos substituted for bullets. Pictures of the opposing team members were then sent back to the master, who decided who won. Drawing from urban game innovators Blast Theory (UK), *Shoot me if you can* consisted of members running around a busy shopping district of Seoul, Myeong-Dong.

While in some ways being a simple appropriation of an FPS game into an urban setting, *Shoot me if you can* reflected some not-so-simple conundrums facing contemporary ICTs. Some photos arrived at the master's phone later than they should due to conflicting telecommunication service providers. Also, human error meant that often delays were caused. In short, *Shoot me if you can* highlights that in an age of immediacy, processes of delay (both intentional and unintentional) are inherent factors. The result was a game in which *both* immediacy and delay were part of the experience, with unexpected moments like 'waiting for immediacy' becoming the poetics of delay. This frustration surrounding technological lag and desires for instantaneity has often played an important part in the gameplay of urban games, and many projects have incorporated this issue as part of the gameplay strategy (Hjorth 2008a). Once again, we are reminded of the disruptive tactics of the *dérive*. Urban mobile games challenge conventions around gaming, and incorporate the relational, contingent and fleeting. This is further extended by the phoneur tactics of LBMGs.

Location-based Mobile Games

Location-based mobile games (LBMGs) are played with cell phones that are equipped with location awareness (i.e. GPS) and internet connection. Like urban games, LBMGs use the urban space as their game space. But unlike urban games, LBMGs add the factor of location-aware interconnectivity between players, as well as the linking of information to places. Although LBMGs might have an online component, the game takes place primarily in the physical space. Players can see each other and/or virtual game elements on their mobile screen. Two examples of LBMGs are *CitiTag* and *CitySneak*.

Organized by the Open University's Knowledge Media Institute (KMi) in Bristol in 2004, *CitiTag* has been described as a wireless location-based multiplayer game, designed to enhance spontaneous social interaction and novel experiences. Extending the old schoolyard 'tag' game, players are equipped with a GPS-WiFi-enabled iPaq Pocket PC to help search out opposing team members to tag. Whilst reading the Pocket PC, players need to negotiate the difference between enemies online and offline. If a player gets tagged, they need a friend to set them free. Sometimes innocent bystanders get tagged because they look like they are in the offline position corresponding with the online coordinates. In this way, *CitiTag*'s gameplay openly acknowledges the confusion and delay between online and offline worlds as part of the game, serving to further blur the boundaries between game space and physical space through the contingencies of urbanity. The role of the phoneur—as part of the informational network of the city—inverts the *flâneur's* role as the wanderer of the physical cityscape. That is, rather than seeing the city as a physical spectacle, the phoneur navigates the city through the informational network. This inversion can also be seen in the game *CitySneak*.

In Robert Sweeny and Ryan Patton's *CitySneak* in 2008, the goal of the game is to navigate the cityscape without being 'seen' by surveillance cameras (Sweeny and Patton 2009). Equipped with a GPS cell phone, players must observe the cameras in the designated game space. If players move within the designated fields of camera visibility, their phone 'controller' notifies them that they have been 'seen', and the game is over. According to Sweeny and Patton, 'CitySneak is designed to enable understanding and navigation of the urban landscape through play' (2008: n.p.). Here, the surveillance experienced by the phoneur in a typical US cityspace-come-informational-network becomes part of an inversion of contemporary urban big brother. HRG further extend this phoneur gameplay of the informational, online networks, fusing with the physical space by deploying 3D virtual worlds.

Hybrid Reality Games

Hybrid reality games (HRGs) draw from both urban games and LBMGs, transforming the city into the game canvas through player interaction in a physical space. However, the key difference is that HRGs have a 3D virtual world component that corresponds with the physical space. The shared game experience among multiple users is what creates the hybrid reality. As urban mobile gaming expert Adriana de Souza e Silva (2009) notes, HRG have three main characteristics: (1) they are mobile, (2) they are multi-user, and (3) they create a new spatial logic in gaming that circumnavigates physical and virtual spaces simultaneously.

One of the pioneering groups in HRGs is the British group Blast Theory, and two of their key projects were *Can you see me now?* and *I like Frank. Can you see me now?* was initiated at The University of Nottingham's Mixed Reality Lab in 2001 and continued to be played—at different times—in various city context such as London, Tokyo and Barcelona until 2008. In what is viewed as the first HRG, street players chase online players who are also running the streets—equipped with a GPS device, a walkie-talkie and a handheld computer, which shows a

2D map of the city and the position of online players. Online players are at remote computer terminals that show 3D representations of the same city space, and use their avatars to show the street players where they are. As de Souza e Silva (2009) suggests, both types of players, although occupying differentiated spaces—one physical, the other virtual—can meet in the same hybrid space created by the game.

In 2004, Blast Theory conducted a residency in Adelaide (Australia) at the Australian Network for Art and Technology (ANAT) that provided a platform for another Blast Theory and Mixed Reality Lab collaboration, *I like Frank*. In order to play, people had to register with Blast Theory for a 60-minute experience as street players. The game included street players (who used the mobile phone interface to navigate the physical cityscape of Adelaide through a 2D onscreen map), as well as online players. Online players could play from anywhere in the world using a home computer, internet connection and web interface to navigate a digital 3D model of Adelaide in which they could locate the position of street players in the 3D world and communicate with them via text messages. The goal of the game for both types of players was to find the character/player named Frank in his office. Guided by the online players, the street players try to find the office. Blast Theory's projects not only show how the urban space can be experienced differently through the coordination of the online but also that these games have an impact on how we conceptualize mobility and play. They use technologies to provide new layers of data and experience to the urban landscape, as well as making us rethink routes and everyday urban practices that might seem too familiar.

Finally, there was *Mogi*, the first commercial HRG. Released in Japan and developed by NewtGames from 2003 to 2006, Mogi deployed mobile phones (*keitai*) equipped with GPS or cellular positioning. Using the player's relative position in physical space to construct a game space in Tokyo, the aim of *Mogi* was to collect virtual creatures and objects, spread out in the city, with the cell phone, in order to form a collection. Players could collect these virtual objects and creatures when they were within 400 meters of them. Additionally, these collected virtual artefacts could be exchanged between players. In 2004, *Mogi* had 1,000 active users who paid just under two dollars a month to subscribe, and whose activities amounted to over 70,000 objects collected and messages sent during the first year. While users could log in anytime, the 'hunt time' generally occurred during the day, from 7.00 a.m. to 6.00 p.m., while the mail and trade peak occurred after 8.00 p.m. (Licoppe and Guillot 2006; Licoppe and Inada 2006). In *Mogi*, the phoneur gameplay tactics help to rediscover the role of community in informing a sense of place.

Having outlined the three main genres of urban mobile gaming, we now turn to the case study of the South Korean group Dotplay. Through this study we can gain an insight into some of the subversive qualities of urban mobile gaming, as well as how this re-enacts older hacking and experimental practices (such as the New Games Movement and *dérive*) that help to found key principles within video games. Here we see that technologies are open to social, linguistic and cultural nuances that shape the ways in which the technologies are used—highlighting that games and play are inevitably linked to, and shaped by, the local.

THE SOFT POWER OF HACKING: A CASE STUDY OF THE SOUTH KOREAN COLLECTIVE DOTPLAY

Heralded for its innovation around ICTs, and as a key example of a twenty-first-century ubiquitous city boasting some of the highest broadband rates in the world (OECD 2006), Seoul has often been held up as an example of the future in the present. With supposedly some of the world's best techno-nationalist (see Chapter 4 for definition) policies (West 2007), Seoul provides a perfect backdrop for exploring the possibilities and limits of urban mobile gaming. This fact was clearly acknowledged and exploited by the Korean collaborative group INP. INP is an interdisciplinary group committed to questioning boundaries around gaming and mobile technologies and practices. Their work is strongly political insofar as they adopt art avant-garde tactics of SI to challenge the importance of new technologies. While their aforementioned *Urban Vibe* project in 2005 clearly engaged with urban mobile gaming tropes through games such as *Shoot me if you can*, it was their latter group

Dotplay which really challenged the boundaries between mobile media and play through political and technological subversion of mobile hardware and software. Dotplay, in a previous incarnation under INP, conducted some of the key urban mobile games in Seoul with the new media centre Nabi in 2005. INP then formed Dotplay as a group focused upon public workshops and community collaboration that sought to challenge conventions around mobile media and games, especially by evoking 'hacktivist' and subversive techniques akin to the *dérive* notion discussed earlier.

Dotplay: An Example of a Media Collective that Deploys Both the Political and Art

From the outset, Dotplay is undoubtedly political. The idea of hacking mobile technologies is specifically political in a country in which mobile technologies have figured greatly in techno-nationalist agendas, and to which the symbol of the mobile phone is a motif for national modernity. The rhetoric of Dotplay's quasi-manifesto (see next box) is reminiscent of avant-garde tactics—a hybrid between Dadaist, Surrealist and SI strategies (see Chapter 3 for discussion of these avant-garde movements in the context of game art). The appropriation of the notion of organization in their quasi-manifesto not only parodies the overtly corporate world of mobile technologies but is also a nod to such pivotal new media groups in South Korea as Young Hae Chang Heavy Industries. There is a long history of art and new media movements (especially avant-garde) in challenging institutional dogma, as discussed in Chapter 3 (also see Flanagan 2009).

In December 2006, INP received a grant from the Arts Council Korea to conduct a 'Mobile Hacking Workshop', and thus Dotplay was begun. By April 2007, a Mobile Technology Workshop was held under the title, *Understanding Mobile Hardware* (conducted by Sungmin Huh from Mobion Inc.); and by May, the group had renamed itself Dotplay. By July, Dotplay was participating in symposia such as *Dislocate 07* (an international symposium on art, technology and locality) and *DAUM YouthVoice Media Conference*. At both the *DAUM conference* and later in the month of August, Dotplay expanded its repertoire via various mobile hacking workshops. Throughout these activities, the mobile phone as both a symbol and a technology comes under scrutiny in the expanding group of Dotplay, especially through the discursive, participatory practice of workshops. Dotplay's series of workshops fused pedagogy with politics, re-energizing the possibilities of play in challenging the role of technology within society.

Dotplay: An Alternative Organization Dedicated to Media Technology

> Dotplay ... is a network of local and international media artists, engineers, cultural researchers, and participants; maintains a critical perspective on media technology by delivering creative alternatives to the mobile culture; explores and challenges through various forms of happenings, participatory workshops, open source manuals, exhibitions, performances, and online publications; prefers process-oriented creation rather than final outcome; welcomes sponsorship and collaboration with art institutions and corporations ... Dotplay is not a research center for media technology, nor mobile contents design firm; Dotplay does not work for art institutions or corporation; Dotplay deliberately displaces utopian fantasies based on technology; Dotplay disagrees with media art that just uses technology or imitates other art. (2007: n.p.)

Dotplay aims to provide an 'ideal and imaginative' Telecom Service in which priority is given to engineering a 'politically correct and culturally free service' rather than a 'traditional emphasis on economic efficiency (investment wise)' (2007: n.p.). For Dotplay, it is important to recognize, deviate from and revolt against the capitalist and 'technocentric fantasy' (2007: n.p.) by defining new infrastructures—different kinds of services for different kinds of users. Working towards an official opening and beta service by 2009, Dotplay's group is growing as a creative commons for mobile media. The ideas presented in the workshop are the business strategy of Dotplay Telecom.

Moreover, Dotplay is a great example of teasing out one of the central tenets of new media debates—what role technology should play in constructions of society, culture and art. Dotplay is a network of media artists, technologists and cultural researchers, and forms the virtual (fictional) mobile telecommunication organization known as Dotplay Telecom. The core members—Yangachi, Jaekyung Shim, Miyoun Kim, Soni Park, Saye Min, Hyeri Rhee and Taeyoon Choi—all provide real free services. The members are both pragmatic and yet ironic in their development of DIY workshops for mobile hackers. The idea of users as hackers plays on the so-called UCC revolution—of which South Korea is supposed to be one of the world leaders. According to the website, 'Dotplay Workshop provides access to hack mobile phones, physically, and conceptually to intervene into mobile device, environment in a physical, social, cultural, political manner in order to creatively re-intervene the mobile' (2007: n.p.).

As one of the most intimate and personal technologies, it is often hard to construct a critical space in which people can reflect upon the role of mobile technologies in everyday life. It is often easier to return to older, remediated technologies such as the landline in order to comment on communications and media via new technologies. Arguably, a new technology becomes fully democratized when it witnesses its first breed of 'hackivists' challenging corporate dogma. As we explored in Chapter 2, the history of gaming, like that of computers, has been one innovated by hackers and hobbyists. As we have seen in this chapter, the importance of hacking and subversion as a political voice for the people was also an important part of SI and the New Games Movement and can be seen, more recently, in the culture jamming work of new media groups such as e-toys. The much publicized example of hacking as a voice for the people against corporations saw the new media group 'e-toys' take on the corporate giant E-toys when the company tried to shut down e-toys' website. This led to a demonstration of people power jamming the E-toys website at the busiest time of year (Christmas), leading to the demise and bankruptcy of the company.

While much of the rhetoric around UCC and mobile convergent technologies seems to suggest media for 'the people', the reality of this 'democratic' media—comparable to the webcam revolution—is notably different in practice. Examples of 'people power' are repeated constantly—from the camera journalists of the London bombings to the political texting revolutions of Korea (Kim 2003) and the Philippines (Rafael 2003).Yet the realities of everyday life and growing precarious labour, along with trends towards 'full-time intimacy', provide little space for mobile media literacy and political action. In the case of South Korea, hacking mobile phones—and particularly holding workshops through which to teach budding hackivists—sends not only a symbolic message. The action also has practical implications that could have disastrous outcomes in terms of accidentally making contact with North Korea (an offense that could lead to court-marshal). From transformer-like toys to sculptures (see Figure 6.1), the works of Dotplay demonstrate that there is much more to mobile media, as new media, than is currently being deployed. For Dotplay, the 'end-user' is as yet far from the user-agency idea of a prosumer or 'produser' (Bruns 2005) as discussed in Chapter 4. Rather, telecommunication companies still exert a trickle-down model of industry. For Dotplay, it is important to reinstate a bubble-up, grass-roots model for mobile media as new media.

Dotplay reconnects new media to its important socio-political dimensions—reminding us that technology is as much cultural and social, and thus political, as it is a functional tool. They remind us of earlier practices such as the Surrealism and SI in their subversion of the 'normal' functions of objects and spaces. Dotplay demonstrates that far from the mobile (phone) setting us free, it has further entrapped us into various erosions between work and leisure. But, maybe, through setting the mobile technology free we can, in turn, become more mobile by mobilizing new media.

Figure 6.1: Dotplay workshop 2007. Permission Dotplay 2007.

Through projects such as Dotplay, we can further explore the dimensions of new media as well as investigating the overlap between social, political and creative labour practices so prevalent in contemporary life, as discussed in Chapter 4. As Dotplay exemplifies, the politics of playing with mobile media—from the software and hardware to the use of mobility in a broader sense—highlights that play, games and technology are informed by the sociocultural and local. Urban mobile games thus provide a lens on the history of games, at the same time as they provide a canvas for future practices. Game on?

CONCLUSION: THE ROLE OF HAPTIC PLAY IN GAMES OF BEING MOBILE

In this chapter we have explored the various ways in which urban mobile gaming has emerged as a dominant form of practice in rewriting the intersections between gaming, play and place. With three genres—urban gaming (or big games), LBMGs/LAMGs, and HRG—urban mobile gaming can help to relocate a sense of place that is missing in many video games. They offer a chance to transform an urban setting into a game space, demonstrating that urban spaces are inherently playful (de Souza e Silva 2009).

The game of mobile media—whether it is engaging with camera phone imagery or whether it takes the form of urban mobile gaming in which interactivity and engagement are navigated by both visuality and haptics—is undoubtedly changing how we are thinking about place and new media. Through the lens of paradoxes that encompass virtual and actual, online and offline, haptic and visual, delay and immediacy, some lessons about twentieth-century media and gaming practice can be learnt.

For anyone who has participated in an urban mobile game, they will quickly identify the lack of coherence between online and offline co-presence. As we have seen, this feature often becomes an integral part of gameplay. The more we try to partake in *practices of immediacy,* the more we succumb to *processes of delay.* While LAMG projects are invaluable in demonstrating the importance of place and specificity in a period of global technologies, they also serve to highlight one of the greatest paradoxes of mobile media—that is, the paradox of co-presence. One example can be found in the aims of twentieth-century technology to overcome difference and distance, from the geographic and physical to the cultural and psychological. This attempt to overcome *distance* and *difference* sees the opposite result, the overcoming of *closeness.*

As noted in the introduction to this chapter, a place is only partly constituted by the physical and geographic. The emotional, psychological and social dimensions of place are what give it significance. Australian phenomenologist Michael Arnold therefore argues that mobile media must be understood as inherently janus-faced in nature; that is, they both push and pull us, setting us free to roam and yet attach us to an invisible perpetual leash (2003). For Arnold, the janus-faced phenomenon is an example of what Martin Heidegger characterized as 'un-distance' (distance mediated by closeness). Within un-distance lies the paradox: the more we try to overcome distance, the more we overcome closeness.

Un-distance can be seen today in the practice of mobile media, particularly LAMG/LBMG projects that rely on the so-called immediacy or instantaneity of the networked. However, one could argue that un-distance has been perpetuated by the primacy of the visual within twentieth-century 'tele' media (such as the telephone and television). This phenomenon has arguably been disrupted by mobile media's emphasis on the haptic as a mediator of the online and the offline, and how these practices subvert spaces as well as extending the possibilities of gaming. On this basis, Richardson disavows the dominance of the ocular-centrism (visual) prevalent in 'new media screen technologies' in favour of 'the spatial, perceptual and ontic effects' (2007: 205) of mobile media. Departing from what Lucas Introna and Fernando Ilharco characterize as the multiple 'screen-ness' (2004) inhabiting contemporary life, Richardson instead argues that the mobile screen challenges 'any notion of a disembodied telepresence' deployed by much screen-based media (2007: 210); and in turn, we can 'see emergent spatial ontologies of a kind never before experienced in such a collective and interactive fashion' (2007: 214).

Although Richardson argues for a future in mobile media, particularly LAMGs, where the virtual and the actual become seamless in their 'glaze-like' engagement, there is much debate about the correlation between online and offline identity, and around how this is tailored by the local. It is undoubtedly these features that give the mobile its sense of place in the world and which, in turn, make them exciting propositions for gaming. Far from the death of geography, place (and boundaries) has never been stronger as communicative and gaming practices with mobile technologies burgeon.

Genres such as HRG can therefore help us to reconsider the relationship between the online and offline, the here and there and the immediacy and delay that are apparent in contemporary techno-cultures. The idea of mobility and immobility, central within urban mobile gaming, will be further explored in the following chapter when we examine two very different models of gaming—Japan and Korea. Here we continue to consider how place informs gameplay and how this manifests through the various modes of mobility—technological and geographic to name but two.

Summary

- There are three main genres of urban mobile gaming: urban gaming or big games, location-aware/based (LBMGs/LAMGs) and hybrid reality (HRG).
- Urban mobile games can be seen to extend earlier models of cultural practice and intervention from the New Games Movement of the 1970s to the SI techniques of *dérive*. They also highlight the ways in which the shaping and experiences of the urban have been transformed from the nineteenth-century vision of the *flâneur* to the twenty-first-century image of the phoneur as part of the informational city (de Souza e Silva and Hjorth 2009).
- Also, urban mobile games make us rethink the relationship between the online and offline, and challenge us to think about place as not only physical and geographic but also as an accumulation of stories, memories and social practices. These issues have often been missing from single player video games.
- Often urban games have the paradox of immediacy and delay factored into their gameplay. This serves to remind us of the relationship between technology as a practice and as a concept.
- Blurring the boundaries of where the magic circle of the game space and the non-game space begins and ends, urban mobile games constantly provide insight into the particularities of place and locality.

7 GAMING IN THE ASIA-PACIFIC: TWO FUTURES FOR GAMING—ONLINE GAMING VERSUS ELECTRONIC INDIVIDUALISM

Within the global games industry, we can see a variety of directions; each location adopts and adapts particular types of games and gameplay that reflect the specificities of the place and its associated techno-culture. Amongst the diversity, some dominant trends and phenomena have appeared—in particular, the rise of online and mobile gaming. In some contexts, especially through ubiquitous media, these two areas have converged. Devices such as PSP and iPhone are exemplary of this convergence.

While mobility may be a key feature of one of the directions—in the form of PSP, Wii, iPhone, Nintendo DS—the types of mobility, often accompanied by immobility, are subject to the cultural context. Mobility can take numerous forms—technological, geographic and capital, to name a few. In the previous chapter we explored some of these new forms of mobility and immobility being performed through urban mobile gaming. We also saw the importance of the particular techno-culture in which the games are being played, in providing a key component in influencing the gameplay. Within each techno-culture, different factors—cultural, linguistic, social, technological—inform the types of games as well as the context in which they are played.

In some locations, where an emphasis is placed on collectivity and community, games are often played in semi-public realms with other (online) players also present offline. In South Korea (henceforth Korea), the history of *bangs* (rooms) for a variety of functions has played a pivotal role in the uptake and success of online games (Chee 2005; Huhh 2009). These *bang* spaces operate in between the public and the private, highlighting the significance of collectivity and community in Korean culture, which, in turn, informs the types of games played. In other locations, in which long periods of time are spent in confined public spaces and travelling, such as Tokyo, the significance of the mobile, individuated device is apparent. Here, the importance of the mobile device remains on one having a sense of individual space that does not intrude upon others—a notion that has been encapsulated by Japanese personal technologies and their focus upon 'electronic individualism' (Kogawa 1984) from the Sony Walkman onwards. The minimalist mantra of 'context as content' seen in the late-twentieth-century art movements like installation (see Chapter 3) is indeed applicable when it comes to understanding the specific *ways*, and *where*, games are played.

However, the mobility of the device deflects some of the key issues in the uptake of these games—most notably, *where* these games are played. Just because a player uses a PSP or iPhone, it cannot be assumed that their contexts of gameplay are being mobilized in a public space. Indeed, in some cultural contexts, game consoles such as PSP are still played predominantly in the private and domestic sphere. For Chan, citing a 2006 study of Japanese casual mobile games, most are played in the domestic sphere in 'sedentary domestic contexts' (2008: 23). So whilst burgeoning networked and ubiquitous technologies might be seen to suggest a future in which various forms of mobility are performed across technological, spatial, geographic, virtual and temporal realms, we can also find forms of immobility—such as physical, spatial, cultural—coming to the forefront. These tensions, between mobility and immobility, are unquestionably informed by the local. Given this characteristic, it is important to locate the gameplay within specific cultural contexts.

In this chapter we explore two of the dominant gaming trends—the online and the mobile—within the context of two locations that have been heralded as representing centres for these phenomena, Seoul (Korea) and Tokyo (Japan). Both locations have been seen as both 'mobile centres' and 'gaming centres', which the world looks towards as examples of the future in the present. Unlike Japan, which pioneered the *keitai* (mobile) IT revolution and mobile consoles such as PlayStation 2, South Korea—branded one of the most broadbanded countries in the world (OECD 2006)—has become a centre for MMO games played predominantly in the social space of PC rooms (PC *bangs*).

Adorned with over 20,000 PC *bangs* in Seoul alone, and with professional players (pro-leagues) making as much as US$1 million per year, locations such as Korea have been lauded as an example of gaming as a mainstream social activity. In a period marked by convergent technologies, Korea and Japan represent two opposing directions for gaming—Korea emphasizes MMO games played on stationary PCs in social spaces (PC *bangs*), whilst Japan pioneers the mobile (privatized) convergent devices.

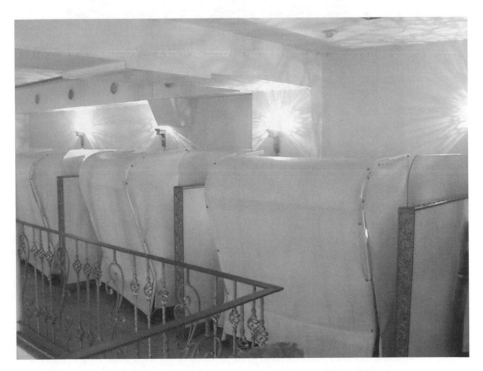

Figure 7.1a and 7.1b: Two examples of 'love' PC *bangs* in Korea. Photo: Hjorth.

These two distinct examples, with histories embroiled in conflict and imperialism, clearly demonstrate the importance of locality in the uptake of specific games and gameplay. As Brian Sutton-Smith (1997) argued, *game* spaces are *social* spaces. These social spaces have histories that are imbued by the local. Moreover, these two locations demonstrate the various ways in which mobility and immobility—across the technological, geographic, sociocultural, physical, spatial—are very much subject to the cultural context of gameplay. In this chapter, as a case study of two divergent gaming cultures, we will explore two futures for gaming—online gaming (Seoul) versus electronic individualism (Tokyo)—with particular focus on contextualizing the specific techno-cultures in order to understand why these two very different types of gaming cultures occurred.

Figure 7.2: Japanese girl with mobile phone game at *Tokyo Game Show* 2005. Photo: Hjorth.

In the case of Japan, mobility, personalization and individualization are three key factors influencing the types of evolving game consoles and communities. Alternatively, in Korea, immobility and collectivity are central features in the current burgeoning of online games, the rise of which cannot be separated from the emergence of the group spaces of the PC *bang* (Huhh 2009; Chee 2005). In this chapter we discuss the current mobile, networked gaming cultures of Japan as extending Williams's concept of 'mobile privatization' (1974; see Chapter 2) and also the specific ways in which personalization and mobility operate within Japan as distinct from other cultures.

For Korea, current gaming cultures will be discussed in terms of 'immobile socialization' (Bakardjieva 2003) in which users negotiate online and offline communities often through a domesticated and social space such as the PC *bang*. As Maria Bakardjieva argues, rather than online technologies mobilizing us on various levels, one can find numerous forms of immobility which function to socialize and localize the technology. Often, online socialization is reflected in the types of offline social contexts, and vice versa. The central role of the *bang* in Korean culture, as a form of 'immobile socialization', is important when comprehending why games, and particularly MMOs—whereby guilds often play together in the same offline spaces—have been so successful. These are but two examples of the diversity of gaming cultures that can help us to understand some of the various localized factors influencing the growth of, and yet divergence in, games globally. This chapter will conclude with some of the prevalent lessons we can learn from putting games, and their associated gameplay, back in their appropriate contexts.

LOCATING THE REGION: THE TECHNO-CULTURES OF THE ASIA-PACIFIC

Japan's role in developing console-based videogames culture is unquestionable. The Nintendo Corporation was responsible for the global distribution and mass popularisation of NES, SNES and Nintendo 64 videogames as well as portable Game Boy games in the late 1980s and early 1990s. Sony entered into the videogames market with PlayStation in 1994; and currently enjoys nearly unrivalled international market dominance with the PlayStation 2 console and its associated games. This continued emphasis on developing videogame consoles and videogames for both domestic and international markets has arguably come at the expense of both stand-alone PC games and online computer games in the Japanese context. By contrast, online games currently tend to dominate in South Korea, Taiwan and Mainland China. (Chan 2006: n.p.)

As noted in the previous chapter, what constitutes a region like the Asia-Pacific is contested and perpetually changing. According to Arjun Appadurai, a more useful model of regionality could take the form of the 'Pacific Rim' (2000)—echoing the cartography of the international dateline. In such a model, regionality would take the form of temporal, rather than geographic, clusters. This interrogation of region-ality is exemplified in the arguments surrounding the Asia-Pacific, as witnessed in debates around the appropriate term to depict the dynamic and contesting spaces it claims to represent. One can find numerous examples such as 'Asia-Pacific', 'Asia-Pacific region', 'Asia/Pacific', 'Asian Pacific' and 'Asia and the Pacific'.

At the turn of the twenty-first century, named by some as the century of the 'Global South' (Dirlik 2007), the Asia-Pacific gained the global attention of the games industry. This attention once took the form of a focus on the new media technologies 'centre', Japan. Since the 1970s, Japan has led the way in the rise of personal tech-nologies globally from the worldwide uptake of the Sony Walkman to the innovation of the DoCoMo i-mode that became known as the 'mobile IT revolution' (Matsuda 2005) by way of its convergence between mobile telephony and the internet. Ito et al. (2005) characterized this phenomenon as the dominance of the 'Portable, Personal and Pedestrian', qualities of Japanese mobile technologies exemplified by the *keitai* (mobile phone). For Tetsuo Kogawa, the significance and success of Japanese personal and portable technologies lie in their 'electronic individualism' (1984), which reflects a specifically Japanese notion of individualism that is linked to forms of nationalism. Embedded within Japanese techno-national policies and the 'personal technologies' industry of Japan, this association between individualism and nationalism has also been identified by McVeigh (2003a) and Fujimoto (2005).

In the games industry, Japan has played a dominant role in the production of both hardware and software, as we explored in Chapter 2. The legacy created by Japan in the histories of gaming has only been paralleled by that of the United States. How-ever, given language and cultural differences, Japan has long escaped the microscope of game studies, which has instead focused upon English-speaking countries like the United States, United Kingdom and Australia, as well as locations in which English is spoken widely such as Scandinavia and other parts of Europe. Japan, whilst being recognized as one of the pioneers in the field, is often sidelined due to language and cultural differences that do not lend themselves to quick translation (Hjorth and Chan 2009). The need to address the gap in English-language literature on Japanese gaming has started to be recognized, although there is still a long way to go. Such books as Chris Kohler's *Power-Up: How Japanese Video Games Gave the World an Extra Life* (2004) attempt to reorient the focus of game studies away from Western-centrism. However, they neglect to fully contextualize the specific techno-culture in which the particular games industry evolved.

Techno-orientalism

Technological 'centres' such as Japan have long been seen as repositories for the fetishization of new technologies—a form of techno-nationalism equated with 'techno-orientalism' (Morley and Robins 1995; Yoshimi 1999), by which the Occident (the 'West') sees technologically developed locations such as Tokyo (particularly the distinct of Akihabara) as a 'default' sci-fi backdrop (Nakamura 2002). Techno-orientalism grew out of the West's attempt to grapple with Japan's quick 'soft power' rise, from the 1970s onwards, through its production of innovative technologies—from the Sony Walkman to video games.

Techno-orientalism is a form of Orientalism. As Edward Said (1978) noted in his pioneering study, *Orientalism*, the 'Orient' was a construction of the Occident's imagination. The Orient was defined as 'other' by the West; everything of the West was seen as being in opposition to Japan. According to David Morley and Kevin Robins (1995), the Western stereotypes of 'Japan' define them as 'other' to the humanism of the West; this form of xenophobia was particularly prevalent when Japan excelled in the global electronics industry from 1970s onwards and the West tried to justify its own failure.

For a long time the residue of techno-orientalism overshadowed conceptualizations of Japan's continuing power in global techno-cultures. It has only been recently that Japan's innovation in technology-related industries has been contextualized within a techno-culture that no longer 'defaults' to Western precepts or models of culture and society. Although Japanese transnational companies such as Atari and Nintendo dominated the gaming market until the mid 1980s crash, it was not until the economic resurgence of Japan in the 1990s that a new Japan techno-culture took form (McVeigh 2003b). However, now, in the wake of transnational flows such as the Korean popular culture wave (*Hallyu*) and the burgeoning role of China in the production and consumption of ICTs, the shifting game of twenty-first-century neo-regionalism begins.

As a region, we see heterogeneous models for gaming production and consumption in the Asia-Pacific. In a period marked by transnational flows of people, ideas and capital, the politics of regionality is indeed a vexed issue. As noted in Chapter 4, the 'imagined community' (Anderson 1983) of various nations is no longer defined by the co-present (here and there) role of print-press media. Rather, the characteristic of new media communities is that they are, on the one hand, governed by 'mobile privatization' (Williams 1974) and, on the other hand, anchored by 'immobile socialization' (Bakardjieva 2003) in which users negotiate online and offline communities, often through a domesticated and social space. The role of the PC *bang* (PC room) in Korea is indicative of this phenomenon.

In the Asia-Pacific, the transnational 'communities of consumers' (Chua 2006) are all-pervasive, exemplified by various competing transnational game cultures that are simultaneously immobile/mobile, intimate/social, private/public. Once, a US-centred political and socio-economic discourse awkwardly subsumed the multiple histories, cultures, and subjectivities of the region under a synthetic rubric of 'community'. Now the region has grown to encapsulate the new 'Global South' (Dirlik 2007), in which the global axis shifts from the north (i.e. US-centred focus in the twentieth century) towards locations such as China.

As Dirlik (2007) trenchantly noted, the sun has now set on the twentieth century, and with it, the domination of the United States and Europe is decreasing. With the dawn of the twenty-first century, the sun rises on the shores of the South—the new 'Global South'. Just as the region's consumption and production patterns have evolved and transformed, so too have the ways in which modernity in the region has been conceptualized. From the Confucius revivalisms of the late 1990s in search of 'Asian' values—which were criticized for homogenizing diversity, self-Orientalization (Dirlik 1999b) and essentialism—the region attempted to think beyond Western and Eurocentric tropes through the lens of 'alternative modernities'. For Dirlik, in this search for identity and cultural modernity in an age of mobility and reformations of the nation-state, it was important that the region not deny its own history of cultural imperialism and colonial conflicts (2000).

In his analysis of the intra-Asian games networks through Chinese virtual agricultural enterprises harvesting online game prizes, Chan (2009, 2006) notes that the transnational, and yet localized, gaming communities provide great insight into the ever-evolving and nebulous notion of the Asia-Pacific. Chan observes that while there is growing transnationalism between the locations (such as Chinese players consuming Korean online games), this is done in a manner that reasserts new notions of nationalism. Through these gaming cultures, the various forms of 'Asianness' are explored, challenged and redefined. The region is not alone, but rather it offers an example of the ways in which gaming cultures rehearse transnational flows and at the same time reinforce new notions of the national. Indeed, as the gaming industries become increasingly visible players in the global creative industries, the undeniably tenacious force of localization emerges. Gameplay, as if we ever doubted it, is not only about the local and the sociocultural. It is about the politics of space.

Reflection

What constitutions a region? Is it a community of people that shares a common culture, language or geography? Can you think of some examples of contested regions? And how do you think gaming reflects a player's region?

As noted in *Gaming Cultures and Place* (Hjorth and Chan 2009), the Asia-Pacific region can be read as 'a geo-political and economic construct'. Encompassing East and South East Asia, as well as countries such as Australia and New Zealand, the regional category was largely the making of 'a post–World War II political and economic imaginary, as opposed to a purely geographic cartography' (2009: 1). Drawing upon Jen Webb's notion of 'the Asia-Pacific effect' as a 'real thing' composed in language by … national and geopolitical entities, we noted that the region was no longer a mere colonial image but rather a diversity of cultural practices and productions that have their own forms of agency and transnational synergies (Hjorth and Chan 2009: 116). As we observe, Webb's 'Asia-Pacific effect' is, in the case of social media and gaming cultures, best understood as the 'Asia-Pacific *affect*'.

> In an age of Web 2.0, SNS and UCC, the various techno-cultural localities might be best defined as the Asia-Pacific 'affect'. To appropriate and expand Webb's words, the Asia-Pacific clearly also has an affect that informs experiences of it as a 'Real thing'—impacting on networks of production, circulation and consumption, as well as emotive registers of performativity, subjectivity, and community. (Hjorth and Chan 2009: 12)

Once a discursive geopolitical rubric, the Asia-Pacific—a site for contesting local identities and transnational flows of people, media, goods and capital—has come under much radical revision and reconceptualization (Arrighi 1994; Arrighi et al. 2003; Wilson 2000). This has led theorists such as Robert Wilson to utilize 'Asia/Pacific' as 'not just an ideological recuperated term' but an imagined geo-political space that has a double reading as both 'situated yet ambivalent' (2000: 567). In their anthology *Asia/Pacific as Space of Cultural Production* (1995), Wilson and Dirlik challenge the 'hegemonic Euro-American' construction underpinning the Asia-Pacific, in order to arrive at new ways of conceptualizing regionalism. In particular, they use the configuration 'Asia/Pacific' to discuss the region as a space of cultural production, social migration and transnational innovation, whereby 'the slash would signify linkage yet difference' (1995: 6). Specifically, the diverse and perpetually changing relationships constituting the Asia-Pacific have been repositioned as a contested space for multiple forms of identity.

Moreover, the global role of the Asia-Pacific has shifted dramatically since the region's economic crisis of 1997. Over the course of this period, the region has witnessed the rise of industrial/technological/economic power concurrent with its growing role in the global gaming industries. This is not an accident. Indeed, through industries such as gaming the region has transformed its economic and technological prowess into a powerful concoction of global cultural capital. GNP (Gross National Product) becomes 'Gross National Cool' (McGray, 2002), and 'soft' power finds itself conveniently located in the development of software. Given the region's ongoing significance in the creative industries, and boasting some of the highest technological infrastructure such as broadband, it provides a great example of governmental strategies and industrial IT policies that have informed its movement into this century's 'participatory media' such as Web 2.0. Consuming 'Asia', within and outside the region, transnationally and globally, is big business. Global consumption takes gameplay to a new level.

Within this consuming 'Asia' phenomenon of games, Japan and Korea have constantly been featured. While China is burgeoning in this field, both Japan's and Korea's presence and significance are still prevalent. In order to understand the two different techno-cultures of Japan and Korea, we will briefly turn to a couple of studies comparing the two countries' internet and mobile usage to each other. Then we will turn to the specific locations to discuss each context's particularities.

In Lee et al.'s 'A Cross-cultural Study on the Value Structure of Mobile Internet Usage: Comparison between Korea and Japan' (2002), they concluded that there are major differing cultural values between Korean and Japanese society that are played out in the adoption and adaptation of the mobile internet. In Korea, there is more emphasis on sharing entertainment content—from music to video games—and on the fact that public use exchange of this material via the personal computer is the norm. Peer-to-peer sharing and what has been dubbed 'scooping' (Yoon 2006), that is, copying and transferring of content on blogs, are popular practices—while less intrusive modes such as mobile e-mail are not so popular. Alternatively, in Japan, mobile internet is convenient but not a main mode for socializing, with mobile e-mailing being a dominant application.

According to McCartney (2004), in Japan there is a preference for sending self-generated pictures and video mail in place of direct calling in public places, whereas in Korea, direct voice calling in public spaces is acceptable. For Kenichi Ishii (2004), there is a distinct difference between the usage of the mobile internet and PC internet in Japan. He argues that, while high numbers of users of PC internet tend to spend less time with family and friends, high numbers of users of mobile internet are the opposite, tending towards very active interpersonal skills and socializing capacity (Ishii 2004: 56). Moreover, users of mobile phones tend to be upfront about their identity, and there is a more seamless relationship between online and offline identity and relationships. According to Daisuke Tsuji and Shunji Mikami (2001), mobile e-mail usage between university students enhances sociability, although McVeigh (2003a) argues this comes at the cost of shrinking social capital, or what Ichiyo Habuchi has dubbed 'tele-cocooning' (2005).

One parallel that is interesting in this compelling and controversial argument about the two very different techno-cultures is that the role of mobile technologies in both Japan and Korea have, in their own way, been carefully orchestrated at both a governmental and industry level into gated communities that nurture local industry. Japan's NTT i-mode and Korea's SK Telecom, Samsung and LG have been able to thrive in the strong local market without the threat of imports. Deploying a different mobile system to other countries ensured prosperity for local companies to invest in innovations, both in terms of software and hardware, that could be then exported into other markets (e.g. i-mode's adoption outside of Japan, Samsung's 8-megapixel camera phones, SK Telecom working with MySpace for mobile content). Unlike Korea, where the internet is still mainly associated with the computer (ensured by phenomena such as PC *bangs*), in Japan, general and cheap internet access was only ensured with the introduction of mobile phone (*keitai*) internet services such as i-mode in 1999.

As Lee et al. (2002) note, the differences between Korean and Japanese relationships to the internet could be gleaned from the types of content that are downloaded, and the modes of UCC they disseminated. In their study, Lee et al. observe that Japanese mobile internet users tended to prefer UCC material such as camera phone images and video, in order to compensate for the fact that mobile voice calls in public were not the norm. They also note that Korean users tend towards 'scooping' content rather than making their own. However, since 2002, the rise of SNSs such as minihompy in Korea and mixi in Japan has obviously been about a shift in those perceptions and uses.

The birth of UCC sites such as PandoraTV and aficeca in Korea (which, though similar to YouTube, allow users to set up their own mobile TV channel), and the rise of 'powerblogging', have dismantled Kyongwon Yoon's (2003, 2006) claim that Korean users are just accessing already existing content. 'Powerblogging'—consisting of blogs often about everyday events such as cooking and also fan sites of pop stars—has come to epitomize a type of UCC agency in which some successful bloggers go on to become famous and even make money (in some rare cases they even gain a profitable career). Powerblogging denotes a new stage in blogging after the political blogs that characterized the internet in South Korea. While Seoul has its example of powerblogging as a form of successful UCC, Tokyo has its counterpart in the *keitai shôsetsu* (mobile phone novels) phenomenon. Whilst powerblogging tends to be written and read on the computer, *keitai shôsetsu* are mostly read on the mobile phone. This shapes not only the content—*keitai shôsetsu* are characterized by short, compressed paragraphs which are meant to be viewed on the small, mobile screen—but also the contexts of reception (train, home, PC room, etc.). These new forms of UCC participation, in which readers are given an active voice and play an important role in the success of the writers, highlight just one of the differences between Korea's collective immobile socialization and Japan's mobile, electronic individualism.

Whereas both Korean and Japanese mobile internet users tend towards being more socially active than non-users, the divide between PC internet users and mobile internet users in terms of the sociality identified by Ishii (2004) is more apparent in the case of Japan than in Korea. As Florence Chee (2005) notes in her study on PC *bangs*, they are incredibly social spaces in which the online and offline are seamlessly negotiated. These spaces operate as 'third spaces' (Chee 2005) in between home and work/school. The fact that Koreans need to register for such services as minihompy using their citizen number does ensure a clear correlation between one's online and offline identity—and this is witnessed in users' online presentation (Hjorth and Kim 2005). It is also helped by the fact that Korea's broadband services are the fastest in the world, alleviating lagging or waiting time. In Japan, this is not the case; rather, the aforementioned *keitai* is what afforded general and cheap internet access, and dominant sites such as BBS 2ch (as mentioned in Chapter 5) are accessed, and contributed to, anonymously. Even SNSs such as mixi, which are built around social capital and cultural capital affiliations, still allow users to remain partly anonymous if they wish.

Having outlined some of the research comparing the two very different techno-cultures, we now turn to each specific case study. First, we explore the particularities of Tokyo and its associated forms of 'electronic individualism', and then move on to Seoul, with its own flavour of online gaming and the associated immobile socialization—in the form of PC *bangs*—in which the games are played.

MOBILE, ELECTRONIC INDIVIDUALISM: TOKYO, JAPAN

Japan's key role in producing technologies, and, more specifically, domestic technologies, for global markets since 1970 is well documented. Behind the global images of techno-savvy youth adorned with the latest technological gadgets in 'electric cities' such as Akihabara, Japan's role in producing and consuming new technologies—from the Sony Walkman and Atari games console to PlayStation and the *keitai* (mobile) IT revolution—has been crucial. For Ito et al. (2005), the market success of Japanese technologies can be best explained by characteristics of the aforementioned three P's—Pedestrian, Personal and Portable. The significance of these three P's is that they transform technological gadgets into sociocultural artefacts by relocating them within the dynamic space of cultural production. These three P's have played a key role, ensuring Japan's success in global gaming cultures, through orchestrating a type of electronic individualism around mobile and personalized media devices such as Game & Watch (handheld electronic games by Nintendo available since 1980).

This particular form of localized personalization was exemplified by Tokyo's '*keitai* IT revolution' at the turn of the twenty-first century. It seemed impossible to avoid the *keitai* IT revolution when Japan's telecommunication giant, NTT DoCoMo, released the i-mode; that is, the mobile phone with internet. The i-mode was not just a mobile phone (or *keitai denwa*, abbreviated to '*keitai*', meaning 'portable'); it was a key example of twenty-first-century mobile media, converging telephony and the internet. As mentioned in the last section, the relatively slow uptake of the internet in Japan in the 1990s afforded Japan the opportunity to leapfrog into the twenty-first-century convergence—mobile internet—with ease. Thus, in the context of Japan, it is impossible to separate the emergence and rise of mobile media from that of the internet. Suddenly, the internet—or i-mode's walled version of it— was being accessed by tens of millions of Japanese everyday. This phenomenon was marked by sharp changes in the generational and gendered patterns of use. Whereas, in 1995, 90 per cent of *keitai* users were the archetype—the salaryman (*oyaji*)— within two years the *shôjo* (young female) had become the dominant user. It seemed that Japan, via the mobile internet 'revolution', had regained its techno-soft cultural power after the economic slump of the 1990s.

Since World War II, Japan's role as a centre for technological innovation has assured a sense of cultural power, particularly in the region. In the wake of Japan's faded imperialism in the Asia-Pacific, NICs (newly industrialized countries) such as Taiwan and Hong Kong have acquired an ambivalent awe of Japan's superpower economy, and its cultural capital associated with products such as *anime* (animation) and *manga* (comics), while in locations such as Korea the memory of Japanese imperialism still remains fresh. Given the history of Japan's cultural, and more recently technological, imperialism, Japan has often found itself the subject of the aforementioned sci-fi 'default setting' (Nakamura 2002), and various manifestations of 'techno-orientalism' (Morley and Robins 1995; Yoshimi 1999).

To understand the new media practices that informed the rise of Japan's gaming cultures, we need to appreciate a context for Japan's specific deployment of personalization that can be mapped back to the Sony Walkman in the 1970s. As Kogawa notes, a key feature of Japanese technologies and the central role of personalization has been 'electronic individualism' (1984). Kogawa argues that electronic individualism has been integral to Japanese techno-nationalism from the Walkman onwards (1984). For Fujimoto, *keitai* cultures and the significance of electronic individualism, as played out in Japan's various gaming console technologies (from Game & Watch to PSP and Wii), need to be considered in terms of specific forms of localized mobilism that can be traced historically. In 'The Third-Stage Paradigm: Territory Machine from the Girls' Pager Revolution to Mobile Aesthetics' (2005), Fujimoto evokes Williams's 'mobile privatization' (1974) through the distinctly Japanese practice of *nagara* mobilism (Fujimoto 2005: 80)—*nagara* referring to an activity that is done 'whilst-doing-something-else' (see Chapter 5).

As Richardson (2009) notes in the case of the iPhone and gaming, users often move between different types of immersion, engagement and distraction. These different modes of engagement and disengagement are the result of not only the device's particular 'stickiness' (ability to immerse; see Chapter 6) but also the specific game and the context in which it is played. Indeed, playing at home alone will create a different type of stickiness than a game played on a busy train. However Fujimoto's (2005) *nagara* mobilism signals a broader phenomenon, not just particular to Japan; that is, with the rise of participatory culture, we are also seeing the emergence of a field called 'notification' research, which studies the various multitasking activities operating within most people's usage of online technologies and social media. The recent work of French sociologist Christian Licoppe (2009) clearly captures this new field attempting to understand modes of engagement and embodiment, beyond just the binary of engagement/disengagement.

For Fujimoto, the 'third-stage paradigm' theory is 'a hypothetical model for mobilising historical facts for theory building, and is one thread for understanding the backdrop to the girl's pager revolution' (2005: 80). In situating the paradigm within the East Asian context, Fujimoto argues that the increase in *keitai* cultures and new identities must be understood in terms of broader techno-cultural shifts that were symbolized by the shift from military (soldier) to business (salaryman) to socialization (youth). This movement makes sense of how personal technologies and gaming cultures started to prevail in the 1970s, and then burgeon concurrently with the demise of the 'salaryman' as national icon.

Nagara mobilism is re-enacted in the visibility and agency by *kôgyaru* (fashionable, youthful female) and *shôjo* users against the hegemony of the *oyaji* (Fujimoto 2005: 80). According to Fujimoto, through the *nagara* mobilism of *keitai* cultures, the conflict between traditional Japan and modern Japan was orchestrated by the shift of attention away from the *oyaji* towards the *kôgyaru*. For Fujimoto, however, this contestation was far from nascent. Rather, Fujimoto argues that this tension between the 'two' Japans—the traditional and the contemporary—has its genealogy in the rise of Japan's export industry that can be linked back to the mid-eighteenth century, with the mobilization of trade routes.

Fujimoto (2005) also argues that the export of *keitai* culture can be linked to the export of other luxury goods, *shikôhin*. Fujimoto utilizes many analogies—from the use of uniform to the use of tea—to differentiate the Japanese *keitai* from Western adaptations of mobile media. The importance of subcultural reappropriation of *keitai* cultures is pivotal to Fujimoto's discussion of Japan's dominance as a global exporter of both hardware and software—including i-mode, *kawaii* (cute) icons, *keitai* straps,

Densha Otoko (Train Man) Case Study: Gender and Media

Since the turn of the new millennium, there has even been a covert implementation of the *otaku* (Japanese media-obsessed fans) as a positive symbol of 'pure love' in Japan (Freedman 2009); this has taken place through popular media stories such as the *Densha Otoko* (Train Man) that sparked the imagination of the Japanese general public. However, recent events such as the knife-wielding man (Kato Tomohiro, who murdered three random people in Akihabara in June 2008 on the seventh anniversary of Osaka Ikeda Elementary killings) in the 'home of the *otaku*', Akihabara, have muddied the waters (Freedman 2009). The symbol of the *otaku*, once denigrated as a social misfit, has, like the gentrification of Akihabara post–*Densha Otoko*, been reconfigured as a positive icon of Japanese culture—both locally and globally. As the story goes, an *otaku* saved a young lady (Hermés) on a train whilst she was being harassed. The *otaku* then wrote about the incident and his love for her on the biggest BBS forum 2ch and, before long, it was the longest and most talked about posting. It became a series of *manga*, feature films and, most important, part of the urban mythology.

The phenomenon of *Densha Otoko* marked a pivotal shift in which Japan reinvented the once denigrated character of the *otaku* to become a twenty-first-century male icon (Freedman 2009). In doing so, it mobilized a nation yearning for romance. This phenomenon not only sought to construct the *otaku* as the new unsung hero of Japan but also positioned him as the ideal man for the professional woman (blamed for the decreasing birth and marriage rates). These gender scriptings around media—as part of the broader shift towards socialization and youth cultures through technologies—are, according to Fujimoto (2005), distinctive to Japan and cannot be compared with European shifts.

wallpapers and ring tones, as well as digital font styles capable of 'unconventional combination[s] of existing characters and symbols named *gyaru-moji* (girl's alphabet) and *heta-moji* (awkward alphabet)' so fundamental to the *gyaru's* reappropriation of mobile media (2005: 87).

For Fujimoto, the distinctively Japanese use of the *keitai* as more than a mere technology has ensured its export overseas (2005: 87). He extends the aesthetic paradigm of the *keitai* by invoking the analogy of traditional tea practices and *shikôhin* (pleasurable favourites) as foregrounding the rituals and relationship between the *keitai* and the everyday. As Fujimoto notes, just as the *shikôhin* were never seen as mere luxury goods—or as he puts it, *shikôkin*—but were embedded in rituals, so too is the *keitai* part of the rituals of the everyday in which customization plays a central role.

Drawing upon the work of historian Sakae Tsunoyama, who traced the history of tea in the aesthetics of Japanese everyday life and then its export to the West, Fujimoto parallels this genealogy with the consumption and exportation of the *keitai* culture. 'The expanded palette of *shikôhin*' grew through eighteenth-century exports and souvenirs (Fujimoto 2005: 90). Fujimoto suggests that rather than seeing *keitai* cultures as a distinct break in Japanese traditional cultures—as symbolized by the notion of *shikôhin*—he argues that the emerging phenomenon of *keitai* cultures (in which customization is intrinsic) could be viewed as *keitai shikôhin*. As Fujimoto notes:

> It is widely recognized that international products such as tobacco, coffee, and tea have been sophisticated informational and media commodities for the past four hundred years, since the emergence of commodity markets in modern Europe. While taking new forms, these basic products have remained resilient through global shifts towards urbanization and informational flows...*Keitai* are less like books, which tend to be decontextualized, de-localized, and escapist media, and more like *shikôhin*, as objects of recontextualization, relocalization, and actual media objects. (2005: 90–1)

For Fujimoto, Japanese customizing is, like *shikôhin* objects, about contextualization. This is exemplified by the role played by *kawaii* customization. He explains:

> Japan has had a tendency to enjoy *shikôhin* not in isolation but within the totality of associated objects, tools, and media. These objects, tools, and media often exist separate from the *shikôhin* themselves and take on their own independent gadget identities in the form of *kawaii* (little, pretty, cute) stationery, fashion accessories, and character goods. (Fujimoto 2005: 91)

The role of *kawaii* customization of the *keitai* to fulfil the sensory experience can be seen as an extension of the legacy of *shikôhin* in Japanese culture. Thus, *kawaii keitai* cultures are part of processes particular to Japanese culture. By drawing upon forms of *nagara* mobilism, popular trends and *shikôhin* cultures, Fujimoto suggests that an analysis of *keitai* culture demonstrates 'Japan's resistance to cultural globalization as well as Japan's leadership role in certain aspects of globalization' (2005: 92–3). As Fujimoto persuasively argues, the rise of *keitai* cultures in Japan must be contextualized in terms of Japanese modernity and nationalism that preceded the introduction of Western modernity, and links to a time in which Japan participated in the regional trade routes and their attendant forms of transnationalism (Arrighi et al. 2003). Thus the role of personalization—particularly in mobile media—must be understood as linking into broader formations of modernity and nationalism.

For others, this personalization is equally intertwined with localized notions of individualization. Tomoyuki Okada notes that this shift parallels the history of landlines in Japan, and identifies the 'dimensions of personalization also related to the individualization of television, radio, and other forms of mass media since the 1970s' (2005: 46). Here, the relationship between domestic technologies and the unilateral domestication between the user and the device are clearly integral to personalization and individualization (McVeigh 2003a). This process occurs across the various platforms and genres of the *keitai*—namely visuality, as in camera phones (Ito and Okabe 2003, 2005), texting (Okada 2005) and aurality, as in ring tones (Okada 2005).

As Kenji Kohiyama notes in 'A Decade in the Development of Mobile Communications in Japan (1993–2002)', the importance of personalization as the central trend has dictated future trends by focusing on the personalization of devices, connectivity and services (2005: 70). For Kohiyama, 'the personalization of mobile communication in Japan began with the pager' (2005: 71). One of the dominant forms of personalization can be traced through the evolving socializing and individualizing techniques of techno-cute from the pager to the *keitai*. As discussed in Chapter 5, both were originally marketed to the *oyaji*, and then appropriated by the female user and inscribed with *kawaii* customization in the form of cute characters adorning and dressing up the device with 'kitten writing' and heavy usage of *emoji*, i.e. emoticons (Kinsella 1995).

In 'Individualization, individuality, interiority, and the Internet' (2003a), McVeigh explores the usage of the internet through mobile telephony in Japan. Conducting case studies based on interviews with Japanese university students, McVeigh focuses on what he argues is the dominant 'cyberstructure', in which the role of 'individualization' is central to this logic and practice. McVeigh's argument foreshadows Castells et al.'s assessment that 'individualism, rather than mobility, becomes the defining trend of the mobile society' (2007: 251). McVeigh argues that mobile internet technologies are indeed leading to a shrinking of social capital in which users only contact a small range of existing friends, a phenomenon Habuchi has defined as 'tele-cocooning' whereby new technologies shrink, rather than extend, existing offline social capital (2005).

Thus the pivotal role played by electronic individualism technologies such as the *keitai* and convergent gaming consoles is linked to the fact that they operated, as noted earlier, as one of the first—and thus dominant—portals for the internet. According to a Ministry of Information Affairs and Communication (MIC) survey in 2006, the highest rate of internet subscriptions—amongst the population of 116 million—was via the *keitai*, with over 80 per cent of the population subscribing. Whereas internet access was difficult and expensive in the early to mid 1990s, this latency allowed Japanese users to jump a step in the convergence chain. Having never reached high penetration rates for internet access via PCs, Japan was able to leapfrog to high levels of internet access via the *keitai*. Behind this adoption was a clear demonstration of the interrelationship between personal technologies and electronic individualism.

The internet was first introduced in Japan in 1984, with the JUNET connecting Keio University, the Tokyo Institute of Technology and the University of Tokyo.

In 1994, the prime minister's office established a section for policy management group as an IT policy management group, which in 1998, under the rule of Prime Minister Mori, was given the title of IT Strategic Headquarters (ITSHQ). By 1997, the telecommunications giant NTT initiated i-mode walled garden versions of the internet nationwide. In 2000, ITSHQ drafted an action plan entitled 'e-Japan Strategy'. By September 2001, SoftBank (Yahoo!) had opened Japan's ADSL service. However, the popular use of the internet really came with the introduction of mobile internet services in 1999 (spearheaded by i-mode, which allowed users to access the internet whether they had a PC or not). To this day, the *keitai* remains the most popular way of accessing the internet. The role of the internet in Japan's grappling with twenty-first-century postmodernity—and reconfiguring the projected imagined communities—was an important issue throughout the development of the MIC.

In 2001, its policies were defined by 'the accelerating IT revolution: a broadband-driven IT renaissance'. This was followed in 2003 by MIC focusing upon 'building a new, Japan-inspired IT society' in order to position Japan globally as a key player. By December 2004, MIC announced its policy aim of achieving a '"ubiquitous network society" (u-Japan) in which "anything and anyone" can easily access networks and freely transmit information "from anywhere at any time" by 2010' (MIC 2006: n.p.). These techno-nationalism policies were pivotal in supporting the widespread adoption of the internet in Japan, which, in turn, led to the rise of online gaming and other forms of social media. It is important to understand that the uptake of such a phenomenon as online gaming is dependent upon a variety of factors such as infrastructure and sociocultural nuances.

This example of technological ubiquity, on various levels of hardware and software, has demonstrated a very different pathway for twenty-first-century urban ubiquity from that of Korea. One way of highlighting these two very different centres for gaming and technological ubiquity can be seen in the form of mobility and immobility—Tokyo representing the mobility of electronic individualism, while Seoul symbolizes immobile socialization. Now we will turn to the particular model presented by Seoul.

IMMOBILE SOCIALIZATION: SEOUL, KOREA

The Korean online game market has rapidly emerged as one of the most dynamic in the world. Within a relatively short period of time, Korea has become known for widespread broadband deployment to households, along with a technologically receptive and literate public, which has resulted in the rapid growth in online gaming. Ever since Nexon, a Korean games corporation, introduced the world's first graphic massively multiplayer online game *Kingdom of the Winds* in 1996, Korea has played a central role in the PC-based online game market and digital economy. In 2005, the Korean online game market was worth $1.4 billion, accounting for 56% of the entire Asia Pacific market share. The Korean online game market is expected to continually grow about 20% annually, reaching $2.9 billion by 2009. Due to the rapid growth of users, the structure and dynamics of the interactive game business becomes a key node in the networked environment of virtual capitalism. (Jin and Chee 2009: 19)

In 'The Politics of Online Gaming' (2009), Jin and Chee explore the geo-political, economic, cultural and social dimensions of Korea's creative industries in the form of online gaming. As Jin and Chee highlight, there were various reasons as to why the online gaming phenomenon has been orchestrated to represent Korea both locally and globally. Signposting Jun-Sok Huhh's discussion of the pivotal role of the PC *bang*—as both a culture and a business—in the rise and success of online gaming in Korea, Jin and Chee identify how this local success story was projected onto a global setting. The rise of the PC *bang* was a shift concurrent with the growth of the internet and gaming cultures—in 1997 there were only 100 PC *bangs*; by 2002 this number had exploded to 25,000 (Jin and Chee 2009). The growth of *StarCraft* also witnessed the concurrent emergence of eSports in 1998, and the advent of three TV cable channels, dedicated to gaming, led to it quickly becoming a success story—whereby the top pro-leagues (professional league players) could earn US$1 million per year.

ESports (Electronic Sports)

ESports is the conflation of the two words 'electronic' and 'sport'. It is the term used to describe the playing of video games competitively. Played at both amateur and professional levels, eSports in Korea has been adopted as a popular pastime for youth to watch and enjoy in live and televised tournaments held regularly.

Behind this success story is a narrative informed by strong techno-nationalism. After the 1997 economic crisis of the region, in which Korea ended up being bailed out by the IMF (International Monetary Fund), the Korean government quickly put much of its focus into technology through the Korean Information Infrastructure (KII). By 2003, it not only boasted the highest broadband rates in the world (OECD) but went on to become an example of one of the 'best' governments for IT policy (West 2007). It was therefore no accident that, also by 2003, Korea represented the highest proportion of online gamers per capita in the world (Chou 2003). By 2007, 93 per cent of households had broadband (MIC 2007).

Given its symbolism as one of the dominant examples of twenty-first-century modernity, it is easy to forget that Korea's rise has been relatively recent. Having experienced a tumultuous twentieth century of Japanese rule and the UN-imposed 38th parallel, to then being bailed out by the IMF, Korea has since grown to have the ninth-largest GDP in the world, and the third-strongest economy in the region. Part of its rapid rise has been thanks to the governmental and industry focus on technologies. With the world's highly integrated IT policies, the IT industry in Korea represents over 15 per cent of GDP (MIC 2007)—and this is dominated by the games industry. As Jin and Chee observe, online games have played 'a unique role in Korea's transition towards a digital economy' (2009: 21). They go on to point out that, 'in 2006, the domestic online game market accounted for as much as 81.5% ($1.77 billion), from 76.2% in 2005, of the total game market ($2.17 billion), including console, online, PC and mobile games' (2009: 21). Jin and Chee (2009) also observe that the online game market increased by 41.3 per cent between 2004 and 2005, and by 2007 Korean online games constituted 32 per cent of the world's online gaming market.

With over 2,000 development houses, 65 per cent of Korea's online industry has been dominated by eight companies, including NCsoft, Nexon, Neowiz, NHN and CJ Internet (Lee and Ryu 2006). In 1998, NCsoft released one of Korea's most successful online games, *Lineage*, which was then surpassed in 2006 with the highly successful 'casual' online game *Kart Rider* (Hjorth 2006a). With *Kart Rider*, NCsoft realized the untapped potential of casual online gaming in capturing the interest of the population—especially female players. NCsoft has gone on to specialize in casual online games aimed at female players, and even hosts female-only games nights to cater to this burgeoning demographic.

Central to this vignette is the image of 'turbo-capitalism' (Luttwak 1999) in which online gaming has proliferated; that is, gaming has been deployed within Korea's own version of techno-culture. By 'turbo-captalism' we mean a type of highly accelerated growth in capitalism—especially given that only a few decades ago Korea was viewed as a developing country. Boasting one of the oldest SNSs, Cyworld mini-hompy, which is accessed by over one-third (18 million out of 48 million) of the population daily, an active blogosphere (Park and Kluver 2009) and netizen media such as *OnMyNews*, Korea provides a pivotal model for twenty-first-century techno-culture. Indeed, one of Korea's most famous industries is online gaming, and its attendant industries such as eSports have enamoured the global gaming industry as a possible future model.

In Korea, internet and mobile telephonic spaces are helping to advance Korean forms of democracy (Kim 2003). For Korean sociologists Shin Dong Kim (2003) and feminist anthropologist Hae-Joang Cho (2004), the rise of a specific type of democracy in Korea has been supported in part by new technologies such as mobile phones. In particular, in Seoul, one can find two types of youth sociality predicated upon two convergent technological spaces: first, that of the mobile phone (*haendupon*), and, second, that of the internet, through virtual communities (such as Cyworld's mini-hompy) and online multiplayer games and their attendant social spaces (i.e. PC *bang*). This usage of technological spaces is *not* about substituting the virtual for the actual, but rather it is about supplementing actual relationships (Hjorth and Kim 2005). The relevance of the technology is intrinsically linked to maintaining face-to-face social capital. As Kyongwon Yoon observes, the rise of *haendupon* technology in Korea after 1997 was linked to the rise of youth cultures, and their often-subversive use that saw them labelled 'Confucian cyberkids' (Yoon 2006). By using 'Confucian cyberkids', Yoon invokes the cultural stereotyping reminiscent of techno-orientalism—whereby the 'orient' is associated with technological production—as well as also highlighting the region's prevalent self-orientalizing with its rise in economic and ideological power globally. Parallels can be made between the 'youth problems' associated with the rise of mobile technologies in both Korea (Yoon 2003) and Japan (Matsuda 2005) and the reorientation by government and industry to rectify the negative press.

Gracing the second floor of most commercial buildings in the bustling city of Seoul is a PC *bang*. These rooms are not the equivalent of 'internet cafés'—why would you need one in a city dubbed the most broadbanded country in the world (OECD 2006)? Rather, PC *bangs* fuse game cultures with social spaces, functioning as a 'third space' in between work/school and home (Chee 2005). Huhh (2009) notes that the 'culture and industry' of PC *bangs* have been integral in the nurturing and growth of Korea's most famous gaming genre, MMOGs (see Chapter 4). In the socio-technological fabric of Korea, games function as a vital industry for the Korean youth of today. And yet, like much of the global games industry, it is still dominated by men—as players, as makers, as professionals.

As a burgeoning centre for innovative technologies, and with a conspicuous usage of technologies in the everyday, South Korea's capital, Seoul, could be viewed as a showcase of techno-nationalism as discussed eloquently by Jin and Chee (2009). The projection of 'dynamic Korea' (the tourism slogan used from 2005 to 2007) is one that has infused notions of technological innovation with the rise of power associated with Korea as a nation. In September 2006, approximately 6.4 million PC *bangs* operated on the dominant Korean internet portal, Daum. Almost 80 per cent of Koreans use these PC *bangs* as a social space, participating both online and offline for an average of over six hours per week (NIDA 2006).

The rise of online communities through internet cafés from 1999 to 2002 was perhaps epitomized by *pyeins* (geeks) using the online community site Cyworld (dubbed '*cypyeins*', cy-geeks). The importance of Cyworld ('Cy' meaning 'between' worlds or 'relationship' world) can be witnessed in the fact that over one-third of South Korea's 48 million people regularly use and visit their and friends' mini-hompys. In Cyworld friends are called *ilchons*, a concept used to denote one degree of distance from family members in traditional Korean kinship (e.g. one's mother is one *chon*).

This phenomenon of virtuality goes hand in hand with South Korea's rise as one of the most broadbanded countries in the world. In 2006, Cyworld was expected to generate over US$140 million in sales (Jacobs 2006). Cyworld's success has been, in part, attributed to the dominant lifestyle trends in South Korea—the high-rise identical blocks of flats, and an easy accessibility of broadband coverage. For Korean youth, most of whom still live at home before (and even after) getting married, the third spaces of PC *bangs* operate as private spaces to connect with other people.

Reflection: PC *Bang* as Third Space

In Korea, PC *bangs* operate as third spaces in between work/school and home (Chee 2005). They are highly social spaces. Do you have a similar space as the PC *bang*? Do you play online games with people who are also, simultaneously, in your offline space? How do you think this influences how a game, especially a MMOG, is played?

The popularity of these spaces has in turn led to an expansion of the types of PC *bangs*—such as dating and health (no smoking) PC *bangs* aimed at female and non-traditional PC *bang* goers (Hjorth, Na and Huhh 2009)—as well as the general growth of *bang* genres such as DVD *bangs*.

As Korea turns a new chapter in its turbo-capitalism, and while its games industry continues to grow unabated with burgeoning new genres such as casual online games aimed specifically at female non-traditional players, some things remain unchanged. As noted in a case study (Hjorth, Na and Huhh 2009), many females in PC *bangs* refute the title of 'girl gamers'—this is partly to do with the fact that often they will do many things in a PC *bang* such as homework, minihompy and e-mailing, along with playing casual games. Games are not seen as separate from the other activities. Rather, games are part of the techno-culture that keeps them returning to PC *bangs* daily. This also has to do with the ongoing stigma of games as a 'boy' or male-orientated activity. Despite the reality of the growing female gamer population, this stereotype is hard to shift, both inside and outside Korea.

THE BIG BANG:
CONTEXTUALIZING GAMES

Over the past decade we have witnessed the rise in divergent localized, regional and transnational forms of gaming, and this is particularly prevalent in the Asia-Pacific. The region is unrecognizable in relation to US-centric notions of gaming 'communities' (Wilson and Dirlik 1995). As a region, it has orchestrated a continuous rise in economic power in which technologies have played a key role, and translated GNP into soft cultural capital. Japan of the 1970s and 1980s was indicative of this, as are Korea and mainland China now. These multiple localities of divergent soft power repudiate any fixed notion of the region as the new game of the twenty-first century begins.

This has led historians and theorists such as Giovanni Arrighi (1996, 1998, 2005) and Dirlik (1992, 1999a, 1999b) to argue that the end of the twentieth century was, and much of the twenty-first will be, marked by the resurgence of East Asian capitalism. The transnational flows of gaming cultures in the region highlight emerging cultural capital currencies that are bound by economic, political industrial cultural and social practices.

Through the localized cultures of gaming, we can not only reconceptualize the contested idea of the Asia-Pacific but also the significance of the local in contextualizing global, transnational gaming cultures. In looking at these localized case studies of gaming, we can examine the relationships between the local and global, and explore the pivotal nature of the contexts in which games are played. As Dovey and Kennedy note, the role of 'technicity' (2006) is considerable in influencing game cultures and associated gameplay. 'Technicity', for Dovey and Kennedy, is not composed of merely technological skills and infrastructure. Rather, it is the way in which people engage with the technology—i.e. *how* the technology is contextualized, and thus rendered part of a techno-culture—that constitutes technicity. Thus, the technicity of gaming cultures needs to be located within the relevant techno-culture in order to understand how the technology shapes, and is shaped by, how we view ourselves and others.

As this chapter has illustrated, gaming cultures can be seen as an allegory for a location's shifting power relations at economic, cultural and ideological levels. Here, we see the importance of locating gaming cultures within the techno-cultures from which they emerge, if we are to understand the diversity of gaming cultures and associated forms of gameplay constituting the global games industry. This chapter has focused upon two dominant, and yet often misunderstood, cultures in order to locate gaming within its cultural context. Moreover, by focusing on Tokyo and Seoul, this chapter has provided case studies outside the often-cited US, UK and European contexts.

Lastly, through the ideas of mobility and immobility, this chapter has explored how gaming cultures can manifest across different terrains—technological, cultural, geographic, social, spatial, temporal and ideological. The two case studies have highlighted that mobility is always accompanied by forms of immobility, and that these forces influence gameplay.

Summary

- To understand the reasons why particular games cultures occur, it is important to comprehend the cultural context from which they sprang. As gaming centres, Tokyo and Seoul have complex techno-cultures that have ensured the success of games. Within each context, particular factors such as the cultural, social, economic, political and governmental all inform the associated gaming culture.
- In Tokyo and Seoul we can see two very different examples of gaming cultures. They mark the two directions of gaming—online and mobile. In these locations, we can find different forms of mobility and immobility that manifest within the types of games, as well as the dominant context of play.
- Games can be transnational but they also serve to highlight the differences between localities of gameplay. For example, the consumption of Korean games in China is transnational; however, the ways in which it is played and consumed operate to reinforce the local.

8 CONCLUSION: GAMING IN THE TWENTY-FIRST CENTURY

> Spending the winter of 2006–07 in New York City, I was beginning to lose count of the times I had heard the same story: somebody had taken their new Nintendo Wii video game system home to parents, grandparents, partner, none of whom had ever expressed any interest whatsoever in video games, and these non-players of video games had been enthralled by the physical activity of the simple sports games, had enjoyed themselves, and had even asked that the video game be brought along for the next gathering. What was going on? (Juul 2009: 1)

Given that we have approached the closure of the first decade of the twenty-first century, it seems fitting to reflect upon some of the shifts that have occurred in gaming during this period. The decade could be seen as initiating some of the trends and shifts in gaming that will continue to burgeon. Some of the dominant movements have included the rise of networked, mobile and casual gaming that have, in turn, recruited new breeds of traditionally non-players. From user-friendly devices such as Nintendo Wii and the explosion of games available on the iPhone to the rise of casual online games associated with SNSs (games such *Mafia Wars* and *Happy Farm*; see Chapter 4), games have become part of the global popular cultural imaginary. While players have expanded from male youth to include more people from all types of socio-demographic backgrounds, the growth in experimental and educational games—especially around urban gaming—has been exponential. These shifts have marked the need to rethink understandings of players and gaming in more complex and divergent ways.

Indeed, in an age of participatory media, the rise of 'playbour' (Kücklich 2005) modes of creativity has fed into new models of engagement and agency. Not only is the distinction between casual and hardcore gamers changing, in what Juul has called the 'casual revolution' (2009), but the modes of attentiveness, immersion and distraction involved in gameplay are also shifting. Social media games, characterized by the sandbox genre that parallels the domestic, ongoing 'flow' once occupied by TV's soap opera, continue to grow in number. In doing so, the role of social, creative and emotional labour on behalf of the player and their community expand. What now constitutes 'playbour' activities is much more than what Kücklich (2005) identified in modding; as a result, gaming has become an integral part of popular culture, no longer the prerogative of young males. With the rise of games as part of everyday sociality, new forms of ancillary playbour activities—such as eSports ('electronic sports'; see Chapter 7 for description) and cosplay ('costume play'; see Chapter 5 for definition)—have been developed. Alongside these shifts, gaming has seen two dominant directions emerge (often also converging)—the online and the mobile versions. Such devices as the Wii and the iPhone helped entice new players into the realm of games, recruiting the young and the old.

Games as Water Coolers

As games became an integral part of popular culture, gaming terms and practices were co-opted into the vernacular in many locations globally. Whereas TV once occupied a 'water cooler' position in everyday conversations (the subject of chat and gossip in collective social spaces), games have increasingly become the subject of twenty-first-century water cooler conversations (it is not by accident that the term has already been deployed for games, see http://www.bogost.com/watercoolergames/). Games were no longer seen as being antisocial, rather they epitomized the opposite—they were seen as a key vehicle connecting different players from different demographic backgrounds and cultural contexts. This phenomenon has been characterized by the realization 'that everybody can be a video game player' (Juul 2009: 2).

In this chapter we summarize some of these emergent trends, in order to reflect upon the possible futures of gaming. This chapter, by drawing on the first decade of this century, hopes to provide students with some future directions and paradigms for games in the twenty-first century. Throughout this book, each of the chapters has explored some of the prevalent issues that have defined, and continue to shape, the history and future directions of gaming. Whilst this chapter will review some of the issues raised in each of the chapters, it will also consider more broadly, and somewhat speculatively, future trends for gaming. It is important not to succumb to the techno-fetishism that surrounds much new media—that is, predictions of the future—while also acknowledging some of the previous pathways that games, as new media, have traversed. By outlining several of the dominant trends in the recent decade of global gaming cultures, this chapter will therefore use these changing patterns and practices to inform how we should think about gaming in the past, now and in the future.

This concluding chapter will therefore focus upon some specific trends—such as the rise of the casual player within the mobile and social media gaming worlds, along with playbour activities such as eSports and cosplay—to illustrate new player agency and expansions of gaming. Through these case studies, this chapter will suggest some of the considerations to be made in defining (and redefining) games, and thus game studies, in the twenty-first century.

CASUALLY HARDCORE: GAMES AND NEW TYPES OF ENGAGEMENT AND DISTRACTION

> Games as well as players can be flexible or inflexible: where a casual game is flexible towards different types of players and uses, a hardcore game makes inflexible and unconditional demands on the skill and commitment of a player. Conversely, where a casual player is inflexible toward doing what a game requires, a hardcore player is flexible toward making whatever commitment a game may demand. This explains the seeming paradox of the casual players making non-casual time commitments: a casual game is sufficiently flexible to be played with a hardcore time commitment, but a hardcore game is too inflexible to be played with a casual time commitment. (Juul 2009: 10)

> Even in the seemingly committed practice of game-play, mobile phone engagement is characterised by interruption, and sporadic or split attention in the midst of other activities, a behaviour quite distinct even from handheld console game-play on the Nintendo DualScreen (DS) or PlayStation Portable (PSP). This is recognized by the growing mobile phone game industry and its labelling of a key market as 'casual gamers', who play at most for five minutes at a time and at irregular intervals; it seems mobile phone gamers don't want immersion. (Richardson 2007: 210)

The above quotations indicate how the types of engagement and commitment required by players are changing as the temporal and spatial organization around gameplay are transforming. Through the rise of casual mobile games on networked mobile and convergent devices such as the iPhone, along with an increase in social media usage in which games such as *Happy Farm* and *Mafia Wars* are recruiting non-players and turning them into enthusiastic users, we are witnessing new types of games, gameplay and players that challenge casual versus hardcore distinctions. As the contexts (technological, spatial, sociocultural) for gameplay change and expand, so too do modes of immersion, engagement, distraction and attentiveness, requiring us to rethink what constitutes gameplay.

Casual versus Hardcore Games

Most casual games can be found on handheld devices, especially mobile phones. Games such as *Golf*, *Solitaire* and *Snake* allow users to play quick, often repetitive, games in moments of waiting. Casual games were characterized by being easy and quick—and thus often addictive. Most casual gamers would never see themselves as 'gamers', a term that has been traditionally deemed as a 'hardcore' preoccupation. Hardcore games are ones in which the time and energy investment on behalf of the player is high. The games associated with this type of engagement were online games—especially MMOs. However, these divisions, like gaming, have dramatically changed and blurred.

As discussed in Chapter 6, the expansion of gaming cultures is requiring us to reconceptualize engagement with games beyond twentieth-century models such as the glance and the gaze. Rather, the immersion and involvement of other senses such as the haptic (most prevalent in the case of Wii and iPhone games) demand that we move beyond ocular-centric (visually focused) models. We need to address the diversity of the senses, as well as the ways in which engagement and attention are changing through ubiquitous, 'always on,' anywhere, anytime technologies. This phenomenon has led to shifts in the temporal and socio-spatial dynamics surrounding gameplay: that is, they can be played across a variety of public and private contexts, whilst players are simultaneously maintaining co-presence in both online and offline spaces. In a study of iPhone users in Australia, Richardson (2009) noted that most users played casual mobile games whilst waiting for friends in public places or while travelling on public transport. This means that mobile games involve a type of engagement that negotiates a 'solitary co-presence' whilst being a 'body-in-waiting' (Bissell 2007). As discussed in previous chapters (see Chapters 5–7), the role of co-presence is important within the practices associated with ICTs. Increasingly casual games prey on those 'in-between' or 'waiting' moments—from momentarily breaking from work-related documents onscreen to checking on an SNS game to waiting for appointments. This 'body-in-waiting', or in a semi-engaged attentiveness, is expanding as one of the dominant modes of media practice within contemporary culture. This requires us to rethink definitions and examples of what constitutes 'engagement' and 'participation' as discussed in Chapter 4.

Reflection

Think about all the different times, spaces and circumstances in which you have played games and consider how the type of engagement differ in each context.

Just as online spaces expand for gameplay, so too do these online contexts impact upon offline engagement and immersion. For example, SNS games tend to lend themselves to an ambient context in which the player may be online all day (and all night) in both work and leisure times, as well as simultaneously acting in offline contexts. The games often regain the attention of players if new players (such as friends) come online. Moreover, given that these games tend to reward those users who remain online for long periods, a key component of gameplay is being perpetually semi-present.

As we saw in Chapter 4, in the game *Happy Farm* (like Facebook's *FarmVille*—popular in the Philippines) players can steal from other players when they are not online. This encourages players to not only stay online all the time (to avoid being stolen from) but also to get online at low-peak times (i.e. the middle of the night or early morning) so that they can steal from the vacant farms (i.e. of users not online). Whilst defined as a casual game, by converging with online social media, the game actually taxes players' time and concentration more—via its ambient characteristics—on a par to that of a hardcore game. Although hardcore games supposedly require the total immersion and engagement of the player, often these casual games are played in a context that suggests that players are semi-engaged (i.e. whilst doing something else). This 'in-between' state is increasingly becoming a key attribute of contemporary media culture in which we often have multiple screens (i.e. mobile, PC) competing for attention, and within those screens there are numerous simultaneous applications/tasks warranting notice (i.e. e-mail, messenger and SNS—to name a few—all open on the desktop).

Reflection

In what ways might this situation of engaging simultaneously with different screens, applications and ICTs generally—and the multitasking it can imply—enhance life, perhaps making tasks easier? Alternatively, how can it make it more difficult to achieve certain goals?

In Chapter 6 we explored the case of mobile gaming whereby coexisting modes of being present, not-present and in-between are all evoked when playing casual mobile games in both public and domestic spaces. Increasingly, mobile technologies (from mobile phones such as the iPhone to PSP) use a haptic relation between the user and their mobile phone, which influences the consequent modes of (located) presence, co-presence and telepresence (Hjorth and Richardson 2009). Telepresence, referring to the kind of 'distant presence' that has been enabled and enhanced by ICT extends the physical limits of the body, whilst also distracting attention from those physical limits via televisual and telephonic media. These examples indicate that within contemporary screen cultures there are multiple, competing screens, operating to both momentarily engage users, whilst also distracting them. Just as mobile devices and ICTs have been defined as 'janus-faced' (Arnold 2003) in their ability to both set us free and be a leash (as discussed in Chapter 6), many types of online games—once the prerogative of hardcore or serious gaming—have now become *immersive by distraction*.

Although seemingly contradictory, immersion and distraction have become an integral part of contemporary everyday life, whereby paying attention to rival screens has become the norm. Even the notion of 'distraction' is janus-faced in its origin— derived from the Latin word *distrahere* that means to pull in different directions. Being telepresent, and occupied by 'distracted immersion', means that perception is divided between the 'here' and 'there', such that we can *know* different times and spaces simultaneously—an effect which shifts the boundaries of what counts as social immediacy, and how it is defined and experienced. These emerging 'in-between' modes of attention and distraction can be witnessed in the various gaming trends considered throughout the previous chapters—from social media games and mobile games to urban gaming. We will now reflect briefly upon online social media, then mobile gaming, followed by a re-examination of 'playbour' and some new types of labour and ancillary gaming practices.

GAME 2.0: ONLINE AND SOCIAL

As noted in Chapter 4, the rise of the internet and social media have led to an expansion of the types of games and their associated players in global gaming cultures. Instead of networked media detracting from a sense of place, we are witnessing a re-assertion of the importance of locality. Just as urban games are subject to the sociocultural, linguistic, geographic and technological nuances of a place, so too are online games strengthening the local and contingent. As we explored in Chapter 7, in each location we see various technological and sociocultural factors informing the types of games that are embraced, as well as how they are contextualized. One example explored in Chapter 7 highlighted the fact that, often, MMO guilds in South Korea play the games whilst occupying the same PC *bang*. This practice illustrates the point that the offline is not replacing the online, but rather it is offline cultural practices and presence that inform how online communities perform and interrelate.

The genre of the online game, once understood to be attached to the hardcore player, is becoming increasingly common with the rise of social media. Sites such as Facebook, Renren (once Xiaonei), Cyworld minihompy and mixi (see Chapters 4 and 7) are some of the foremost contexts for recruiting new players. Games become an extension of the already existing social networks, providing new ways to interact and engage frequently with friends, acquaintances and even strangers. These games also function across platforms—such as the PC and mobile phone—to further provide always-on playability for users. With the rise of cross-platform media, it has been games that have most profited from this phenomenon, and, in turn, the types of game genres and player engagement have shifted.

Certainly, the emergence of cross-platformed, convergent media has been instrumental in the rise of SNS-related games. This cross-platforming provides more contexts for players, in different spaces and occupying different lifestyle patterns. These contexts—both in terms of divergent consoles and media frames, as well as the space outside the frame such as public transport, home and work—inform a variety of new ways of engaging in games, as well as co-opting new players from non-traditional demographics. If we are to understand the future of gaming, then understanding issues of media *convergence* is therefore pertinent.

We saw how for Jenkins, contemporary culture is characterized as *Convergence Culture* (2006a) in which media is no longer produced for consumers, but rather consumers (or 'produsers'; see Bruns 2005) play an active role in what he has defined as 'participatory' media (2006b). As Jenkins observes, this media and technological convergence in a participatory culture is occurring simultaneously with sociocultural divergence (such as localized communities of players). The uptake of convergent mobile media is inextricably linked to local considerations. For Goggin, 'convergence indicates the merging of media and cultural industries associated with forms of twentieth century media such as radio, television, newspapers, magazines that came to be relatively well established in their cultural bearings' (2006: 143). Convergence—along with its twin, divergence—are therefore central in understanding the rise of online gaming through SNSs.

From Facebook, Xiaonei, MySpace, Flikr, YouTube, LinkedIn, Twitter and Cyworld to mixi and QQ/Tencent, myriad active social networking sites continue to burgeon globally. As digital ethnographers such as Ito have argued, within the rise of networked social media and gaming we see new forms of youth-driven sociality (Ito et al. 2008). In this phenomenon—encompassing new means of media literacy, creativity and collaboration—practices of 'vernacular creativity' (Burgess 2008) within the UCC and ancillary gaming areas become apparent. From new forms of eSports to SNS games like Renren's *Happy Farm*, *Happy Farmer*, *Friends for Sale* and *Parking War*, users are finding new ways to express themselves and share amongst specific communities.

SNS Games

There are many examples of the same type of SNS game that are given different names. For example, Renren's *Happy Farm* (China) is very similar to Facebook's *FarmVille*. These games involve the players' social network and can be played casually throughout the day whilst doing other activities (i.e. open on the screen while doing other things on the PC). The undisputed success of SNSs has been due to the fact that they tap into established online communities and provide novel ways for socializing through the act of play. SNS games tend to be sandbox in design for non-linear, procedural play. Other examples of SNS games include *Mafia Wars*.

The sharing aspect is pivotal, as it creates a type of collaboration between writer/designer/player/artist/audience like none that has preceded it. Moreover, these sharing activities highlight the significance that 'community' continues to play, especially through social media games, in developing communal forms of creativity, literacy and politics. In any given locality or geographic space, offline communities utilize networked social media games in different ways—subject to the locality's social, cultural, linguistic and national norms, as well as policies and regulations surrounding media technologies. These specific offline conditions inform the online communities. Just as the roles of place and the offline have been reinforced by the new generation of social media games, so too have mobile media increasingly strengthened a sense of place.

MOBILE MEDIA: THE GAME OF BEING MOBILE

One of the key attributes of mobile media that has ensured its success as one of this century's dominant forms of techno-culture is the way that they have operated to enhance notions of place and community. In the deluge of applications that has accompanied the mobile phone's shift from a mere extension of the landline telephone to becoming this century's multimedia Swiss Army Knife (Boyd 2005), games have been central. Whilst the mobile phone was initially viewed as a communications device, mobile media have expanded the forms of communication available through convergence (i.e. becoming an internet portal). This shift sees mobile technologies transforming into mobile media. They have also extended the ways that communications can take place through the sharing of multimedia (i.e. camera phone images), and participation in online entertainment such as games with others elsewhere. This extension of mobile media has, in turn, informed new types of gaming genres and modes of playing.

A key aspect of this has been the rise of haptic screens—most exploited by particular games such as urban mobile games (see Chapter 6). Urban games require the screen to become a physical component of the gameplay, whilst players negotiate online and offline spaces simultaneously.

Urban Games and Touch Screens

As discussed in Chapter 6, there are many subgenres of urban games that use the mobile device (phone or otherwise) in their gameplay. The rise of touch screen devices—from mobile phones such as iPhone and LG Prada to portable game consoles such as Nintendo DS and PSP—brings the haptic into the networked mix. This dimension provides more exciting possibilities for urban gaming.

But even games for the mobile—once the epitome of casual gaming—have grown to make the most of the particularities afforded by mobile media through the use of haptic screens. Whilst the game console Wii has made the haptic a key part of its unique gameplay, mobile media such as the iPhone have also started to 'play up' the integral haptic feature. South Korean companies such as LG, in collaboration with telecommunications giant SK (as discussed in Chapter 7), have long understood the significance of haptic screens for the mobile phone user, and hence have understood the need to speak to this unique feature within mobile phone games. Examples of haptic mobile games were launched as early as 2004 (the now-defunct Gomid company was one of the producers of haptic games for the mobile phone). In sum, whilst twentieth-century screens were all about the visual, twenty-first-century screens are all about the haptic.

Just one glance at the current models of mobile media such as the iPhone and LG Prada underlines this point that the screen is no longer about visuality; it is about haptics—haptic screens to be precise. The engagement of mobile media is not visual as in the case of the gaze or the glance, but rather akin to what Chesher (2004) characterizes as the 'glaze', as discussed in Chapter 6. To reiterate his argument, Chesher draws upon console games cultures to identify three types of glaze spaces—the glazed over, sticky and identity-reflective. These three modes identify different types of immersion and engagement between the device, the gameplay and the player. For Chesher, these three 'dimensions' of the glaze move beyond a visual engagement, using the other senses such as the aural and the haptic.

The haptic has often been under-theorized and overlooked in favour of the once much-privileged visual. Within the twentieth-century canon, media approaches and practices have been preoccupied by the visual and the screen—highlighted by the prevalence of 'tele' technologies such as TV. Accordingly, much of the rhetoric around mobile media and convergence has still been focused upon the frame and visuali·

Figure 8.1: Example of Korean haptic racing game for mobile phone. Photo: Hjorth 2004.

despite movements towards 'cross-platforming'. With the increase in the ubiquity of mobile technologies however, we have also witnessed a concurrent rise in the pervasiveness of the haptic dimension. The number of haptic-type games available on Wii, PSP and iPhones has risen dramatically. Accordingly, in twenty-first-century media, the screen is no longer (just) visual, especially in the context of mobile technologies that accompany the movements and gestures of the body, and perform a different type of embodiment. In contexts of simultaneous online and offline co-presence, being both 'here' and 'there' is so much part of these everyday technologies that it becomes manifest in a growing number of games genres. In these emerging genres we can see an interplay between the engagement of both body and mind. These factors are not only transforming the modes of games available, and expanding the types of potential players and gameplay contexts; they are repositioning the role games can play in the future of media cultures and attendant forms of media literacy.

As noted in Chapter 6, Mäyrä (2003) has argued that many of the earlier video games neglected to engage two pivotal components of gameplay—a negotiation of *place* (co-presence between the gamespace and outside, or between online and offline, here and there) and the associated *mobility* (i.e. emotional, psychological, virtual) that is required to partake in the 'magic circle' of gameplay. In Chapter 6 we explored the role of big/urban/location-aware games in uncovering the significance of place and people in the negotiation of co-presence. The potentiality of these 'big games' to expose and comment on practices of co-presence—traversing virtual and actual, here and there, in contemporary media cultures—has gained much attention. This is because these games highlight some of the key modes of co-presence of everyday life, including ways of negotiating virtual and actual places, online and offline spaces, cerebral and haptic embodiment, and the delay and immediacy of attention.

Alongside these new forms of engagement, we are seeing ways in which ideas about the role of the player—their agency, participation, creativity and labour—are changing. As gaming takes centre stage, we are witnessing the emergence of ancillary forms of media practice and 'playbour'. As was discussed in Chapter 4, with shifts in media consumption and fandom towards participatory modes such as the 'produser', emerging forms of lifestyle practices are being initiated. Some examples include eSports and cosplay, as explored below.

PLAYBOUR: THE RISE OF PLAYERS, NEW MODES OF LABOUR AND ANCILLARY GAMING AREAS

As noted in Chapters 3 and 4 in detail, the relationship between players and game makers is also shifting. Just as the notion of 'the fan' has transformed through the rise of participatory cultures such as social media (Jenkins 1992, 2006a), we are now seeing types of player labour (emotional, affective, social and creative) being dramatically redefined. These new types of 'playbour' have not only blurred the boundaries between the production and consumption of games; they have also given rise to emergent ancillary gaming cultures such as eSports and cosplaying. These ancillary realms allow players to become 'produsers' and, in some cases, become producers or game makers in more formal settings. This is especially the case in cosplaying for female gamers, where an emerging rite of passage in games programs appears to be some young female game players becoming cosplayers, then 'produsers', then game makers (Hjorth 2009c).

Therefore, cosplayers are a key example of the fan as a co-producer in interpreting and adapting game characters into the offline world. Cosplay highlights the boundaries between fans, players and those in creative roles such as designers and producers, which are transforming as a result of media cultures' 'participatory' character (Jenkins 1992, 2006b).

Figure 8.2a and 8.2b: Some cosplayers at the 'Mecca' of cosplay conventions, *Tokyo Game Show*. Photo: Hjorth 2007.

Cosplayers rewrite the role of fandom, as well as acting as examples of twenty-first-century transmedia storytelling (Jenkins 2006a). They transform the relations between gaming and other media while forming various social networks from blogs to offline communities and conventions. However, cosplay must be understood as stemming from the context of Japan and the particular media environment that includes prolific *anime* and *manga* cultures as discussed in the previous chapter. In Chapter 7 we considered some of the broader factors informing Japan's specific techno-culture—such as the role of 'electronic individualism' (Kogawa 1984) and the 'pedestrian, portable and personal' (Ito et al. 2005)—that can be mapped through the historical rise of Japanese technologies and media such as gaming globally. We also reflected upon the particular role of gender within the use and symbolism of technology and media practice in Japan and how the models of gender performativity (discussed in Chapter 5) have expanded dramatically. These models have been co-opted by non-Japanese youth cultures—especially in the Asia-Pacific region—as a way of exploring gendered identity and media practice. Paralleling the role of the avatar as both an extension of one's identity and also as being forms of expression allowing one to depart from one's offline identity (as discussed in Chapter 5), cosplaying provides a vehicle to experiment with gendered performativity outside of cultural norms.

In this way cosplayers have become a key part of the expanding media cultures surrounding gaming. The process of dressing up as game characters affords new types of gender performativity for the likes of 'kogals' (Miller 2005). These kogals deploy irony, often combining the *kawaii* and feminine with the masculine. Kogals, like cosplayers, transgress gender types and de-centre the male role of the *otaku* as prime game consumer (see Chapter 7). Transformation and subversion are all part of the game as cosplayers play fantasies and fictions, bringing media versions of 'techno-cuteness' (McVeigh 2000) into the offline, corporeal world.

However, it is important to recognize that, within Japan, gender scripting around technologies has been incredibly prescriptive. In Japan, the phenomenon that has resulted in *kawaii* culture represents a paradoxical tension between industry personalization and UCC—epitomized by the high school girl pager revolution (Hjorth 2003a, 2003b). Many of the techno-national policies (as discussed in Chapter 7) in Japan have recognized the gendering of technologies—symbolized by the *kôgyaru* (fashionable, youthful female) and the male equivalent, the *otaku* (male technology geek). Both have represented extreme media usage—the *kôgyaru* was famous for her often-subversive use of the *keitai* (mobile phone) while the *otaku* became the icon of Japan's gaming culture. As noted in Chapter 7, such stories as the *Train Man* phenomenon have been fundamental in rescripting more positive narratives of male usage of media in the form of the *otaku* (Freedman 2009).

Figure 8.3a, 8.3b, and 8.3c: Cosplayers at the *Tokyo Game Show*. Photo: Hjorth 2007.

Concurrent to this rescripting of the *otaku* was the rise of the female *kôgyaru* in which new technologies such as the *keitai* (mobile phone) were deployed as part of her diet of restructured femininity. In the latter part of the twentieth century, Japan's national icon, the *oyaji* ('salaryman' as discussed in Chapter 7), had been displaced by the *kôgyaru* (Matsuda 2005). In her disavowal of traditional notions of femininity as passive, she demonstrated through vicarious consumption that she did not need a man—thus gaining much negative press in Japan. In 2005 and 2006, the rise of *keitai* creative industries—and the dominance of female creators and fans in such areas as *keitai shôsetsu* (mobile phone novels)—has highlighted that ongoing role of women (as both makers and consumers) in alternative (indie) media in Japan (Freedman 2009). The *kôgyaru*, like the kogal, are two models of female representation that resist traditional 'feminine' labels and have provided empowered roles for women within new media cultures such as cosplay.

The emergence of cosplayers has highlighted the growing interest and agency of female game players. Emerging from Japanese game and *anime* cultures, the phenomenon has spread globally providing a platform for female fans and gamers to participate actively in the process of gaming cultures and, specifically, to support Japan's role as a 'gaming centre'. As gaming becomes increasingly mainstream, it is ancillary cultures—such as cosplaying—that are demonstrating the aforementioned new forms of gendered performativity. In turn, they reconfigure Japan's role in interactive entertainment in the twenty-first century. The circulation of images of cosplayers takes place across transnational borders, complicating the role of 'consuming Japan' globally. Often, cosplayers outside of Japan draw from their favourite Japanese cosplayer before they role model an actual game character. Increasingly, as more women enter the games industry as both players and producers/designers, so too has the phenomenon of cosplay grown.

Cosplaying is exemplary of the 'produser', that is, emerging forms of creativity and expression within contemporary networked media. As noted in a case study of cosplayers in Melbourne (Australia), the role of consuming Japanese gaming cultures—as part of broader media scapes and digital literacies—is providing ways for young female gamers to role play and shift, as noted earlier, from *player* to *produser* to *producer* (Hjorth 2009c). Indeed, within games programs in Australia, there is a sizable number of young female students who either engage in cosplay or are interested in cosplay as part of their general preoccupation with Japan as an alternative site for gaming. Through cosplay, these young women are provided with an avenue to re-imagine their role in the games industry as they move from consumer to active fan to games designer/producer. For many, cosplaying is synonymous with both Japan and gaming, and thus to partake in cosplaying is to enter into a world in which interpretations of gaming and of Japan are continuously called into question. In the relatively male-dominated industry, cosplaying provides female gamers with a way to explore and

Figure 8.4: Cosplayers in Melbourne. Photo: Hjorth 2007.

express themselves within gaming genres, which, in turn, informs how they contextualize themselves within the games industry.

For non-Japanese, such forms of fashion and self-expression through the *kawaii*—characterized by youthful feminine or androgynous styles (especially in the 1980s)—have provided an avenue for creative identity formation and gender performativity that seemingly transcends the gender tropes within Western culture and the associated gender stereotypes in games. This phenomenon has been part of the success in the adoption of cosplaying outside of Japan whereby youth cultures can subvert their gender performativity by appropriating the 'playful' mode of *kawaii*.

Just as cosplay can be seen as a dominant avenue for predominantly female players to participate and engage in gaming, so too is eSports providing a vehicle for mostly male game players to become stars and icons. Just as Japan provides the material for transnational cosplay playbour, South Korea is exemplary as a centre for the massive growth of eSports gaming. In locations such as Korea, with two TV channels dedicated to gaming (Ongamenet and MBC Game), five IP TVs, and two Web portals, eSports is a lucrative and popular activity with top pro-league players earning up to US$1 million per year (see Chapter 7). In Korea, pro-league players are treated like celebrities, gathering thousands of fans and gaining large corporate sponsorship deals. Since hosting the first 'World Cyber Games (WCG)' in Seoul in 2001, often viewed as the Olympics of Computer Games, Korea has become a model for new avenues for playbour in which financial remuneration and public exposure are part of the package. This suggests a more positive avenue for playbour empowerment than Kücklich's (2005) modding example, where the emotional, creative and affective labour of players can be seen sometimes as a form of exploitation by game companies (see Chapter 4).

For Jin (2010), eSports is complex because it evolves from various cultural and economic factors. As Jin observes, eSports neither fits comfortably as a cultural genre nor as a sporting event. Rather, it converges culture with technology, sport and business. Jin observes that eSports is exemplary of digital convergence, highlighting the ways in which converging media (TV, the internet, the mobile phone) can be deployed in new ways to provide sources for audience participation. Beginning with local *StarCraft* tournaments in 2000, the phenomenon of eSports as a dominant form of popular media culture in Korea has continued unabated. The rise of eSports has been concurrent with the shift of online games into mainstream culture. ESports has both contributed to and been a product of this rise of online gaming. As Peichi Chung notes, the popularity of eSports works to merge different social interest groups, industry players and online game consumers (2008: 313).

ESports did not begin with online gaming, however. Rather, online gaming afforded new models for competition and business that were not earlier provided by non-networked gaming. The first versions of eSports can be seen as early as 1981 with the arcade game *Twin Galaxies*, which allowed players to keep track of their scores against previous players. However, the context of reception was limited to those at the arcade, and the competition only offered a-synchronous gameplay. A second development was in 1983, when a US National Video Game Team was founded and toured to Europe and Asia.

But it was in 1997, with the internet becoming more pervasive in some countries, that eSports took on more growth and formalization. Through the internet, more audiences were able to watch and participate, thus ensuring the expansion of the genre. Whilst countries such as Germany, the United Kingdom and France have attempted to found cable TV programmes or channels dedicated to eSports, none have replicated the successful mainstream model of Korea. Various factors have ensured its success, as discussed in the case study of Korea in Chapter 7, in which we explored the significant role of techno-nationalist policy and the sociocultural phenomenon of the PC *bang* (which Huhh [2009] would also define as a business).

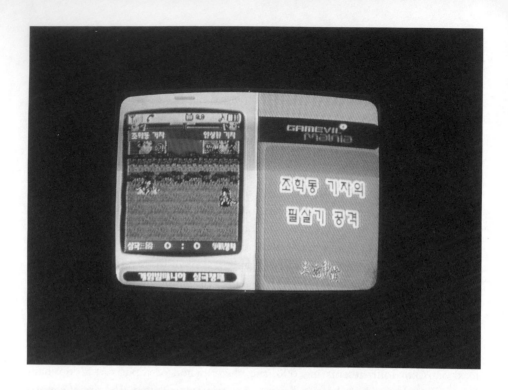

Figure 8.5a and 8.5b: Screenshots of casual games being competitive played in Seoul. Photo: Hjorth 2005.

Both cosplaying and eSports not only attest to the increased popularity of games within mainstream culture, they have also contributed to a new type of playbour agency and engagement that will continue to grow. With these new types of labour and ancillary gaming areas, distinctions between players and produsers are shifting. In the case of cosplaying, this is providing predominantly young females with new avenues to express themselves creatively within gaming cultures and, in some cases, advance to becoming game designers and makers. For eSports in Korea, dominated by male players (good female players tend to become coaches), these pro-league players can transcend the social stigma of hardcore playing and become celebrities with hundreds of female fans.

While these emergent ancillary areas provide exciting new possibilities for a range of playbour practices contributing to empowerment and agency, the role of gender remains relatively fixed. This was noted in a study conducted on young women who play games in Korea—they refuse to be called game players because of the male and antisocial reference, despite the fact they are actively involved in everyday gaming (Hjorth, Na and Huhh 2009). Whilst avenues such as cosplaying are affording many young females entrance into gaming beyond being a player, the industry is still relatively unreflexive with respect to people from numerous demographic backgrounds who can now be deemed to be players. Indeed, as Cassell and Jenkins (1998) and Kafai et al. (2008) have noted, despite the increase of female players and women entering the industry, the stereotypes and the industry itself still need major renovations. As gaming increasingly becomes marked by mainstream and yet divergent demographics in which the rise of ancillary areas can be identified, there are still some disparities between the multiplicity of gaming cultures, modes of player agency and engagement and how they are addressed by the industry.

CONCLUSION: TWENTY-FIRST CENTURY GAMING CULTURES

As we approach the end of the first decade in the twenty-first century, games are providing a variety of alternative and mainstream forms of storytelling. Relationships between players and industry are no longer distinct, as modes of playbour become increasingly pervasive. With games moving onto centre stage as a dominant form of creative and social media, the demographics of players have dramatically expanded to include young and old and male and female in what has been called a 'casual revolution'. In this chapter we have explored some of the key trends in twenty-first-century gaming—the erosion of hardcore and casual categories, the emergence of gaming as one of the most pervasive forms of global popular culture (attaching diverse demographies of players that contest old game player stereotypes), the growing significance of features such as the haptic dimension within screen cultures and the emergence of ancillary gaming cultures such as cosplay and eSports. As the ubiquity of online and mobile devices increases within everyday cultures, we are seeing not only the casualization and socialization of online games through SNSs but also new contexts for playing and modes of player engagement. All these changes mark positive steps in the future of games in the twenty-first century.

Whilst the games industry both globally and locally appears to become all-inclusive, and provides ever-expanding possibilities for new forms of storytelling, authorship, collaboration and community, there are still some problems. In particular, despite gaming becoming popular across the genders and generations, there has been one major hangover from its inception—the far from equal distribution of women within the industry. Whilst this problem has been acknowledged, and attempts have been made to address this through changes to education and recruitment policies within the industry, the fact that female game developers constitute only 12 per cent of those worldwide (International Game Developers Association 2008) suggests that much more work needs to be done if Game 2.0 is going to succeed.

Reflection

Can you think of reasons why a greater proportion of women in the industry might make a difference to the nature of gaming? Would this change the types of games made? How?

As we noted in Chapter 2, thinking about game studies in terms of the domestication approach not only makes us consider the social, cultural and economic dimensions of games but also the ongoing role that *context* plays in informing the *content*, meanings and practices around gameplay. As the stay-at-home vacation ('staycation') and user-friendly consoles such as the Wii play key roles in the rise of family gaming, it is important to consider the way in which the domestic sphere has functioned to construct particular modes of gendered behaviour, and how technologies such as TV, and now games, are constructing different types of gendered and generational modes of interaction. Notwithstanding the body of literature in game studies exploring gendered gaming consumption and production (Cassell and Jenkins 1998)—particularly around types of gendered representation and role models (Kennedy 2002)—the gendered domain of the context of gameplay (i.e. at home, in an internet café) is still in need of analysis.

So too, as gendered genres/platforms such as 'casual' mobile phone games become more compelling and divergent, concurrent with the rise of networked, multimedia devices such as the iPhone, there need to be more studies on gendered modes of gaming and the role of multiple screen engagement. Indeed, to explore 'casual' mobile gaming is, according to the Casual Games Association (2008), a gendered issue, with around 74 per cent of paying customers being female. Mobile convergent, cross-platform devices such as the iPhone have become key repositories for new types of game storytelling with a female focus (Richardson and Hjorth 2009). Within one year of its release in 2008, the iPhone had already more than 1,500 game titles from which to choose—from both mainstream and independent companies. As of December 2008, more than 50 million iPhone games had been downloaded (Moses 2008). This growth signals a need for more female game developers. For Game 2.0 to be as successful as Web 2.0 in developing new avenues for creativity, authorship and collaboration for a variety of communities and individuals, it needs to make clearer inroads into addressing the gender inequalities in which female 'playbour'—and its various forms of social, creative, affective and emotional labour—continues to be a site for industry exploitation rather than empowerment. Game on?

Summary

- As games increasingly become part of the global popular imaginary, this is expanding the types of games played, the contexts in which they are played and the modes of player engagement, as well as bearing witness to the emergence of new ancillary genres such as cosplaying and eSports.
- Some of the key attributes defining gaming in the twenty-first century have been the demise of hardcore and casual categories, the emergence of mobile media (haptic games for mobile phones as well as the more experimental urban games) and playbour realms such as cosplaying and eSports.
- Whilst gaming has shifted from being the preoccupation of young males into being fully embraced by the mainstream, the industry still needs to be more proactive in reflecting the diverse demographics of players (such as women).

ANNOTATED GUIDE TO FURTHER READING

Chapter 1: Introduction

Game studies has emerged from an interdisciplinary background. There are many ways to analyse games, gaming cultures and gameplay. For two key introductory game studies textbooks, see Egenfeldt Nielsen, Smith and Tosca's (2008) *Understanding Video Games: The Essential Introduction* and Mäyrä's (2008) *Introduction to Game Studies: Games in Culture*. For game design students, two of the 'bibles' are Salen and Zimmerman's (2003) *Rules of Play: Game Design Fundamentals* and (2005) *The Game Design Reader*. For readers on both game studies theory and history, Wolf's three books provide a great overview of pivotal texts and movements with the history of games. See Wolf (2001) *The Medium of the Video Game,* Wolf and Perron (eds) (2003*) The Video Game Theory Reader* and the revised 2008 *The Video Game Theory Reader 2*. Also see Raessens and Goldstein's (eds) (2005) *Handbook of Computer Game Studies*.

As for game studies journals, there are four main journals: *Games and Culture* (http://www.gamesandculture.com/news/); *Simulations and Gaming* (www.unice. fr/sg/)*; Games Studies journal* (http://gamestudies.org/); *Journal of Game Development* (http://www.jogd.com/). There are also a few new media journals that often feature important game-related articles: *New Media and Society* (http://www.new-media-and-society.com/); *Convergence* (http://www.luton.ac.uk/Convergence/); *Fibreculture journal* (gaming issue, 2006), http://journal.fibreculture.org/. There are two main international game studies associations relevant for games studies students: Digital Games Research Association (DiGRA), www.digra.org; International Simulation and Gaming Association (ISAGA), www.isaga.info. DiGRA hosts a conference every second year in a different location, www.gamesconference. org. For examples of a game-related video presentations, see http://www.gamesand storytelling.net/.

Chapter 2: The Histories of Gaming

Along with the key reference texts cited under Chapter One, Haddon's (1999) 'The Development of Interactive Games' provides a great contextualization of games within the domestication tradition.

As noted in the summary of approaches towards media technologies and ICTs in Chapter 2, dominant models have included the substantive (McLuhan 1964) and SCOT (social construction of technology) (MacKenzie and Wajcman 1999). In the chapter we explored the impact of the domestication approach (see Hirsch and Silverstone 1992), digital ethnography (Wesch 2008) and virtual ethnography (see Hine 2000) within game studies. For a key example of ethnography, particularly prevalent within the studies of online gaming, see Taylor's (2006a) *Play between Worlds: Exploring Online Game Cultures* and Boellstorff's (2006) 'A Ludicrous Discipline? Ethnography and Game Studies'. Dovey and Kennedy's (2006) *Game Cultures* is very useful in revising game studies within this cultural studies tradition.

For key texts relating to the ludology versus narratology debate, see the work of Frasca, Juul and Aarseth. In particular, see Frasca's (1999) 'Narratology meets Ludology: Similitude and Differences Between (Video)games and Narrative' and (2003) 'Simulation versus Narrative', as well as Juul's (one of the most defiant ludologists) (1999/2001) 'A Clash Between Game and Narrative: A Thesis on Computer Games and Interactive Fiction' (2001 English translation from Danish) and (2005) *Half-Real: Video Games between Real Rules and Fictional Worlds*.

One of the issues when exploring gaming is the role of play. Definitions of play are integral to the *ludus* and *paidia* discussion—see Caillois's (1961) *Man, Play and Games* and also Huizinga's ([1938]1955) *Homo ludens: A study of the play element in culture*. Sutton-Smith (1997) offers a wonderful revision in *The Ambiguity of Play*.

Chapter 3: Games as New Media

For general new media references, not necessarily focused specifically upon gaming, see the influential Bolter and Grusin's (1999) *Remediation: Understanding New Media*, Jenkins's (2006a) *Convergence Culture: Where Old and New Media Intersect* and Manovich's (2001) *The Language of New Media*. For references that explore the intersection between new media and gaming, see Waldrip-Fruin and Harrigan's (2004) (eds) *First Person: New Media as Story, Performance, and Game,* Darley's (2000) *Visual Digital Culture: Surface Play and Spectacle in New Media Genres*, Dovey and Kennedy's (2006) *Game Cultures* and Lister's (2002) *New Media: A Critical Introduction*.

Given the pervasiveness of games as both a cultural practice and artefact, they have become tools of experimentation for such new media groups as UK's Igloo (i.e. Swan Quake), Swedish artist Tobias Bernstrup (http://bernstrup.com/), Australian Julian

Oliver (http://julianoliver.com/) and US artists Cody Arcangel (http://www.beige
records.com/cory/), Eddo Stern (http://www.c-level.cc/tekken1.html; http://waco.
c-level.org/) and Brody Condon. Moreover, the integral role that hacking has played
in the birth and growth of gaming can be found in the variety of player-driven UCC
genres such as machinima and modding (computer modifications). For an example
of mainstream, professional machinima, see Rooster Teeth (specifically *Red vs. Blue*,
which was adapted from the *Halo* game engine http://www.roosterteeth.com).

As gaming has increasingly become prevalent in popular and mainstream culture,
we can also see the rise of indie (independent), political and educational games, of
which a variety of examples can be found. The 'water cooler' games (http://www.
bogost.com/watercoolergames/) are exemplary of this burgeoning field. The spirit
of hacking and the indie gamer has continued throughout the rise of gaming to
mainstream culture. As discussed earlier, examples such as modding and machinima
highlight the strong drive of players and their labour practices. Festivals such as
Indie Games Con (http://www.indiegamescon.com) have been important in bringing together programmers, artists, designers, musicians and produsers ('producers
plus users', Bruns 2005) to foster independent discussion and debate around the
games industry.

Chapter 4: Web 2.0, Social Media and Online Games

In the rise of 'participatory' and 'networked' social media such as Web 2.0 and online
gaming, we are seeing emerging, and yet remediated, forms of new media. Through
the rubric of online gaming communities, we can begin to reconceptualize what
these emergent modes of participation, engagement, creativity and collaboration entail. In this chapter we explored the contested terrain that is Web 2.0. Characterized
by collaboration, sharing and distribution sites like YouTube, Flickr and Social Networking Sites (SNSs), Web 2.0 and its associated social media is having a dramatic
impact upon games genres, modes of play and recruiting larger player audiences
across a variety of demographics.

In this chapter we explored some of the ways in which games are impacting upon
the social fabric of the online, and how social media such as SNSs like Facebook were
recruiting new players at the same time as converting the types of games played. We
also considered how MMOGs, once the preoccupation of 'hardcore' gamers, have
now become casualized (Juul 2009) and part of the daily diet of many millions of
SNS users. In Singapore, Facebook users are now becoming synonymous with *Mafia
Wars* players; in China, Renren (formerly Xiaonei) and Kaixin users are constantly
keeping an eye on their farms and livestock in *Happy Farm*. In sum, online games are
recruiting the young and the old as key forms of everyday sociality and play.

While Web 2.0 has often been wrongly assigned to Tim O'Reilly as the creator, its distinguishing features include 'participatory', 'dynamic' and 'user-centred'. For two journal special issues, see Munster and Murphie's 'Web 2.0: Before, during and after the Event', *Fibreculture journal* 14 and Goggin and Hjorth's (2009) 'Waiting to participate', *Communication, Politics & Culture*, 42 (2). For further reading on SNSs, see boyd (http://www.danah.org/SNSResearch.html), Shirky (2008) and Hjorth (2007, 2009a, with Kim 2005). For discussions on social media and games, see Malaby (2006), Taylor (2003b, 2006a, 2006b) and Williams et al. (2006).

Chapter 5: The Politics of the Personal: Avatar Representation, Identity and Beyond

Since the inception of cyberspace as a 'consensual hallucination' by famous sci-fi writer Gibson in his pioneering book *Neuromancer* (1984), the way in which the online has been conceptualized, imagined and practiced has grown to encompass various communities and networks. As a metaphor for the internet, 'cyberspace' was often used to refer to the digital networked spaces of the online rather than the hardware and software that are also associated with the internet.

For early debates, see some of the 1990s poststructuralist feminists such as Haraway (1985), Turkle (1995), Stone (1995), Nakamura (2002) and Wajcman (1991) who identified the ways in which identity was constructed across online and offline spaces in the face of various inequalities, and how cyberspace's consensual hallucination has taken on numerous guises.

One of the ways in which users express themselves online is through 'avatars'. As a concept, the avatar has come under much revision, but avatars can be defined as personal representations used by individuals in digital environments. For discussion of avatars as bodies and identities, see Taylor (2003a) and Pearce (2009). Discussions of avatars often draw explicitly upon poststructural analyses of identity and lifeworlds—see in particular Butler (1991) in the case of gender and Luckmann (1983) in the case of lifeworlds.

In this chapter we explored a case study of the avatar through the role of cute character culture. We focused upon the history of cute culture through the context of Japanese *kawaii* (cute) culture. For further details on *kawaii* culture, see Kinsella (1995), Allison (2003) and Hjorth (2003a).

Chapter 6: Glaze Cultures: Urban and Location-aware Gaming

Vodafone magazine, an online magazine dedicated to mobile media (www.receiver. vodafone.com), has featured many important articles on urban and hybrid reality gaming. Some of the articles include Adams (2004), Lantz (2006), Mäyrä (2003) and Galloway (2004a, 2004b). For discussions on the emerging modes of engagement and mobile media, see Chesher's (2004) 'Neither Gaze nor Glance, but Glaze: Relating to Console Game Screens', Richardson's (2007) 'Pocket Technoscapes: The bodily Incorporation of Mobile Media' and Hjorth's (2008b) 'Being Real in the Mobile Reel'.

De Souza e Silva and Sutko edited one of the first publications devoted to locative media—see (2009) *Digital Cityscapes: Merging Digital and Urban Playspaces*. As one of the experts in the various areas, some key texts of de Souza e Silva's include (2006a) 'Interfaces of Hybrid Spaces', (2006b) 'From Cyber to Hybrid: Mobile Technologies as Interfaces of Hybrid Spaces' and (2004) 'Art by Telephone: From Static to Mobile Interfaces'.

The case studies explored throughout the chapter include the following URLs for games references: Dotplay: INP (2005–2007) http://www.tyshow.org/web/dotplay telecom/dotplay_telecom.html; *Big Urban Game (B.U.G.)*: (2003) http://gothamist. com/2003/09/04/bug_big_urban_game.php; *Can you see me now?*: Blast Theory and The Mixed Reality Lab (2001–2004) http://www.canyouseemenow.co.uk; *CitySneak* http://www.untwine.net/webpage/CitySneak_index.htm; *CitiTag*: Centre For New Media (2004) http://cnm.open.ac.uk/projects/CitiTag/; Geocaching: http://www.geocaching.com/; *I like Frank*: Blast Theory and The Mixed Reality Lab (2004) http://www.ilikefrank.com; *Mogi*: NewtGames (2003–2006) http://www. MogiMogi.com; *Pac-Manhattan*: http://pacmanhattan.com/; *Shoot me if you can* INP (2005) http://eng.nabi.or.kr/project/view.asp?prjlearn_idx=119.

Chapter 7: Gaming in the Asia-Pacific: Two Futures for Gaming—Online Gaming versus Electronic Individualism

There are still relatively few texts focusing specifically upon the Asia-Pacific region available in English, despite the significance of locations such as Japan, South Korea and China in the consumption and production of games. Two examples that include a sampling of case studies and approaches focusing upon the region are Hjorth and Chan (2009) (eds) *Gaming Cultures and Place in Asia-Pacific*, and a special issue of *Games & Culture* (2008) 3 (3) edited by Hjorth.

QUESTIONS AND EXERCISES

Chapter 1: Introduction

Exercise 1: The Art of Adaptation

Working in pairs, take an example of a non-computer game such as chess or mah-jong and think about how you would implement and present it differently for playing on two different devices—the personal computer and mobile phone.

Then consider how you would redesign it for playing in another cultural context, perhaps a location where the game was less familiar. What factors would you need to consider? Reflect upon the cultural, technological, linguistic and social issues that you might have to take into account.

Once you have adapted the game for a different cultural context, you now need to think about how you would redesign/market it for two different age groups—one for teenagers (13–16 years) and the other for people in their fifties.

Exercise 2: What Types of Games Have You Played?

Draw up a personal history of the games you have played throughout your life and discuss the different types of gameplay and context.

Questions

1. Twenty-first-century media have been characterized as 'conversation' (Jenkins 2005), as opposed to twentieth-century 'packaged' media. This transformation is epitomized by the rise of user created content (UCC). Discuss this evolution and what this means for conceptualizing media practices, and especially games.
2. How do place, gender, ethnicity and age impacts upon the types of game played? Choose one of the notions (e.g. place) and find two diverse examples to compare and contrast (e.g. a 'typical' male and female game). Try to move beyond stereotypes by being specific and detailed.

Chapter 2: The Histories of Gaming

Exercise

This exercise will take the form of a class debate. Divide the class into two groups—those who are arguing for 'ludology' and those arguing against (taking a narratology approach). Try to find as many working examples of games to illustrate your argument. You may wish to look at different genres (e.g. sandbox) or specific games like *GTA*. Clarify your definition of narrative and consider the relationship between *ludus* and *paidia*.

Questions

1. What are some of the ways in which play and game have been defined? Starting with the pivotal ludology versus narratology debate, discuss some of the limits and advances to the various approaches around 'games' and 'play'.
2. As noted in Chapter 2, we need to think of the history of games as multiple and divergent. In turn, the interdisciplinary nature of game studies demonstrates many approaches. Choose one of the approaches covered (such as domestication) and discuss the limits and possibilities afforded by such a methodology in understanding games.
3. The media effects model tends to be ascribed to any new media. Like TV, games have attracted much negative press from the mass media in which stories about game addiction have dominated. Take some key examples of such 'media effects' stories and analyse the text. Discuss how the story positions games as media and the agency (or lack thereof) of players. What factors does the story neglect to address?

Chapter 3: Games as New Media

Exercises

Machinima is a neologism for 'machine cinema' and it is characterized by use of a game engine. Machinima offers a genre in which to critique the normal assumptions implicit in gameplay and in stereotypes about gaming. In this class exercise, students will be asked to form groups of 2–4 people. This assignment asks groups to make a machinima that explores and critiques some myths around gaming.

Here are some examples of myths you may wish to subvert:

- Gaming causes violence
- Girls don't play FPS
- Children become violent through playing games
- Old people don't play games

Alternatively, what defines an 'indie' game as opposed to a mainstream one? Take an example of each of the genres and discuss why they are defined under that category.

Questions

1. According to Flanagan (2009), one way in which games and play can be conceptualized is through avant-garde art movements. Do you agree? Outline Flanagan's argument and then find game examples to discuss.
2. One of the key characteristics of new media is that it often borrows from older media. This has led theorists such as Flew to ask, 'what is *new* about new media?' (2002). New media theorists Bolter and Grusin describe this process as 'remediation' (1999). Define remediation and how this notion can be applied to thinking about game studies as new media.
3. What features characterize games as art? How do these differ from non-art games? Analyse some examples of art games and the attributes that render them as 'art'. Is it context? The fact they are made by artists? Is there some content or approach that identifies them as art?

Chapter 4: Web 2.0, Social Media and Online Games

Exercises

In groups, choose a case study in the form of a social networking system (SNS) and discuss one of the associated games available. For example, you may wish to look at Facebook (or the contemporary equivalent) and discuss *Mafia Wars*. Consider the ways in which the game incorporates play, community and social capital and how this extends the existing network and practices of that SNS. You may wish to interview some players and ask them how their usage of the SNS changed and how it repositioned the role of games in their daily life. Reflect upon the SNS games you and your friends play: How do these types of games differ from other online games? You may wish to compare and contrast.

Alternatively, imagine it is five years later—what role do you think SNSs play? Will they continue to thrive? Or is it just a fad? What will the internet look like then? Will it be an extension of what it is today? Or a departure? Justify your vision.

Questions

1. Since Bourdieu first coined the term 'social capital' in 1979, it has come under much revision from theorists such as Colman and Putman. Outline the various definitions and some of the ways it is continuing to change in the face of Web 2.0, online games and social media.

2. The role of ethnography has played a pivotal role in the emerging approaches to analysing online gaming communities as evidenced in the work of Taylor and Pearce. Outline the different subsets of ethnographic approaches and argue as to the validity—limitations and benefits—afforded by the specific methods.

Chapter 5: The Politics of the Personal: Avatar Representation, Identity and Beyond

Exercises

1. In this class exercise each person will contribute one type of avatar they have used at some point. Provide an image of the avatar along with the context in which it functioned (e.g. *World of Warcraft*) and the types of emotions, feelings and thoughts you associate with that avatar. Get into small groups of 4–5 students and discuss the different avatars, especially considering the relationship between aesthetics, ethics and sociocultural considerations.

2. In this class exercise, each group is given a particular gaming environment. These gaming environments should be diverse in terms of the types of aesthetics involved, ranging from highly 'cute' contexts such as *LittleBigPlanet* and Wii, to MMO fantasy games like *World of Warcraft* and *Final Fantasy*, to realism mediascapes provided in *GTA* and *Second Life*. Each user will construct an avatar for the group's gaming environment detailing why they made certain aesthetic choices and how this reflects their relationship to the game and its associated gameplay and community, as well as how it functions as a 'presentation of self' (Goffman 1959).

3. How does design influence the ways in which people relate to their character and play a game? Choose an example of a cute and realistic character you have played and how this impacted upon your experience and engagement with the game. Compare and contrast in groups.

Questions

1. Since the inception of cyberspace as a 'consensual hallucination' by famous sci-fi writer William Gibson (1984), the way in which the online has been conceptualized, imagined and practised has grown to encompass various communities and networks. How has the internet changed over the past three decades? Think of some examples (i.e. hardware, software, graphics, memory, filmic and literary depictions) and discuss.

2. Avatars can be seen as part of a type of online performativity. Some of the ways to conceptualize the role of the avatar have been through Butler's (1991) notion of performativity and Cleland's 'impression management' (2009). For T. L. Taylor, avatars are 'intentional bodies' (2003), whilst for Pearce avatars are 'the primary

forms of expression provided to players' (2009: 111). Discuss some of the ways in which avatars have been theorized and the limits and possibilities afforded by the different approaches. You may wish to use a case study of an online gaming avatar to illustrate your point.

Chapter 6: Glaze Cultures: Urban and Location-aware Gaming

Exercises

1. After reflecting upon some of the examples provided in this chapter, this exercise asks you to work in groups to invent your own urban mobile game. Try to design a game that you believe makes the most of your own specific sociocultural context and urban setting. For example, if you live in a setting in which there is graffiti, you may wish to invent a game that makes players find specific tags by providing camera phone details of the images. Alternatively, you may wish to improvise one of the games discussed in this chapter or, perhaps, redesign a specific video game you already know so that it fits into the context of an urban setting.

    The game can use either advanced technology or simple devices in its gameplay. The simpler ones, of course, will be able to be tested and played, whilst the more technologically advanced will just have to be presented to demonstrate the concept. Consider how your game relates to others in the genre, as well as how it demonstrates good conceptual exploration, clear organization and structuring of ideas and visual material.

2. Alternatively, the rise of mobile phones as networked multimedia devices has made them an increasingly pertinent realm for games. In turn, the context of mobile phones, as an intimate device that accompanies people almost everywhere, anywhere, has impacted upon the types of games made for the device. Discuss some of the key features of mobile phone games and how they might be changing. You may want to focus specifically on the iPhone as a model and explore some of the types of games being made.

Questions

1. What are the different types of urban mobile games? How do they redefine the experience of the urban? Provide some examples beyond the ones in the chapter to illustrate your point.

2. What are some of the ways urban mobile games affect players? You may wish to consider the difference between one of the examples provided (i.e. *Pac-Manhattan*) and how it differs from *Pac-Man*. Discuss the role of paradoxes such online/offline and cerebral/haptic games have within the gaming space.

3. Drawing on Ellis's (1992) discussion of TV as glance and film as gaze culture, Chesher (2004) uses the notion of the glaze to discuss engagement with games. Are there types of engagement that differ between games and other media? Are there forms that are similar? Outline the theories around engagement and analyse through a case study of specific games and their attendant consoles.

Chapter 7: Gaming in the Asia-Pacific: Two Futures for Gaming—Online Gaming versus Electronic Individualism

Exercise

In groups take one well-known game from both Japan and South Korea and compare and contrast them. Consider the different types of gameplay, engagement, game content and context of reception (i.e. PC, PSP) and discuss how you think these games reflect specific characteristics of each location.

Questions

1. In this chapter we explored the two very different case studies of Tokyo and Seoul to see how gaming cultures are subject to various factors at the level of the local. Choose another cultural context (such as China or the United Kingdom) and discuss the various specific factors at play such as regulation (government and industry), socioculture, language and economy.
2. Discuss some of the differences (i.e. gameplay, context, immersion and community) between online games and games for mobile devices such as PSP. You may wish to focus upon a game from each genre to discuss in detail.

Chapter 8: Conclusion: Gaming in the Twenty-first Century

Exercise

How do you imagine the future of games? Working in small groups, make a list of some of the issues and directions you see developing in the games industry. Describe a typical playing scene you could imagine in five years' time.

Questions

1. Choose one of the ancillary areas such as cosplay or eSports to reflect upon, consider and revise in light of the notion of 'playbour'. What types of player's skills and labour are being utilized? How does it reflect and expand upon the role of gaming as a medium? You may wish to choose a particular case study to explore (i.e. *StarCraft*, eSports or cosplaying groups in your cultural context).

2. Investigate some of the current haptic games available across a variety of consoles. Choose some of the dominant examples and discuss the role of haptics within gameplay, as well as how that might inform different types of gameplay and player engagement. Which game do you think is the most successful in exploiting the characteristics of gaming within haptic screens and why?

3. Do you agree with Juul's (2009) assertion that there is a 'casual revolution' in which everyone can become a player? Develop an argument for and against Juul's claim.

4. Is it possible to talk about types of gameplay in terms of engagement and distraction? What are some of the various modes of attentiveness and participation across the different consoles and playing contexts? Make a list of types of engagement (full, semi, distracted), co-presence (online and offline, here and there) and the possible playing contexts (train, bedroom, classroom). Consider some of the variables. You may wish to analyse in the context of particular case studies.

5. The shift of online games from being hardcore, as in MMOGs such as *Lineage* and *WoW*, towards the prevalence of casual online games linked to social media such as Facebook is noticeable. Take a SNS game such as *Mafia Wars* and compare it to a more traditional MMOG within a similar genre.

BIBLIOGRAPHY

Aarseth, E. (1997), *Cybertext: Perspectives on Ergodic Literature,* Baltimore: Johns Hopkins University Press.

Adams, M. (2004), 'Experiments in Mixed Reality', *receiver* 09, www.receiver.vodafone.com (accessed 3 July 2008).

Allen, M. (2009), 'Tim O'Reilly and Web 2.0: The Economics of Memetic Liberty and Control', in G. Goggin and L. Hjorth (eds), special issue of *Communication, Politics & Culture,* 'Waiting to Participate', 42 (2): 6–23.

Allison, A. (2003), 'Portable Monsters and Commodity Cuteness; *Pokémon* as Japan's New Global Power', *Postcolonial Studies,* 6 (3): 381–98.

Anderson, B. (1983), *Imagined Communities: Reflections on the Origin and Spread of Nationalism,* London: Verso.

Ang, I. (1985), *Watching* Dallas*: Soap Opera and Melodramatic Imagination,* London: Routledge.

Appadurai, A. (2000), 'Grassroots Globalisation and the Research Imagination', *Public Culture,* 12 (1): 1–19.

Ariés, P. (1962), *Centuries of Childhood: A Social History of Family Life*, trans. R. Baldick, New York: Knopf.

Arnold, M. (2003), 'On the Phenomenology of Technology: The "Janus-faces" of Mobile Phones', *Information and Organization,* 13: 231–56.

Arnold, M. (2007), 'The Concept of Community and the Character of Networks', *Journal of Community Informatics,* 3 (2), http://www.ci-journal.net/index.php/ciej/article/view/327/355 (accessed 20 October 2008).

Arrighi, G. (1994), *The Long Twentieth Century: Money, Power, and the Origins f Our Times,* New York: Verso.

Arrighi, G. (1996), 'The Rise of East Asia and the Withering Away of the Interstate System', *Journal of World Systems Research,* 2 (15), http://jwsr.ucr.edu/archive/vol2/v2_nf.php (accessed 5 July 2007).

Arrighi, G. (1998), 'Globalization and the Rise of East Asia', *International Sociology,* 13 (1): 59–77.

Arrighi, G. (2005), 'States, Markets and Capitalism, East and West', Semináro Internacional Alternativa Globalização UNESCO, Rio de Janeiro, October.

Arrighi, G., Hamashita, T. and Selden, M. (eds) (2003), *The Resurgence of East Asia: 500, 150, 50 Year Perspectives,* London: Routledge.

Bakardjieva, M. (2003), 'Virtual Togetherness: An Everyday-life Perspective', *Media Culture Society,* 5: 291–313.

Baym, N. K. (1995), 'The Emergence of Community in Computer-Mediated Communication', in S. Jones (ed), *Cybersociety,* Newbury, CA: Sage, pp. 138–63.

Beck, U., and Beck-Gernsheim, E. (2002), *Individualization: Institutionalized Individualism and Its Social and Political Consequences,* London: Sage.

Befu, H. (2003), 'Globalization Theory from the Bottom Up: Japan's Contribution', *Japanese Studies,* 23 (1): 1–22.

Bell, D., and Kennedy, B. (2000), *The Cybercultures Reader,* London: Routledge.

Berlant, L. (1998), 'Intimacy', in L. Berlant (ed), special issue of *Critical Inquiry,* 'Intimacy', 24 (2): 281–88.

Berners-Lee, T. (2006), 'Interviewed by Scott Laningham', *developerWorks,* http://www.ibm.com/developerworks/podcast/dwi/cm-int082206txt.html (accessed 10 September 2009).

Bittanti, M., and Quaranta, D. (eds) (2006), *GameScenes: Art in the Age of Videogames,* Milano, Italy: John & Levi.

Bissell, D. (2007), 'Animating Suspension: Waiting for Mobilities', *Mobilities,* 2 (2): 277–98.

Blast Theory (2005), *Can You See Me Now?,* http://www.blasttheory.co.uk/bt/work_cysmn.html (accessed 8 November 2005).

Boellstorff, T. (2006), 'A Ludicrous Discipline? Ethnography and Game Studies', *Games & Culture,* 1 (1): 29–35.

Boellstorff, T. (2008), *Coming of Age in Second Life: An Anthropologist Explores the Virtually Human,* Princeton: NJ: Princeton University Press.

Bolter, J., and Grusin, R. (1999), *Remediation: Understanding New Media,* Cambridge, MA: MIT Press.

Bourdieu, P. (1984 [1979]), *Distinction: A Social Critique of the Judgment of Taste,* trans. R. Nice, Cambridge, MA: Harvard University Press.

Bourriaud, N. (2002), *Relational Aesthetics,* trans. S. Pleasance and F. Woods, Dijon: Les Presses du Réel.

boyd, d. http://www.danah.org/SNSResearch.html.

boyd, d. (2003), 'Reflections on Friendster, Trust and Intimacy', School of Information Management & Systems (SIMS), University of California, Berkeley.

boyd, d. (2004), 'Revenge of the User: Lessons from Creator/ User Battles', *O'Reilly Emerging Technology Conference,* February, http://www.danah.org/papers/Etech2004.html (accessed 5 March 2006) Presses du Réel.

boyd, d. (2006), 'Friends, Friendsters, and MySpace Top 8: Writing Community into Being on Social Network Sites', *First Monday* 11:12, December, www.firstmonday.org.issues/issue11_12/boyd/index.html.

boyd, d., and Heer, J. (2006), 'Profiles as Conversation: Networked Identity Performance on Friendster', in *Proceedings of the Hawaii International Conference on Systems Sciences* (HICSS–39), January.

Boyd, J. (2005), 'The Only Gadget You'll Ever Need', *New Scientist,* 5 March: 28.

Bruns, A. (2005), 'Some Exploratory Notes on Produsers and Produsage', *Snurblog,* 3 November 2005, http://snurb.info/index.php?q=node/329 (accessed 10 December 2007).

Butler, J. (1991), *Gender Trouble*, London: Routledge.

Burgess, J. (2008), '"All Your Chocolate Rain Are Belong to Us"? Viral Video, YouTube and the Dynamics of Participatory Culture', in G. Lovink et al. (eds), *The Video Vortex Reader*, Amsterdam: Institute of Network Cultures.

Caillois, R. (1961), *Man, Play and Games*, trans. Meyer Barash, New York: Free Press.

Cassell, J., and Jenkins, H. (eds) (1998), *From Barbie to Mortal Kombat: Gender and Computer Games*, Cambridge, MA: MIT Press.

Castells, M. (1996), *The Rise of the Network Society, The Information Age: Economy, Society and Culture*, vol. 1, Cambridge, MA: Oxford University Press.

Castells, M. (2001), *The Internet Galaxy: Reflections on the Internet, Business, and Society*. Oxford: Oxford University Press.

Castells, M., Fernandez-Ardevol, M., Qiu, J. L. and Sey, A. (2007), *Mobile Communication and Society: A Global Persepective*, Cambridge, MA: MIT Press.

Casual Games Association (CGA) (2008), http://ww.casualgamesassociation.org/ (accessed 5 February 2009).

Chan, D. (2006), 'Negotiating Intra-Asian Games Networks: On Cultural Proximity, East Asian Games Design, and Chinese Farmers', in C. Chesher, A. Crawford and J. Kücklich (eds), special issue of *Fibreculture,* 'gaming networks', 8, http://journal.fibreculture.org/issue8/index.html (accessed 10 October 2007).

Chan, D. (2008), 'Convergence, Connectivity, and the Case of Japanese Mobile Gaming', *Games and Culture,* 3 (1): 13–25.

Chan, D. (2009), 'Beyond the "Great Firewall": The Case of In-game Protests in China', in L. Hjorth and D. Chan (eds), *Gaming Cultures and Place in Asia-Pacific*, London: Routledge, pp. 141–57.

Chasey, J. (2004), 'The Future of Mobile Gaming—Multiplayer Games', *receiver* 11, www.receiver.vodafone.com/11/index.html (accessed 6 April 2006).

Chee, F. (2005), 'Understanding Korean Experiences of Online Game Hype, Identity, and the Menace of the "Wang-tta"', *DIGRA Conference, Changing Views—Worlds in Play*, Canada.

Chesher, C. (2004), 'Neither Gaze nor Glance, but Glaze: Relating to Console game Screens', *SCAN: Journal of Media Arts Culture*, 1 (1), http://scan,net.au/scan/journal (accessed 10 February 2007).

Cho, H.-J. (2004), 'Youth, Internet, and Alternative Public Space', *Urban Imaginaries: An Asia-Pacific Research Symposium*, Lingnan University, Hong Kong.

Cho, H.-J. (2005), 'Reading the "Korean Wave" as a Global Shift', *Korea Journal*, Winter: 147–82.

Chou, Y. (2003), 'G-commerce in East Asia: Evidence and Prospects', *Journal of Interactive Advertising,* 4 (1), http://jiad.org/vol4/no1/chou/.

Chua, B. H. (ed.) (2000), *Consumption in Asia*, London: Routledge.

Chua, B. H. (2006), 'East Asian Pop Culture: Consumer Communities and Politics of the National', *Cultural Space and the Public Sphere: An International Conference*, Seoul, South Korea, March.

Chung, P. (2008), 'New Media for Social Change: The Online Gaming Industries in South Korea and Singapore', *Journal of Science, Technology and Society,* 13: 303–23.

Chung, P. (2009), 'New Media Globalization in Asia: A Comparative Study of Online Gaming Industries in South Korea and Singapore', in L. Hjorth and D. Chan (eds), *Gaming Cultures and Place in Asia-Pacific*, London: Routledge, pp. 58–77.

Clarke, A., and Mitchell, G. (eds) (2007), *Videogames and Art*, Bristol, UK: Intellect Books.

Cleland, C. (2009), 'Face to Face', in G. Goggin and L. Hjorth (eds), *Mobile Technologies*, New York: Routledge, pp. 217–32.

Clifford J., and Marcus, G. E. (eds) (1986), *Writing Culture: The Poetics and Politics of Ethnography*, Berkeley: University of California Press.

Colman, J. (1988), 'Social Capital in the Creation of Human Capital', *American Journal of Sociology*, 94: 95–120.

Cornell, S. (1995), 'The Ethnography of an Electronic Bar: The Lesbian Café', *Journal of Contemporary Ethnography*, 24 (3): 270–98.

Darley, A. (2000), *Visual Digital Culture: Surface Play and Spectacle in New Media Genres*, London: Routledge.

Davis, A. (2005), 'Mobilising Phone Art', *RealTime*, http://www.realtimearts.net/article/issue66/7782 (accessed 20 August 2005).

Dewdney, A., and Ride, P. (2006), *The New Media Handbook*, London: Routledge.

De Souza e Silva, A. (2004), 'Art by Telephone: from Static to Mobile Interfaces', *Leonardo Electronic Almanac*, 12 (10), http://mitpress2.mit.edu/e-journals/LEA/TEXT/Vol_12/lea_v12_n10.txt (accessed 4 January 2006).

De Souza e Silva, A. (2006a), 'Interfaces of Hybrid Spaces', in A. P. Kavoori and N. Arceneaux (eds), *Cultural Dialectics and the Cell Phone*, New York: Peter Lang.

De Souza e Silva, A. (2006b), 'From Cyber to Hybrid: Mobile Technologies as Interfaces of Hybrid Spaces', *Space & Culture*, 9 (3): 261–78.

De Souza e Silva, A. (2009), 'Hybrid Reality and Location-based Gaming: Redefining Mobility and Game Spaces in Urban Environments', *Simulation and Gaming*, 40 (3): 404–24.

De Souza e Silva, A., and Delacruz, G. (2006), 'Hybrid Reality Games Reframed: Potential Uses in Educational Contexts', *Games and Culture*, 1 (3): 231–51.

De Souza e Silva, A., and Hjorth, L. (2009), 'Playful Urban Spaces: A Historical Approach to Mobile Games', *Simulation and Gaming*, 40 (5): 602–25.

De Souza e Silva, A., and Sutko, D. (eds) (2009), *Digital Cityscapes: Merging Digital and Urban Playspaces*, New York: Peter Lang.

DiNucci, D. (1999), 'Fragmented Future', *Print*, 53 (4): 32, http://www.cdinucci.com/Darcy2/articles/Print/Printarticle7.html.

Dirlik, A. (1992), 'The Asia-Pacific Idea: Reality and Representation in the Invention of a Regional Structure', *Journal of World History*, 3 (1): 55–79.

Dirlik, A. (1995), 'Confucius in the Borderlands: Global Capitalism and the Reinvention of Confucianism, *boundary 2*, 22 (3): 229–73.

Dirlik, A. (1999a), 'Culture against History? The Politics of East Asian Identity', *Development and Society*, 28 (2): 167–90.

Dirlik, A. (1999b), 'Is There History after Eurocentrism? Globalism, Postcolonialism, and the Disavowal of History', *Cultural Critique*, 42 (Spring): 1–34.

Dirlik, A. (2000), 'Globalization as the End and the Beginning of History: The Contradictory Implications of a New Paradigm', http://globalization.mcmaster.ca/wps/dirlik.pdf (accessed 20 June).

Dirlik, A. (2007), 'Global South: Predicament and Promise', *The Global South*, 1 (1): 12–23.

Dovey, J., and Kennedy, H. (2006), *Game Cultures: Computer Games as New Media*, Maidenhead, UK: Open University Press.

Du Gay, P., Hall, S., Janes, L., Mackay, H. and Negus, K. (eds) (1997), *Doing Cultural Studies: The Story of the Walkman*, London: Sage.

Egenfeldt Nielsen, S., Smith, J. and Tosca, S. (2008) *Understanding Video Games: The Essential Introduction*, London: Routledge.

Ehrenreich, B., and Hochschild, A. (eds) (2003), *Global Woman: Nannies, Maids and Sex Workers in the New Economy*, New York: Metropolitan Books.

Ellis, J. ([1982]1992), *Visible fictions*, London: Routledge & Kegan Paul.

Flanagan, M. (2009), *Critical Play: Radical Game Design*, Cambridge, MA: MIT Press.

Flew, T. (2002), *New Media: An Introduction*, South Melbourne, Vic.: Oxford University Press.

Fortunati, L. (2005), 'Mobile Telephone and the Presentation of the Self', in R. Ling and P. E. Pederson (eds), *Mobile Communications: Re-negotiation of the Social Sphere*, London: Springer, pp. 203–18.

Frasca, G. (1999), 'Narratology Meets Ludology: Similitude and Differences between (Video) games and Narrative', *Parnasso*, 3: 365–71.

Frasca, G. (2003), 'Simulation versus Narrative' in M. J. P. Wolf and B. Perron (eds), *The Video Game Theory Reader*, New York: Routledge, pp. 212–36.

Freedman, A. (2009), '*Train Man* and the Gender Politics of Japanese "*Otaku*" Culture: The Rise of New Media, Nerd Heroes and Consumer Communities', in M. McLelland (ed), special issue of *Intersections: Gender and Sexuality in Asia and the Pacific*, 'Japanese Transnational Fandoms and Female Consumers', 20, http://intersections.anu.edu.au/issue20/freedman.htm (accessed 20 July 2009).

Fujimoto, K. (2005), 'The Third-Stage Paradigm: Territory Machine from the Girls' Pager Revolution to Mobile Aesthetics', in M. Ito, D. Okabe and M. Matsuda (eds), *Personal, Portable, Pedestrian: Mobile Phones in Japanese Life*, Cambridge, MA: MIT Press, pp. 77–102.

Galloway, A. (2004a), 'Mobility as World-building/Technologies at Play', *receiver* 10, www.receiver.vodafone.com (accessed 20 February 2006).

Galloway, A. (2004b), *A Brief History of the Future of Urban Computing and Locative Media*, PhD diss., Carleton University, http://www.purselipsquarejaw.org/dissertation.html (accessed 6 July 2005).

Gee, J. P. (2003), *What Video Games Have to Teach Us About Learning and Literacy*, New York: Palgrave Macmillan.

Geertz, C. (1973), *The Interpretation of Cultures*, New York: Basic Books.

Gergen, K. J. (2002), 'The Challenge of Absent Presence', in J. Katz and M. Aakhus (eds), *Perpetual Contact*, Cambridge: Cambridge University Press, pp. 227–41.

Gibson, W. (1984), *Neuromancer,* New York: Bantam Books.

Goffman, E. (1959), *The Presentation of Self in Everyday Life*, Harnmondsworth: Penguin Books.

Goffman, E. (1963), *Behaviour in Public Places: Note on the Social Organisation of Gatherings*, New York: Free Press.

Goggin, G. (2006), *Cell Phone Culture: Mobile Technology in Everyday Life*, London: Routledge.

Goggin, G., and Hjorth, L. (2009), 'Waiting to Participate: Introduction', in G. Goggin and L. Hjorth (eds), special issue of *Communication, Politics & Culture,* 'Waiting to Participate', 42 (2): 1–5.

Goggin, G., and McLelland, M. (eds) (2009), *Internationalizing Internet Studies*, London: Routledge.

Graham, P. (2006), *Interview about Web 2.0,* http://paulgraham.com/web20interview.html (accessed 10 October 2007).

Green, L. (2001), *Technoculture: From Alphabet to Cybersex*, St Leonards, N.S.W.: Allen & Unwin.

Gregg, M. (2007), 'Work Where You Want: The Labour Politics of the Mobile Office', *Mobile Media Conference*, University of Sydney, July.

Gye, L. (2007), 'Picture This', in G. Goggin (ed), special issue of *Continuum: Journal of Media & Cultural Studies,* 21 (2): 279–88.

Habuchi, I. (2005), 'Accelerated Reflexivity', in M. Ito, D. Okabe and M. Matsuda (eds), *Personal, Portable, Pedestrian: Mobile Phones in Japanese Life*, Cambridge, MA: MIT Press, pp. 165–82.

Haddon, L. (1997), *Empirical Research on the Domestic Phone: A Literature Review*, Brighton: University of Sussex.

Haddon, L. (1999), 'The Development of Interactive Games', in H. Mackay and T. O'Sullivan (eds), *The Media Reader: Continuity and Transformation*, Sage: London, pp. 305–27.

Hanson, M. (2004), *The End of Celluloid: Film Futures in the Digital Age*, London: RotoVision.

Haraway, D. (1985/1994), 'A Manifesto for Cyborgs: Science, Technology and Socialist Feminism in the 1980s', in S. Seidman (ed), *The Postmodern Turn*, Cambridge: Cambridge University Press.

Harvey, D. (2001), *Spaces of Capital: Towards a Critical Geography*, New York: Routledge.

Hebdige, D. (1988), *Hiding in the Light*, London: Taylor & Francis.

Hemment, D. (2004), 'Locative Arts', http://www.drewhemment.com/2004/locative_arts.html (accessed 7 November 2005).

Herzfeld, M. (1997), *Cultural Intimacy: Social Poetics in the Nation-State*, London: Routledge.

Hine, C. (1998), 'Virtual Ethnography', *Internet Research and Information for Social Scientists Conference*, University of Bristol, UK, March.

Hine, C. (2000), *Virtual Ethnography*, London: Sage.

Hirsch, E., and Silverstone, R. (eds) (1992), *Consuming Technologies: Media and Information in Domestic Spaces*, London: Routledge.

Hjorth, L. (2003a), 'Cute@keitai', in N. Gottlieb and M. McLelland (eds), *Japanese Cybercultures*, New York: Routledge, pp. 50–9.

Hjorth, L. (2003b), '"Pop" and "Ma": The Landscape of Japanese Commodity Characters and Subjectivity', in F. Martin, A. Yue and C. Berry (eds), *Mobile Cultures: New Media in Queer Asia*, Durham, NC: Duke University Press, pp. 158–79.

Hjorth, L. (2005), 'Odours of Mobility: Japanese Cute Customization in the Asia-Pacific Region', *Journal of Intercultural Studies*, 26: 39–55.

Hjorth, L. (2006a), 'Fast-forwarding Present: The Rise of Personalization and Customization in Mobile Technologies in Japan', *Southern Review,* 38 (3): 23–42.

Hjorth, L. (2006b), '*Playing at Being Mobile*: Gaming, Cute Culture and Mobile Devices in South Korea', in *Fibreculture journal* 8, http://journal.fibreculture.org/ (accessed 10 January 2007).

Hjorth, L. (2007), 'Domesticating New Media: A discussion on locating mobile media', in G. Goggin and L. Hjorth (eds), *Mobile Media Proceedings,* Sydney: University of Sydney.

Hjorth, L. (2008a), *Cybercute@korea:* The Role of Cute Customisation and Gender Performativity in a Case Study of South Korean Virtual Community, Cyworld minihompy', in Y. Kim (ed), *Media Consumption and Everyday Life in Asia*, London: Routledge, pp. 203–16.

Hjorth, L. (2008b), 'Being Real in the Mobile Reel', *Convergence,* 14 (1): 91–104.

Hjorth, L. (2009a) *Mobile Media in the Asia-Pacific: Gender and the Art of Being Mobile*, London: Routledge.

Hjorth, L. (2009b), 'Gifts of Presence: A Case Study of a South Korean Virtual Community, Cyworld's Mini-Hompy', in G. Goggin and M. McLelland (eds), *Internationalizing Internet Studies*, London: Routledge, pp. 237–51.

Hjorth, L. (2009c), 'Game Girl', in M. McLelland and F. Martin (eds), special issue of *Intersections: Gender and Sexuality in Asia and the Pacific Journal*, 20, http://intersections.anu.edu.au/.

Hjorth, L. (2010), 'The Game of Being Social: Social Media and Online Games', *Iowa Journal of Communication,* 42 (1).

Hjorth, L., and Chan, D. (eds) (2009), *Gaming Cultures and Place in Asia-Pacific*, London: Routledge.

Hjorth, L., and Kim, H. (2005), 'Being There and Being Here: Gendered Customising of Mobile 3G Practices through a Case Study in Seoul', *Convergence,* 11: 49–55.

Hjorth, L., Na, B. and Huhh, J-S. (2009), 'Games of Gender: A Case Study on Females Who Play Games in Seoul, South Korea', in L. Hjorth and D. Chan (eds), *Gaming Cultures and Place in Asia-Pacific*, London: Routledge, pp. 251–72.

Hjorth, L., and Richardson, I. (2009), 'The Waiting Game: Complicating Notions of (Tele) presence and Gendered Distraction in Casual Mobile Gaming', in G. Goggin, C. Lloyd and S. Rickard (eds), special issue of *Australian Journal of Communication,* 'Placing Mobile Communication', 36 (1).

Hochschild, A. R. (1983), *The Managed Heart: Commercialization of Human Feeling*, Berkeley: University of California Press.

Hochschild, A. R. (2000), 'Global Care Chains and Emotional Surplus Value', in W. Hutton and A. Giddens (eds), *On The Edge: Living with Global Capitalism*, London: Jonathan Cape, pp. 130–46.

Hochschild, A. R. (2001), *The Time Bind: When Work Becomes Home and Home Becomes Work*, California: Holt Press.

Hochschild, A. R. (2003), *The Commercialization of Intimate Life: Notes from Home and Work*, California: University of Cal. Press.

Huhh, J-S. (2009), 'The "Bang" Where Korean Online Gaming Began: The Culture and Business of the PC *bang* in Korea', in L. Hjorth and D. Chan (eds), *Gaming Cultures and Place in Asia-Pacific*, London: Routledge, pp. 102–16.

Huizinga, J. ([1938]1955), *Homo ludens: A Study of the Play Element in Culture*, Boston: Beacon Press.

Hughes, R. (1981), *The Shock of the New*, London: Thames and Hudson.

Huhtamo, E. (1997), 'From Kaleidoscomaniac to Cybernerd: Notes Toward an Archaeology of the Media', *Leonardo*, 30 (3): 221–24.

Illouz, E. (2007), *Cold Intimacies: The Making of Emotional Capitalism*, Cambridge, UK: Polity Press.

International Game Developers Association (IGDA) (2008), http://www.igda.org (accessed 5 January 2009).

International Labour Organization (ILO) (2008), 'Global Employment Trends for Women', http://www.ilo.org/public/english/employment/strat/global.htm (accessed 2 March 2008).

Introna, L. D., and Ilharco, F. M. (2004), 'The Ontological Screening of Contemporary Life: A Phenomenological Analysis of Screens', *European Journal of Information Systems*, 13: 221–34.

Ishii, K. (2004), 'Internet Use via Mobile Phone in Japan', *Telecommunications Policy*, 28 (1): 43–58.

Ito, M. (2002), 'Mobiles and the Appropriation of Place', *receiver* 08, www.receiver.vodafone.com (accessed 10 December 2003).

Ito, M. (2005), 'Introduction: Personal, Portable, Pedestrian', in M. Ito, D. Okabe and M. Matsuda (eds), *Personal, Portable, Pedestrian: Mobile Phones in Japanese Life*, Cambridge, MA: MIT Press, pp. 1–16.

Ito, M. (2006), 'The Gender Dynamics of the Japanese Media Mix', *Girls 'n' Games*, University of California, Los Angeles, May.

Ito, M., boyd, d. and H. Horst (2008), *Digital Youth Research*, http://digitalyouth.ischool.berkeley.edu/.

Ito, M., and Okabe, D. (2003), 'Camera Phones Changing the Definition of Picture-worthy', *Japan Media Review*, http://www.ojr.org/japan/wireless/1062208524.php (accessed 10 June 2004).

Ito, M., and Okabe, D. (2005), 'Intimate Visual Co-presence', *UbiComp 2005*, Tokyo, Japan, September, http://www.itofisher.com/mito/ (accessed 10 December 2005).

Ito, M., Okabe, D. and Matsuda, M. (eds) (2005), *Personal, Portable, Pedestrian: Mobile Phones in Japanese Life*, Cambridge, MA: MIT Press.

Ito, M. et al. (2008), 'Forword', in W. L. Bennett (ed), *Civic Life Online: Learning How Digital Media Can Engage Youth,* John D. and Catherine T. MacArthur Foundation Series on Digital Media and Learning, Cambridge, MA: MIT Press, pp. vii–ix.

Iwabuchi, K. (2002), *Recentering Globalization: Popular Culture and Japanese Transnationalism*, Durham, NC: Duke University Press.

Jacobs, D. (2006), 'Cyworld Lands on MySpace', *International Business Times*, 31 July. http://www.ibtimes.com/articles/2006731/cyworld-myspace-sktelecom-newscorp.htm (accessed 10 August 2006).

Jamieson, L. (1998), *Intimacy: Personal Relationships in Modern Societies*, Cambridge: Polity Press.

Jamieson, L. (1999), 'Intimacy Transformed: A Critical Look at the "Pure Relationship"', *Sociology*, 33: 477–94.

Jenkins, H. (1992), *Textual Poachers: Television, Fans and Participatory Culture*, New York: Routledge.

Jenkins, H. (2005), 'Welcome to Convergence Culture', *receiver* 12, http://www.receiver.vodafone.com/12/articles/pdf/12_01.pdf (accessed 10 January 2006).

Jenkins, H. (2006a), *Convergence Culture: Where Old and New Media Intersect*, New York: New York University Press.

Jenkins, H. (2006b), *Fans, Bloggers, and Gamers: Essays on Participatory Culture*, New York: New York University Press.

Jin, D. Y. (2010), *Hands On/Hands Off: The Korean State and the Market Liberalization of the Communication Industry*. Cresskill, NJ: Hampton Press.

Jin, D. Y., and Chee, F. (2008), 'Age of New Media Empire: A Critical Interpretation of the Korean Online Game Industry', in L. Hjorth (ed), special issue of *Games and Culture*, 3 (1): 38–58.

Jin, D. Y., and Chee, F. (2009), 'The Politics of Online Gaming', in L. Hjorth and D. Chan (eds), *Gaming Cultures and Place in Asia-Pacific*, London: Routledge, pp. 19–38.

Jungnickel, K. (2004), *Urban Tapestries: Sensing the City and Other Stories*, http://proboscis.org.uk/publications/SNAPSHOTS_sensingthecity.pdf (accessed 10 September 2009).

Juul, J. (1999/2001), 'A Clash between Game and Narrative: A Thesis on Computer Games and Interactive Fiction' (2001 English translation from Danish), Institute of Nordic Languages and Literature, University of Copenhagen, www.jesperjuul.dk/thesis/AClashBetweenGameAndNarrative.pdf.

Juul, J. (2005), *Half-Real: Video Games between Real Rules and Fictional Worlds*, Cambridge, MA: MIT Press.

Juul, J. (2009), *A Casual Revolution: Reinventing Video Games and Their Players*, Cambridge, MA: MIT Press.

Kafai, Y., Heeter, C., Denner, J. and Sun, J. (eds) (2008), *Beyond Barbie and Mortal Kombat: New Perspectives on Gender and Gaming*, Cambridge, MA: MIT Press.

Katsuno, H., and Yano, C. R. (2002), 'Face to Face: On-line Subjectivity in Contemporary Japan', *Asian Studies Review*, 26 (2): 205–31.

Kennedy, H. W. (2002), 'Lara Croft: Feminist Icon or Cyberbimbo? On the Limits of Textual Analysis', *Game Studies*, 2 (2), http://www.gamestudies.org/0202/kennedy/.27 (accessed 20 January 2009).

Kerr, A. (2006), *The Business and Culture of Digital Games: Gamework/Gameplay*, London: Sage.

Kim, S. D. (2003), 'The Shaping of New Politics in the Era of Mobile and Cyber Communication', in K. Nyíri (ed), *Mobile Democracy,* Vienna: Passagen Verlag, pp. 317–26.

Kinsella, S. (1995), 'Cuties in Japan', in L. Skov and B. Moeran (eds), *Women, Media and Consumption in Japan,* Surrey, UK: Curzon Press, pp. 220–54.

Kline, S., Dyer-Witherford, N. and de Peuter, G. (2003), *Digital Play: The Interaction of Technology, Culture, and Marketing,* Montreal: McGill-Queen's University Press.

Koch, P., Koch, B., Huang, K. and Chen, W. (2009), 'Beauty Is in the Eye of the QQ User: Instant Messaging in China', in G. Goggin and M. McLelland (eds), *Internationalizing Internet Studies,* London: Routledge, pp. 265–84.

Kogawa, T. (1984), 'Beyond Electronic Individualism', *Canadian Journal of Political and Social Theory/Revue Canadienne de Thetorie Politique et Sociale,* 8 (3), http://anarchy.trans local.jp/non-japanese/electro.html (accessed 20 July 2007).

Kohiyama, K. (2005), 'A Decade in the Development of Mobile Communications in Japan (1993–2002)', in M. Ito, D. Okabe and M. Matsuda (eds), *Personal, Portable, Pedestrian: Mobile Phones in Japanese Life,* Cambridge, MA: MIT Press, pp. 61–74.

Kohler, C. (2004), *Power-Up: How Japanese Video Games Gave the World an Extra Life,* London: Dorling Kindersley/Brady Games.

Korinets, R. V. (2009), *Netnography: Doing Ethnographic Research Online,* London: Sage.

Kozinets, R.V. (2006), 'Netnography 2.0', in R. W. Belk (ed), *Handbook of Qualitative Research Methods in Marketing,* Northampton, MA: Edward Elgar, pp. 129–42.

Kücklich, J. (2005), 'Precarious Playbour: Modders and the Digital Games Industry', *Fibreculture journal* 5, http://journal.fibreculture.org/issue5/kucklich.html (accessed 20 August 2007).

Koskinen, I. (2007), 'Managing Banality in Mobile Multimedia', in R. Pertierra (ed), *The Social Construction and Usage of Communication Technologies: Asian and European Experiences,* Quezon City: University of the Philippines Press, pp. 48–60.

Kusahara, M. (2001), 'The Art of Creating Subjective Reality: An Analysis of Japanese Digital Pets', *Leonardo,* 34 (4): 299–302.

Lantz, F. (2006), 'Big Games and the Porous Border between the Real and the Mediated', *receiver* 16, http://www.receiver.vodafone.com/16/articles/index07.html (accessed 10 February 2007).

Lasén, A. (2004), 'Affective Technologies—Emotions and Mobile Phones', *receiver* 11, www. receiver.vodafone.com (accessed 5 June 2006).

Latour, B. (1986), *Science in Action,* Reading, UK: Open University Press.

Lee, E. V., and Ryu, S. S. (2006), 'Information Technology Industry Forecast: Contents', *Information Technology Industry Forecast,* 12: 245–77.

Lee, Y., Lee, J. and Kim, H. (2002), 'A Cross-cultural Study on the Value Structure of Mobile Internet Usage: Comparison between Korea and Japan', *Journal of Electronic Commerce Research,* 3 (4): 227–39.

Lefebvre, H. (1991), *The Production of Space,* Cambridge, MA: Blackwell.

Licoppe, C. (2009), 'The Pragmatics of Notification: The Case of the Uses of Instant Messaging at Work', *COST 298: The Good, the Bad and the Challenging conference,* May.

Licoppe, C., and Guillot, R. (2006), 'ICTs and the Engineering of Encounters. A Case Study of the Development of a Mobile Game-based on the Geolocation of Terminal', in J. Urry and M. Sheller (eds), *Mobile Technologies of the City,* London: Routledge, pp. 152–76.

Licoppe, C., and Inada, Y. (2005), '"Seeing" One Another Onscreen and the Construction of Social Order in a Mobile-based Augmented Public Space: The Use of a Geo-localized Mobile Game in Japan', in K. Nyíri (ed), *Proceedings of Seeing, Understanding, Learning in the Mobile Age conference*, Budapest, April.

Licoppe, C., and Inada, Y. (2006), 'Emergent Uses of a Location Aware Multiplayer Game: The Interactional Cnsequences of Mediated Encounters', *Mobilities,* 1 (1): 39–61.

Lister, M. (2002), *New Media: A Critical Introduction*, London: Routledge.

Luckmann, T. (1983), *Life-World and Social Realities*, Oxford, UK: Heinemann Educational Books.

Luke, R. (2006), 'The Phoneur: Mobile Commerce and the Digital Pedagogies of the Wireless Web', in P. Trifonas (ed), *Communities of Difference: Culture, Language, Technology*, Palgrave: London, pp. 185–204.

Luttwak, E. (1999), *Turbo-Capitalism: Winners and Losers in the Global Economy*, London: HarperCollins.

MacKenzie, D., and Wajcman, J. (eds) (1999), *The Social Shaping of Technology*, 2nd edn, Buckingham, UK: Open University Press.

Malaby, T. M. (2006), 'Parlaying Value: Capital in and Beyond Virtual Worlds', *Games and Culture*, 1 (2): 141–62.

Manovich, L. (2001), *The Language of New Media*, Cambridge, MA: MIT Press.

Manovich, L. (2003), 'The Paradoxes of Digital Photography', in L. Wells (ed), *The Photography Reader*, London: Routledge, pp. 240–49.

Margaroni, M., and Yiannopoulou, E. (2005), 'Intimate Transfers: Introduction', *European Journal of English Studies*, 9 (3): 221–28.

Mason, J. (1996), *Qualitative Researching*, London: Sage.

Massey, D. (1993), 'Questions of locality', *Geography,* 78: 142–9.

Massey, D. (1995), *Spatial Divisions of Labor: Social Structures and the Geography of Production,* London: Routledge.

Massey, D. (1999), *City Worlds*, London: Routledge.

Matsuda, M. (2005), 'Discourses of *Keitai* in Japan', in M. Ito, Okabe, D. and M. Matsuda (eds), *Personal, Portable, Pedestrian: Mobile Phones in Japanese Life*, Cambridge, MA: MIT Press, pp. 19–40.

Mauss, M. (1954), *The Gift,* London: Kegan Paul.

Mäyrä, F. (2003), 'The City Shaman Dances with Virtual Wolves—Researching Pervasive Mobile Gaming', *receiver* 12, www.receiver.vodafone.com (accessed 20 May 2005).

Mäyrä, F. (2008), *Introduction to Game Studies: Games in Culture,* London: Sage.

McCartney, N. (2004), 'Cultural Ties Shape Consumer Choices', *Variety,* 4–10 October, http://findarticles.com/p/articles/mi_hb1437/is_2004/ai_n18403236 (accessed 14 June 2006).

McGray, D. (2002), 'Japan's Gross National Cool', *Foreign Policy*, May/June: 44–54.

McKay, D. (2007), '"Sending Dollars Shows Feeling"—Emotions and Economies in Filipino Migration', *Mobilities,* 2 (2): 175–94.

McLelland, M. (2007), 'Socio-cultural Aspects of Mobile Communication Technologies in Asia and the Pacific: A Discussion of the Recent Literature', *Continuum,* 21 (2): 267–77.

McLuhan, M. (1964), *Understanding Media,* New York: Mentor.

McVeigh, B. (2000), 'How Hello Kitty Commodifies the Cute, Cool and Camp: "Consumutopia" versus "Control" in Japan', *Journal of Material Culture,* 5 (2): 291–312.

McVeigh, B. (2003a), 'Individualization, Individuality, Interiority, and the Internet', in N. Gottlieb and M. McLelland (eds), *Japanese Cybercultures,* London: Routledge, pp. 19–33.

McVeigh, B. (2003b), *Nationalisms of Japan: Managing and Mystifying Identity,* New York: Rowman and Littlefield.

Miller, D. (1987), *Material Culture and Mass Consumption,* London: Blackwell.

Miller, D. (ed.) (1988), *Material Cultures: Why Some Things Matter,* Chicago: University of Chicago Press.

Miller, D., and Slater, D. (2000), *The Internet: An Ethnographic Approach,* Oxford: Berg.

Miller, L. (2005), 'Bad Girl Photography', in J. Bardsley and L. Miller (eds), *Bad Girls of Japan,* London: Palgrave Macmillan, pp. 127–42.

Miller, L. (2006), *Beauty Up,* Berkley: University of California Press.

Milne, E. (2004), 'Magic Bits of Paste-board', *M/C journal,* 7 (1), http://journal.media-culture.org.au/ (accessed 10 June 2004).

Ministry of Information Affairs and Communication, Japan (MIC) (2006), *White Papers,* http://wwwjohotsusintokei.soumu.go.jp/statistics/statistics05.html and http://johotsusintokei.soumu.go.jp/english/ (accessed 10 February 2007).

Ministry of Information Affairs and Communication (MIC) (2007), *Broadband IT Korea Vision,* http://www.istat.go.kr/eng/.

Morley, D. (1992), *Television, Audiences, and Cultural Studies,* London: Routledge.

Morley, D. (2003), 'What's "Home" Got to Do with It?', *European Journal of Cultural Studies,* 6 (4): 435–58.

Morley, D., and Robins, K. (1995) *Spaces of Identities: Global Media, Electronic Landscapes and Cultural Boundaries,* New York: Routledge.

Morse, M. (1998), *Virtualities: Television, Media Art, and Cyberculture,* Bloomington: Indiana University Press.

Moses, A. (2008), 'iPhone Games Put the Heat on Sony, Nintendo', *The Sydney Morning Herald,* 24 November, http://www.smh.com.au/news/technology/biztech/iphone-games-pu-the-heat-on-sony-nintendo/2008/11/24/1227491432729.html.

Munster, A., and Murphie, A. (2009), 'Editorial—Web 2.0: Before, during and after the event', *Fibreculture journal* 14, http://journal.fibreculture.org/issue14/ (accessed 10 October 2009).

Murakami, T. (2000), *Superflat Catalogue,* Tokyo: Parco.

Murray, J. H. (1997), *Hamlet on the Holodeck: The Future of Narrative in Cyberspace,* Cambridge, MA: MIT Press.

Nakamura, L. (2002), *Cybertypes: Race, Ethnicity, and Identity on the Internet,* New York: Routledge.

Nardi, B. A (2009), 'Play, Community, and History' in C. Pearce (with Artemesia), *Communities of Play: Emergent Cultures in Multiplayer Games and Virtual Worlds*, Cambridge, MA: MIT Press, pp. x–xi.

National Internet Development Agency of Korea (NIDA) (2006), *Netizen Internet Usage: Press Release*, http://www.nida.go.kr/doc/issue_sum_report.pdf (accessed 20 August 2007).

Nelson, T. (1980 [1990]), *Literary Machines* Sausalito, CA: Mindful Press.

Ng, W.-M. (2006), 'Street Fighter and the King of Fighters in Hong Kong: A Study of Cultural Consumption and Localization of Japanese Games in an Asian Context', *Games Studies: The international journal of computer game research*, 6 (1), http://gamestudies.org/0601/articles/ng (accessed 15 November 2006).

Norman, D. (1988), *The Design of Everyday Things*, New York: Doubleday.

Okada, T. (2005), 'Youth Culture and the Shaping of Japanese Mobile Media: Personalization and the *Keitai* Internet as Multimedia', in M. Ito, D. Okabe and M. Matsuda (eds), *Personal, Portable, Pedestrian: Mobile Phones in Japanese Life*, Cambridge, MA: MIT Press, pp. 41–60.

O'Reilly, T. (2005), 'What Is Web 2.0: Design Patterns and Business Models for the Next Generation of Software', http://oreilly.com/web2/archive/what-is-web-20.html (accessed 10 September 2009).

Organization for Economic Co-operation and Development (OECD) (2006). *OECD Broadband Statistics, 2006*, http://www.oecd.org/sti/ict/broadband (accessed 3 December 2006).

Palmer, D. (2005), 'Mobile Exchanges', ACMI, Vital Signs conference, Melbourne, September.

Parikka, J., and Suominen, J. (2006), 'Victorian Snakes? Towards a Cultural History of Mobile Games and the Experience of Movement', *Games Studies: The international journal of computer game research*, 6 (1), December, URL: http://gamestudies.org/0601 (accessed 20 April 2007).

Park, H. W., and Kluver, R. (2009), 'Affiliation in Political Blogs in South Korea: Comparing Online and Offline Social Networks', in G. Goggin and M. McLelland (eds), *Internationalizing Internet Studies*, London: Routledge, pp. 252–64.

Park, S. Y., and Yoo, S. H. (2003), 'The Effect of the Sense of On-line Community on Website Loyalty and Purchase Intention', *Kyungyounghak Yonku*, 32 (6): 1695–1713.

Parreñas, R. (2001), *Servants of Globalization: Women, Migration, and Domestic Work*, Stanford, CA: Stanford University Press.

Parreñas, R. (2005), *Children of Global Migration: Transnational Families and Gendered Woes*, Stanford, CA: Stanford University Press.

Pearce, C. (with Artemesia) (2009), *Communities of Play: Emergent Cultures in Multiplayer Games and Virtual Worlds*, Cambridge, MA: MIT Press.

Pertierra, R. (2005), 'Mobile Phones, Identity and Discursive Intimacy', *Human Technology*, 1: 23–44.

Pertierra, R. (ed) (2007), *The Social Construction and Usage of Communication Technologies: Asian and European Experiences*, Quezon City: University of the Philippines Press.

Proboscis (2007), 'Public Authoring in the Wireless City', *Urban Tapestries*, http://urbantapestries.net/ (accessed 20 June 2008).

Putnam, R. (2000), *Bowling Alone*, New York: Simon and Schuster.

Qiu, J. (2007), 'The Wireless Leash: Mobile Messaging Service as a Means of Control', *International Journal of Communication*, 1: 74–91.

Qiu, J. (2008), 'Wireless Working-class ICTs and the Chinese Informational City', in special issue of *Journal of Urban Technology*, 'Mobile Media and Urban Technology', 15 (3): 57–77.

Quaranta, D. (2003), Eddo Stern, http://www.gamescenes.org/2009/09/essay-domenico-quaranta-on-eddo-stern.html.

Quaranta, D. (2009), 'Machine animation and animated machines', http://domenicoquaranta.com/2009/09/text-machine-animation-animated-machines/.

Raessens, J., and Goldstein, J. (eds) (2005), *Handbook of Computer Game Studies*, Cambridge, MA: MIT Press.

Rafael, V. (2003), 'The Cell Phone and the Crowd: Messianic Politics in the Contemporary Philippines', *Popular Culture*, 15 (3): 399–425.

Raiti, G. (2007), 'Mobile Intimacy: Theories on the Economics of Emotion with Examples from Asia', in L. Hjorth and O. Khoo (eds), special issue of *M/C Journal*, 'Mobility in the Asia-Pacific', 10 (1), http://journal.media-culture.org.au/0703/02-raiti.php (accessed 10 March 2007).

Richardson, I. (2007), 'Pocket Technoscapes: The Bodily Incorporation of Mobile Media', *Continuum: Journal of Media & Cultural Studies*, 21 (2): 205–16.

Richardson, I. (2009), 'Sticky Games and Hybrid Worlds: A Post-Phenomenology of Mobile Phones, Mobile Gaming and the iPhone', in L. Hjorth and D. Chan (eds), *Gaming Cultures and Place in Asia-Pacific*, London: Routledge, pp. 213–32.

Roach, M. (1999), 'Cute Inc.', *Wired*, 7 (12), http://wired.com/wired/archive/'7.12/cute_pr.html (accessed 7 April 2001).

Robertson, R. (1995), 'Glocalization: Time–Space and Homogeneity–Heterogeneity', in M. Featherstone, S. Lash and R. Robertson (eds), *Global Modernity*, London: Routledge, pp. 24–44.

Rodriguez, H. (2006), 'The Playful and the Serious: An Approximation to Huizinga's Homo Ludens', *Game Studies*, 6 (1), http://gamestudies.org/0601/articles/rodriges (accessed 5 July 2007).

Said, E. (1978), *Orientalism*, New York: Random House.

Salen, K., and Zimmerman, E. (2003), *Rules of Play: Game Design Fundamentals*, Cambridge, MA: MIT Press.

Salen, K., and Zimmerman, E. (2005), *The Game Design Reader*, Cambridge, MA: MIT Press.

Screen Digest (2008), http://www.screendigest.com/reports (accessed 20 December 2008).

Shirky, C. (2008), 'Here Comes Everybody', *Aspen Ideas Festival*, Aspen Colorado, June/July, http://fora.tv/2008/07/06/Clay_Shirky_on_Social_Networks_like_Facebook_and_MySpace#chapter_01 (accessed 20 January 2009).

Silverstone, R., and Haddon, L. (1996), 'Design and Domestication of Information and Communication Technologies: Technical Change and Everyday Life', in R. Silverstone and

R. Mansell (eds), *Communication by Design: The Politics of Information and Communication Technologies*, Oxford, UK: Oxford University Press, pp. 44–74.

Silverstone, R., Hirsch, E. and Morley, D. (1992), 'Information and Communication Technologies and the Moral Economy of the Household', in E. Hirsch and R. Silverstone (eds), *Consuming Technologies: Media and Information in Domestic Spaces*, London: Routledge.

Soja, E. (1989), *Postmodern Geographies: The Reassertion of Space in Critical Social Theory*, New York: Verso.

Stone, A. R. (1995), *The War of Desire and Technology*, Cambridge, MA: MIT Press.

Sutton-Smith, B. (1997), *The Ambiguity of Play*, London: Routledge.

Swalwell, M., and Wilson, J. (eds) (2008), *The Pleasures of Computer Games: Essays on Cultural History, Theory and Aesthetics,* Jefferson, NC: McFarland.

Sweeny, R., and Patton, R. (2008), 'CitySneak: Play, Pedaogy, and Surveillance', http://www.boomboxgames.org/citysneak (accessed 10 October 2008).

Sweeny, R., and Patton, R. (2009), 'CitySneak: Play, Pedaogy, and Surveillance', in A. de Souza e Silva and D. Sutko (eds), *Digital Cityscapes: Merging Digital and Urban Playspaces,* New York: Peter Lang, pp. 204–16.

Tapscott, D. (1995), *The Digital Economy: Promise and Peril in the Age of Networked Intelligence*, New York: McGraw-Hill Books.

Taylor, A., and Harper, R. (2002), 'Age-old Practices in the "New World": A Study of Gift-giving between Teenage Mobile Phone Users', in *Changing Our World, Changing Ourselves*, Proceedings of the SIGCHI Conference on Human Factors in Computing Systems, Minneapolis, pp. 439–46.

Taylor, T. L. (2003a), 'Intentional Bodies: Virtual Environments and the Designers Who Shape Them', *International Journal of Engineering Education*, 19 (1): 25–34.

Taylor, T. L. (2003b), 'Multiple Pleasures: Women and Online Gaming', *Convergence*, 9 (1): 21–46.

Taylor, T. L. (2006a), *Play between Worlds: Exploring Online Game Cultures*, Cambridge, MA: MIT Press.

Taylor, T. L. (2006b), 'Base, and Surveillance Mod Scene Caused Me Pause Does WoW Change Everything?: How a PvP Server, Multinational Player', *Games and Culture*, 1 (4): 318–37.

Toffler, A. (1980), *The Third Wave*, New York: William Morrow.

Tofts, D. (2004), 'Metaphysics and Mash at Harry's Café de Wheels: New media at the Sydney Biennale', in *On Reason and Emotion: 2004 Sydney Biennale catalogue*, Sydney: Sydney Biennale.

Tönnies, F. (1988[1887]), *Community and Society*, trans. from *Gemeinschaft and Gesellschaft*, New Brunswick, NJ.: Transaction Publishers.

Treat, J. W. (1996), 'Japanese Studies into Cultural Studies', in J. W. Treat (ed) *Contemporary Japan and Popular Culture*, Honolulu: University of Hawaii Press, pp. 1–16.

Truong, T. D. (1999), 'The Underbelly of the Tiger: Gender and Demystification of the Asian miracle', *Review of International Political Economy*, 6 (2): 133–65.

Tsuji, D., and Mikami, S. (2001), 'A Preliminary Student Survey on the E-mail Uses of Mobile Phones', *JSICR conference*, Tokyo, June.

Turkle, S. (1995), *Life on the Screen: Identity in the Age of the Internet*, New York: Simon and Schuster.

Turner, B. (2007), 'The Enclave Society: Towards a Sociology of Immobility', *European Journal of Social Theory,* 10 (2): 287–303.

Turner, V. W. (1982), 'Liminal to Liminoid, in Play, Flow, and Ritual: An Essay in Comparative Symbology', in *From Ritual to Theatre: The Human Seriousness of Play*, New York: PAJ Publications, pp. 20–60.

Urban Vibe (2005), Nabi Media Centre, http://eng.nabi.or.kr/project/view.asp?prjlearn_idx=119 (accessed 28 May 2008).

Wajcman, J. (1991), *Feminism Confronts Technology*, Cambridge: Polity Press.

Wajcman, J. (2004), *Technofeminism*, Cambridge: Polity Press.

Wajcman, J., Bittman, M. and Brown, J. (2009), 'Intimate Connections: The Impact of the Mobile Phone on Work Life Boundaries', in G. Goggin and L. Hjorth (eds), *Mobile Technologies*, London: Routledge, pp. 9–22.

Waldrip-Fruin, N., and Harrigan, P. (eds) (2004), *First Person: New Media as Story, Performance, and Game*, Cambridge, MA: MIT Press.

Wei, D., and Qian, T. (2009), 'The Mobile Hearth: A Case Study on New Media Usage and Migrant Workers' Social Relationship', *ANZCA conference*, June.

Weiser, M. (1983), 'Some Computer Science Issues in Ubiquitous Computing', *Communications of the ACM,* 36 (7): 75–84.

Weiser, M. (1991), 'The Computer for the 21st Century', *Scientific American,* 265 (3): 94–104.

Wesch, M. (2008), 'Digital Ethnography', http://mediatedcultures.net/ksudigg/ (accessed 10 September 2009).

West, D. M. (2007), *Global e-government*, Providence, RI: Center for Public Policy, Brown University.

White, M. (1993), *The Material Child: Coming of Age in Japan and America*, New York: Free Press.

Williams, D., Ducheneaut, N., Xiong, L., Zhang, Y., Yee, N. and Nickell, E. (2006), 'From Tree House to Barracks: The Social Life of Guilds in World of Warcraft', *Games and Culture,* 1 (4): 338–61.

Williams, R. (1974), *Television: Technology and Cultural Form*, London: Fontana.

Williams, R. (1983), 'Mobile Privatization', in P. du Gay, S. Hall, J. Lanes, H. Mackay and K. Negus (eds), (1997), *Doing Cultural Studies: The Story of the Sony Walkman*, London: Sage.

Wilson, R. (2000), 'Imagining "Asia-Pacific": Forgetting Politics and Colonialism in the Magical Waters of the Pacific, An Americanist Critique', *Cultural Studies,* 14 (3/4): 562–92.

Wilson, R., and Dirlik, A. (eds) (1995), *Asia/Pacific as Space of Cultural Production*, Durham: Duke University Press.

Winnicott, D. W. (1971), *Playing and Reality*, London: Tavistock.

Wolf, M. J. P. (2001), *The Medium of the Video Game*, Austin: University of Texas.

Wolf, M. J. P., and Perron, B. (eds) (2003), *The Video Game Theory Reader*, New York: Routledge.

Wolf, M. J. P., and Perron, B. (eds) (2008), *The Video Game Theory Reader 2,* New York: Routledge.

Wyeld, T. G., Leavy, B. and P. Crogan (2009), 'The Re-presentation of Country as Virtual Artefact in Australian Aboriginal Cultural Heritage Using a Game Engine', in L. Hjorth and D. Chan (eds), *Gaming Cultures and Place in Asia-Pacific,* London: Routledge, pp. 194–212.

Yoo, S. H. (2009), 'Internet, Internet Culture, and Internet Communities of Korea: Overview and Research Directions', in G. Goggin and M. McLelland (eds), *Internationalizing Internet Studies,* London: Routledge, pp. 217–36.

Yoon, K. (2003), 'Retraditionalizing the Mobile: Young People's Sociality and Mobile Phone Use in Seoul, South Korea', *European Journal of Cultural Studies,* 6: 327–43.

Yoon, K. (2006), 'The Making of Neo-Confucian Cyberkids: Representations of Young Mobile Phone Users in South Korea', *New Media and Society,* 8 (5): 753–71.

Yoshimi, S. (1999), '"Made in Japan": The Cultural Politics of "Home Electrification" in Postwar Japan', *Media, Culture and Society,* 21: 149–71.

Zuckerman, E. (2008), 'Cute Cat Theory of Digital Activism', *O'Reilly E-tech conference,* March, http://en.oreilly.com/et2008/public/schedule/detail/1597 (accessed 14 September 2009).

INDEX